About the Book and Editor

Government deficits, the spiraling imbalance of trade, inconsistencies in foreign policy, illegal immigration, unemployment, the decay of our cities, the abuse of the environment, the staggering cost of elections, and the piracy of special interest groups—these problems and a host of others have led thoughtful citizens to question whether our political system is capable of meeting the challenge of modern governance. We stand in awe of the wise men who framed the Constitution nearly two centuries ago, but as they themselves anticipated, changing circumstances demand a reassessment.

As we approach the bicentennial anniversary of the Constitution, such an assessment is being undertaken by the Committee on the Constitutional System, a group of two hundred prominent citizens (among them present and former members of the Senate and House, Cabinet and White House staff, governors, party officials, members of academia, journalists, lawyers, and labor, business, and financial leaders). *Reforming American Government* includes both a discussion of the problems of modern governance and an assessment of various proposed reforms. Some of the proposals call for changes in party rules for nominating candidates; some for federal statutes to funnel campaign finances through the parties. Others present drafts of Constitutional amendments designed to coordinate the terms of representatives, senators, and the president, to allow legislators to serve in administrative positions, and to provide for new elections in the event of deadlock.

The book presents draft language for each of these proposals and an assessment of "pros and cons." Also included is a discussion of aspects of the French, West German, and English constitutions that shed light on American possibilities for governmental reform.

The Committee, which is nonpartisan and nongovernmental, is chaired by Senator Nancy Landon Kassebaum, Republican of Kansas; C. Douglas Dillon, member of the Eisenhower and Kennedy cabinets; and Lloyd Cutler, former White House Counsel to President Jimmy Carter. It has taken no position on the proposals it has considered. Its purpose is to use the occasion of the bicentennial of the Constitution for a candid assessment of the performance of our governing institutions and to stimulate a nationwide debate about alternative structures and processes.

Donald L. Robinson, editor of the volume, is professor of government at Smith College.

Reforming American Government
The Bicentennial Papers of the Committee on the Constitutional System

edited by
Donald L. Robinson

Westview Press / Boulder and London

Copyright © 1985 by The Committee on the Constitutional System

Published in 1985 in the United States of America by Westview Press, Inc.; Frederick A. Praeger, Publisher; 5500 Central Avenue, Boulder, Colorado 80301

Library of Congress Cataloging in Publication Data
Main entry under title:
Reforming American Government
    Bibliography: p.
    1. United States—Constitutional law. I. Robinson,
Donald L., 1936–   . II. Committee on the Constitutional System.
KF4549.W67 1985   342.73′03   85-3199
ISBN 0-8133-7059-0   347.3023
ISBN 0-8133-7114-7 (pbk.)

Printed and bound in the United States of America
Composition provided by the editor

10   9   8   7   6   5   4   3   2

Table of Contents

Foreword, *Nancy Landon Kassebaum, Lloyd N. Cutler, and
C. Douglas Dillon*, Co-Chairs, Committee on
the Constitutional System...................................... xi
Preface, *Donald L. Robinson*..................................... xiii

Part 1. Diagnoses of the Problem
    Introduction.. 1
1   The Crisis and Its Cure (1974), *Charles Hardin* 3
2   To Form a Government (1980), *Lloyd N. Cutler*................11
3   The Challenge of Modern Governance (1982), *C. Douglas
    Dillon* 24
4   Statement on Campaign Finance (1985), *Nancy Landon
    Kassebaum* 30
5   The Moral Equivalent of Defeat (1981), *Lester Thurow*........ 33
6   Words of Caution About Structural Change (1983),
    Don K. Price 39
7   Leave the Constitution Alone (1982), *Arthur M.
    Schlesinger, Jr.*... 50
8   A Rebuttal to Arthur Schlesinger, Jr. (1983),
    Lloyd N. Cutler and C. Douglas Dillon 55
9   Why Think About Constitutional Reform? (1982),
    James M. Burns....................................... 59
10   A Remedy for Defects in the Federal System (1984),
    Neal R. Pierce....................................... 61
11   Priorities in Governmental Reform (1984), *Elmer Staats*....... 65
12   A Statement of the Problem (1983), *Committee on the
    Constitutional System*................................... 68

Part 2. Reforms of the Electoral System
    Introduction... 73
13   'Tis Done—But 'Tis Never Done (1983),
    Alexander Heard 76
14   Reversing the Decay of Party (1982), *James L. Sundquist*...... 89

15 Party Government Under the Constitution (1985),
   Lloyd N. Cutler 93
16 The Impact of Television (1985), *Newton Minow* 110
   Specific Proposals: Text and Analysis
   A. Bicameral Nominating Convention (party rules) 114
   B. Two-Phase Federal Elections (federal statute) 117
   C. An Option to Vote for Party Slates (federal statute) 119
   D. Public Financing of Campaign Broadcasts
      (federal statute) 120
   E. Campaign Financing Limits (party rules) 122

Part 3. Reducing the Risk of Divided Government
   Introduction 127
17 Cabinet Government in the United States (1879),
   Woodrow Wilson 131
18 In Defense of the Presidential System (1940),
   Harold Laski. 135
19 Cabinet Members on the Floor of Congress (1945),
   Thomas K. Finletter 143
20 Toward a New Constitution (1974), *Charles Hardin* 149
21 To Encourage Cooperation (1979), *Henry Reuss* 155
22 The Power to Lead (1984), *James M. Burns* 157
23 Balance the Budget (1985), *Dick Thornburgh* 164
24 The Single, Six-Year Term for Presidents (1984),
   The Jefferson Foundation 167
   Specific Proposals: Text and Analysis
   A. Coordinated Terms of Office (constitutional
      amendment). 175
   B. The Team Ticket (constitutional amendment) 177
   C. Bonus Seats for Party Winning Presidential
      Election (constitutional amendment) 179
   D. Legislators in the Executive Branch (constitutional
      amendment). 182
   E. Cabinet Secretaries in Congress (constitutional
      amendment) 185
   F. Repeal of Two-Term Limit on the Presidency
      (constitutional amendment). 186

Part 4. Breaking Deadlocks
   Introduction 189
25 An American Parliament (1980), *Kevin Phillips* 191
26 A Coalition Government (1984), *Theodore C. Sorensen* 199
27 Presidential Dissolution (1935), *William Yandell Elliott* 202

28   A Congressional Vote of No Confidence (1975),
      Henry Reuss... 206
29   The Inadequacy of Impeachment (1975), *Hans A. Linde*...... 209
30   The British Experience (1975), *Samuel Beer*................ 215
31   A Critique of the Reuss Proposal (1975), *Allan Sindler*...... 222
32   The Case for an Easier Method to Remove Presidents
      (1975), *James L. Sundquist* 227
33   No-Confidence Will Not Work in America (1976),
      Bob Eckhardt and Charles L. Black, Jr..................... 236
34   *Immigration and Naturalization Service* vs. *Chadha* (1983),
      A Discussion in the Supreme Court 241
35   The Implications of *Chadha* (1983), *James L. Sundquist*....... 248
      Specific Proposals: Text and Analysis
      A. Dissolution and Special Elections
         (constitutional amendment).......................... 254
      B. One-House Override (constitutional amendment) 257
      C. Referendum (constitutional amendment) 258
      D. Item Veto (statute or constitutional amendment)......... 259
      E. Legislative Veto (constitutional amendment) 261
      F. Reduced Majority for Treaty Ratification
         (constitutional amendment)........................... 262

Part 5. The Amending Process
      Introduction 265
36   Why Risk a Constitutional Convention? (1980),
      C. Herman Pritchett.................................... 267
37   What Constitutional Changes Do Americans Want?
      (1984), *Austin Ranney*.................................. 280
38   When States Amend Their Constitutions (1974),
      A. E. Dick Howard..................................... 288

Part 6. Other Constitutions
      Introduction 297
39   Modern European Constitutions and Their Relevance
      in the American Context (1984), *Lloyd N. Cutler* 299
40   Reflections of a Modern Framer (1978), *Michel Debré* 313

Suggestions for Further Reading 328
CCS Board of Directors 333

Nancy Landon Kassebaum,
Lloyd N. Cutler, and C. Douglas Dillon, Co-Chairs,
Committee on the Constitutional System

Foreword

Our society was one of the first to write a Constitution. It reflected the confident conviction of the eighteenth century Enlightenment that explicit written arrangements could be devised to structure a government that would be neither tyrannical nor impotent in its time and to allow for future amendment as experience and change might indicate.

We are all children of this faith in a rational written arrangement for governing. Our faith has encouraged us to adopt occasional changes in our Constitution—for which the framers explicitly allowed—that have assisted us in adjusting to the changes in the world in which the Constitution must function.

As we prepare to celebrate the bicentenary of this remarkable instrument, we must not stand completely in awe. We must not treat it as immutable, like the Ark of the Covenant. We must remember that while it entrenched the Bill of Rights, it also entrenched the institution of slavery, and that only the built-in capacity for amendment enabled us to correct that evil.

The framers were bold and daring men. Twice in their own lifetime, and at great risk to themselves, they changed their own form of government. They left us a charter that can and should be changed with the times. They did not make amendment easy or quick, to suit the whims of a political moment, but they made it possible after enough deliberation so that a lasting consensus for change could be formed. As Thomas Jefferson wrote: "I am certainly not an advocate for frequent and untried changes in laws and constitutions. . . . But I know also that laws and institutions must go hand in hand with progress of the human mind. As that becomes more developed, more enlightened, as new discoveries are made, new truths disclosed, and manners and opinions change with the change of circumstances, institutions must advance also and keep pace with the times."

All of us appreciate the balance and flexibility that the Constitution has built into our system of government. But our appreciation must be honest and clear-eyed. We must see the weaknesses that have appeared over two centuries as well as the enduring strengths. The rarity of constitutional amendments demonstrates how difficult it is to improve on the work of the framers. The same history also demonstrates that when the need is great enough, the required national consensus can be found.

Let us hope and pray that our generation will exercise this critical power in our time as justly and wisely as the framers did in theirs.

Donald L. Robinson

Preface

The political history of the American republic presents a paradox. On the one hand, it has been strikingly conservative. The Constitution, drafted in 1787 and ratified the following year, is the oldest written frame of national government still in operation. During the two centuries of our existence as an independent nation, Great Britain has evolved from a constitutional monarchy, through a classic, bicameral parliamentary government, to a modern prime ministerial state. The United States, meanwhile, has retained its basic form intact, including a bicameral legislature of co-equal branches and a separation of executive and legislative powers. As Daniel Boorstin has remarked, this system has come to be regarded by the American people virtually as "given."

On the other hand, Americans have been remarkably innovative in their approach to political institution-building. Parties are not mentioned anywhere in the Constitution; indeed, the framers hoped to thwart them. Yet, when it became apparent that democracy required political parties, the founding generation went ahead and created them, and their successors proceeded to develop the first modern party system, complete with caucuses, nominating conventions, and primary elections. Similarly, when the regulation of the modern marketplace required agencies that could make rules, enforce them, and adjudicate disputes over them, we set aside the doctrinaire version of the separation of powers and developed "independent regulatory commissions," combining legislative, administrative and judicial powers in a single agency.

These two impulses—conservatism about the basic structure, combined with a willingness to improvise within and around it—have served us well. Whenever the system's constraints have seemed to threaten its continuation, as in the middle of the nineteenth century and during the Great Depression, ways have been found to surmount the crisis without destroying the basic framework.

The ability of the Constitution to adapt to changes is certainly one of its great strengths, but it carries a potential danger. It encourages the assumption that our system will always work, no matter what changes occur in its own environment or in the challenges it must meet from abroad.

Common sense tells us to be wary of this assumption. Our nation has undergone tremendous changes since the end of the eighteenth century, and those changes have accelerated in recent decades. We are no longer a homogeneous, predominantly rural country, isolated from powerful competitors by vast oceans. Our economy is a complicated, delicate mechanism, which is inescapably part of a worldwide economy. The farmer in Iowa and the autoworker in Michigan depend for their livelihood on agreements made in Tokyo and Bonn. Our national defense now entails vast expenditures, and our weapons must be ready for almost instantaneous use. Meanwhile, chronic budget deficits and growing national debt, an unfavorable balance of trade, conflicting diplomatic efforts, decaying urban areas, porous borders, and a host of other problems seem to mock the capacities of our political system.

These facts compel a re-examination of our system of government. It may be that the same government that quarreled for decades about whether it had authority to build a road over the mountains can now strike the balance of a sound industrial policy: encouraging free trade, spurring domestic productivity, and protecting the environment. It may be that a government that had to wait several weeks before learning the outcome of a battle on its frontier can now decide in minutes how to respond to a nuclear attack, without sacrificing democratic account-ability. But these are momentous changes in circumstances. They vastly alter the demands on government, and they create new challenges for a nation that is committed to government of the people, by the people, and for the people.

The Committee on the Constitutional System is a group of men and women who are determined to face up to these questions. Formed in 1982, its participants include present and former senators and repre-sentatives, members of the cabinet and White House staff, officials of the national and state political parties, governors, lawyers, scholars in the fields of law, political science, and history, university and college presidents, journalists, labor officials, business and financial leaders, and other interested citizens from across the nation. It has met in Washington and in regional settings around the country to examine the political system and search for ways to improve its performance.

During its three years of meetings so far, the Committee has considered a number of proposals for improving the American political process. They have ranged from changes in party rules, to statutes, to structural amendments of the Constitution itself. The Committee is not now committed to all, some, or any of these possibilities. But as the nation approaches the two hundredth anniversary of its constitutional system, we seek to promote discussion of these crucial issues of governance and to encourage and assist our fellow-citizens to consider whether we might improve the performance of our government by adjusting its basic structure and processes.

Readers will notice that the Committee has focused on structural matters, such as the shape of the major political institutions and relations between them, rather than questions of rights and liberties, or the judicial interpretation thereof. The Committee's basic concerns have been the effectiveness and accountability of government. Has the governmental system been able to meet the challenges of modern times? Has it been able to agree on a definition of the problems that beset our nation? Can it fashion adequate responses to these challenges and see to their timely implementation? Have the people been able to hold elected officials accountable for the performance of the government?

This book of "working papers" is laid out in six parts. Part 1 contains several pieces that generally explore the need for fundamental structural change in our system of governance.

Parts 2 through 4 examine particular proposals for reform. Part 2 considers changes in party rules and public statutes (measures that would not require constitutional amendment) designed to strengthen the major political parties as instruments of democratic accountability. Part 3 looks at several proposed amendments to the Constitution that would reduce the likelihood of deadlocks developing between the legislative and executive branches of government. Part 4 takes up several possible measures for breaking deadlocks that may occur.

Parts 2 through 4 each include a section devoted to draft language of proposed reforms. These specific, concrete suggestions constitute one of the Committee's most important contributions. It is easy enough to wish that the president and Congress would cooperate more closely in framing and implementing national policy. It is quite another thing to figure out how to accomplish this change without sacrificing the ability of political leaders to check each other's excesses. These drafts will enable citizens to begin the difficult but essential task of refining ideas into specific statutory or constitutional language. Each draft in this collection is followed by a brief summary of "pros and cons," to initiate the discussion that must take place before any such proposals can be taken seriously as potential parts of our organic law.

Part 5 discusses the process of amending the Constitution. Particular attention is paid to the device, outlined in Article V of the Constitution, for calling a modern convention of delegates to draft amendments, which would then be submitted to the states for ratification. As the materials in this part and elsewhere in this volume make clear, most members of the Committee would far prefer to proceed by the traditional method.

Part 6 takes a brief look at the constitutions of several other developed nations to see what suggestions they may contain for reforming the American system of governance. The section includes a memorandum outlining aspects of European constitutions that seem most relevant to American needs, and a speech by Michel Debré, one of the principal framers of the French constitution and a keen and sympathetic observer of American government.

Finally there are suggestions for further reading about the origins and development of the American Constitution and about other proposals for constitutional revision.

This book would not have been possible without the support and encouragement of many people. The Committee owes its existence to the courageous vision and energetic leadership of its founding co-chairs, Lloyd Cutler and C. Douglas Dillon, and much of its continuing vitality to Senator Nancy Landon Kassebaum, of Kansas, who accepted the position of co-chair in early 1984. Intellectual inspiration came from James MacGregor Burns, Charles Hardin, and James Sundquist, three scholars who have shown, by their own example, that we honor the founders best by examining the constitutional system candidly, tracing its faults wherever the evidence leads, and turning our wits, as they did, to the fashioning of remedies that reflect a commitment to the highest principles of constitutional democracy.

Peter Schauffler, coordinator of the Committee's Washington office, assisted by Thomas Burnard and Mary Schauffler, has handled the administration of all its affairs, including the production of earlier editions of these papers, with skill, patience, and good humor. James Sundquist has repeatedly taken time from work on his own related book, scheduled for publication by The Brookings Institution next year, to offer guidance on this one. Gary Born, an associate in the law firm of Wilmer, Cutler and Pickering, and Steven Charnowitz have worked on the drafts of specific proposals. Several women at Smith College—particularly Virginia Risk, Christina Koenig, Catherine Worsley, Doris Lukaszuk, Margaret Trimble, Jennifer Mason, Lara Levison and Susan Im—have given vital secretarial and research assistance.

Financial support has come from The Ford Foundation, The Brookings Institution, and The Rockefeller Foundation. Support for the Committee's work as a whole has been provided by The Dillon Fund and the Hewlett and American Express foundations, and by the contributions of its members. Finally, special thanks are due to Westview Press, particularly to Miriam Gilbert and Dean Birkenkamp, who saw the need for this book and nursed it to existence in its present form.

Ashfield, Massachusetts
May, 1985

Part 1

Diagnoses of the Problem

Debates about the adequacy of the Constitution have been a recurrent theme of American political discourse. Only rarely, however, have these discussions aroused interest outside of academic circles, and even more rarely still have they led to a serious consideration of alternative forms of government.

The abuses of the Johnson and Nixon presidencies, however—what Arthur Schlesinger, Jr., called "the imperial presidency"—led to serious questioning, in and out of government, about whether the safeguards of our eighteenth century Constitution could withstand the strains and temptations of modern governance. The frustrations of the ensuing Ford and Carter administrations led almost immediately to an equal, if opposite, concern: could a government that remained doggedly faithful to constitutional restraints deal with the dangerous rush of modern problems?

For much of the general public, the popularity of the Reagan administration seemed to quell these concerns. Many thoughtful citizens, however, saw the invasion of Grenada as a reminder of the "imperial" potential, and the deadlock over the deficit, the overvaluation of the dollar and the imbalance of trade as an indication that the problems were structural, rather than personal, and seemed likely to persist, no matter who won various electoral contests.

As the analysis ripened, it came to center on the two essential measures of democratic constitutionalism: competence and accountability. Is the government capable of framing and implementing a coherent policy, or does it tend to fall into stalemate and deadlock and then resort to extra-constitutional means to cope with emergencies? Are the mechanisms of popular accountability adequate? Is the electorate capable of rendering an effective verdict on the performance of the government, and is it possible to replace a failed government? These are the questions addressed in Part 1.

The first selection is from a book by Professor Charles Hardin, who convoked several informal meetings of academics and public servants in the late 1970s and early 1980s which were forefunners of CCS. The next two pieces—an article by Lloyd Cutler and an address by C. Douglas Dillon—quite independently gave articulation to similar thoughts. It was these expressions which led to the decision to form CCS, with Cutler and Dillon as founding co-chairs.

A democracy must rest on a candid, confident relationship between elected officials and the living electorate. This relationship is threatened in modern times by the tremendous mobilization of single interest groups, and by television, which enables well-financed individuals to by-pass party organizations and make direct appeals to mass electorates. Senator Nancy Landon Kassebaum, who joined the Committee as co-chair in the spring of 1984, brought a special concern for these problems, and we include a statement from her in this section.

The nation's current economic difficulties have given urgency to the Committee's concerns. These problems produce such dislocations as inflation, rising interest rates, unemployment, budget deficits, trade imbalances, and overvalued currency. They also take the form of longer term problems, such as lagging productivity and low rates of investment. The selection from economist Lester Thurow outlines some of these problems and ends with a call for fundamental reform of governing processes.

Not everyone associated with the Committee believes that the remedy for current difficulties lies in constitutional reform. We include here two writings, by Don K. Price and Arthur M. Schlesinger, Jr., which argue that the problems can best be addressed by changes in culture and political leadership, rather than in the framework of governance. Cutler and Dillon, in a reply to Schlesinger, restate the case for structural change, and political scientist James M. Burns tells why the Committee's work may be useful even though the current odds seem to lie against constitutional amendment.

The pieces by Neal Pierce and Elmer Staats are included to reflect the Committee's ongoing deliberations. Pierce speaks about strains in the federal system, a topic which has been of serious concern to several participants, including Benjamin Read and Henry Reuss. The letter from Staats was written shortly after the September, 1984, national meeting.

The final selection in this Part is a summary of the Committee's position that a consideration of structural changes should be part of the bicentennial of the Constitution.

Charles Hardin

1. The Crisis and Its Cure (1974)

Charles Hardin, a founder of the Committee on the Constitutional System, is professor emeritus of political science at the University of California, Davis. He has served in the Agriculture Department and taught for many years at the University of Chicago. His book, Presidential Power and Accountability: Toward a New Constitution, *of which the following material constitutes the introductory chapter, was published in the wake of the Johnson and Nixon presidencies.*

In 1973 America was gripped by its gravest political crisis since the Civil War. The president all too often was out of control. Unbridled bureaucracies acted with the arrogance befitting their autonomy. Many pressure groups exercised appalling political leverage. Increasingly disorganized, the public felt deceived and disillusioned. The threat of an inquisitorial government's espionage—and even of armed attacks by its minions, regardless of constitutional guarantees—was in the air. A former high official of the Nixon White House, asked by a Senate Watergate Committee member what advice he would give young people inquiring about careers in government, replied—"Stay away!" The audience rocked with cynical laughter. The heritage of Washington, Jefferson, and Lincoln—so long miraculously intact—was crumbling to dust.

A sense of the need for fundamental changes was abroad. Recent presidents—Eisenhower, Kennedy, and Lyndon B. Johnson—had considered and some had urged basic constitutional reforms. In 1973 Richard M. Nixon endorsed a single six-year term for presidents coupled with a four-year term for congressmen. Ironically, his suggestion coincided with the most serious discussion of presidential impeachment since

Reprinted by permission of the University of Chicago Press, from *Presidential Power and Accountability*, by Charles Hardin. Copyright 1974.

Andrew Johnson. The thought of impeachment made many persons shudder. And yet there was the haunting nightmare of a discredited president continuing in office for forty months. Senator Edward M. Kennedy and ABC commentator Howard K. Smith pointed out that the parliamentary system would enable the displacement of a politically disabled president by political means and for political reasons—a great improvement over impeachment. Clark Clifford, formerly special counsel to President Truman and secretary of defense under President Johnson, called for the president and vice-president to resign pursuant to the twenty-fifth amendment. Among those who denounced Clifford was Arthur H. Dean, formerly negotiator at Panmunjom for the United States and sixteen other nations, American ambassador to South Korea, and holder of many other distinguished assignments. But all that was in the summer; by November 1973 Vice-President Spiro T. Agnew had resigned, the House of Representatives was inquiring through its committee on the judiciary into the evidence for impeaching the president, and the chorus of voices calling for the president to resign had swelled while those opposing resignation had fallen virtually silent.

In this period a number of people, including CBS commentator Eric Sevareid, urged Congress to reassert itself, forgetting that Congress had repeatedly proven unable to provide the concerted leadership required by the times. Former Senator Eugene McCarthy advocated "depersonalizing" the presidency in order to free the energies, "intellectual, spiritual, and moral," of the people. In reality what emerged from the people was a collective sense of the inevitable and virtually ubiquitous crookedness of politicians.

In this situation, two facts were of first importance. First, the crisis of 1973 had been foreshadowed. Presidential abuse of power, though seriously worsened, had been visible for decades; the inadequacy of Congress to provide an alternative to presidential government had been shown from the close of the Civil War to the end of the nineteenth century and fitfully demonstrated again thereafter; and the malaise of public opinion had appeared in the late 1960s. In other words, the problems were long-standing and were rooted in structural faults; they were not associated with one adminstration and one series of events. Second, there was—there is—a way out, painful, difficult, and dangerous as it may be. It will require constitutional surgery at least as severe as that of 1787. The end result can be briefly stated as "presidential power and accountability" or, to put it another way, as presidential leadership and party government.

It will be useful to set forth the diagnosis and the prescription in an outline:

1. A foremost requirement of a great power is strong executive leadership. The political demand for it, manifest world-wide, arises from the present condition of international relationships, given the state of the military arts; from the inexorable need to develop and use science to maintain national security; and from the nature of modern economic and social organization especially when coupled with emergent ecological considerations.

2. America met the first requirement by its presidency; but in recent decades the presidency has escaped the political controls essential to constitutional, i.e., *limited*, government. New controls must be found.

3. The search for controls is complicated by the danger that curbs may diminish the effectiveness of the presidency. The executive needs energy today at least as much as in the critical years immediately following 1787 when the framers concluded that it should be wielded by a single pair of hands to achieve the "decision, activity, secrecy [yes, secrecy!], and despatch" essential in safeguarding the republic. How to maintain the full force and effect of the presidency and yet to restrain those presidential excesses so generously demonstrated in this century?

4. The beginning of the answer lies in the relationship between the president and the people. The controlling principle had been *vox populi, vox dei*. The voice of the people is the voice of God. This has been the major premise of our theory of representation; for the people cannot govern, and the president has become their surrogate. Accordingly, he personifies their political authority. When he speaks *ex cathedra* from atop his pyramid of forty million votes, with the bulk of the populace reportedly behind him, he is awe-inspiring. His infallibility especially impresses those closest to him whose approval if not their adulation convinces him that he is larger than life. And yet all this authority may dissolve if the public turns against him. The people's choice becomes the people's curse. We have seen it happen four times in this century. The results of an abrupt decline in presidential power are often unfortunate and may be disastrous.

5. It follows (although the logic may be clear only after further reading and reflection) that a measure of control over the president can be provided by subjecting him to the criticism of an organized, focused opposition with leadership centered in one person who will be continuously visible and vocal as the alternative to the president. As the presidency is unified, so should the opposition be unified. As the president speaks with a single voice, so should he be answered by a single voice instead of a clamor of discordant

and little-known voices in a legislative body whose present genius is the dispersion of power. If a focused opposition can be achieved, the crucial relationship between the public and its government will begin to change.

6. To establish an opposition we must turn to Congress, and the first step is to contradict the myth that the end of providing greater controls over the president without unduly undermining his power may be accomplished merely by increasing the weight of Congress. When powers are separated they are ordinarily less shared than displaced. Either power resides in the presidency with some congressional criticism and subject to some bargaining, or it shifts to the bureaucracy, defined as comprising a conglomerate of power among agencies, strategic congressmen, and interest groups. It must be understood that the genius of Congress is opposite to that of the presidency. Where the presidency comes to life in the unification of power, Congress disperses power among a hundred leaders each with his own base in seniority and in sectional jurisdiction (over taxation, finance, transportation, military, labor, and judiciary or whatever). It appears to be impossible to organize in Congress a concentration of power sufficient to provide an orchestrated and programmatic opposition—let alone a centralized executive government.

7. The nature of Congress is strongly influenced by the manner of its selection—staggered terms for senators, two-year terms for representatives. As with the president, this situation induces a particular relationship between Congress and the public. Where the president is elected as the nonpareil, the father, the leader, the magic helper, the incarnation of the infallible goodness and wisdom of the people, congressmen and senators tend to be chosen as a means of assuring their constituents' shares of national largesse. Henry Adams cynically wrote, "A congressman is like a hog. You have to kick him in the snout." The grain of truth in his statement exists by virtue of the congressman's expression of the sacred demands of the public. The voter's political obligation in electing congressmen is held to be exhausted when he communicates his wants to government. The voter has no share in the responsibility of government. Indeed, the "responsible electorate" has been authoritatively defined as one that knows on which side its bread is buttered. The logical outcome for public opinion is that Congress "as a whole" is despised because congressmen are generally seen as serving the interests of others— but individual congressmen are typically admired and appreciated by the active and knowledgeable among their constituents.

8. The first reform then must strike at the relationships not only between president and Congress but also between both and the public. The president and Congress should be elected for simultaneous four-year terms. In addition, the defeated candidate for the presidency should have a seat in the House of Representatives, priority in committees and on the floor, and a staff, offices, and other prerequisites suitable to his position as the leader of the opposition.

9. Candidates for Congress of both parties, including a generous slate of candidates running at large on a national ticket, should constitute the nominating conventions for presidential candidates so that when people vote or otherwise share in nominations of congressmen they know that they are also naming those who will nominate for the presidency. The office of vice-president should be abolished. Other reforms will be explained in the last chapter [see page 000]—especially the steps to reduce the political leverage of the Senate; the introduction of national at-large candidates in a manner that will ensure the winning presidential candidate a working majority in the House of Representatives; and the provision that the minority party in Congress may remove the defeated presidential candidate as leader of the opposition but that it must replace him with another leader.

10. These changes should give the voters a new sense of their function and of their relationship to government. They will be able to realize a political responsibility that the present constitution denies them, namely, that they share in the selection of a government—or, equally important, of an opposition. This action is rich in significance. *First*, it will cause a salutary change in a basic premise of American political thought. Implicit in the new electoral system is the realization that government—far from being "the greatest of all reflections on human nature"—is a necessity if people are to dwell, as they must as human beings, in communities. *Second*, these changes will give voters the experience that will vindicate an improved theory of representation. Instead of perpetuating the myth that people in general are in position and sufficiently informed to make all political decisions—the idea of the General Will and of the initiative and referendum dear to the Progressives—the new assumption will be in accordance with a sensible division of political labor: the people will elect a government—and an opposition—and hold them accountable, the one for governing, the other for systematically criticizing government during its term in office. A workable theory of representative democracy should emerge. *Third*, an extremely significant step will be taken to restore

political controls over the president without diminishing his essential power. He would be seen as the necessary and legitimate leader for a given period rather than as the personification of the deity domiciled in the collective breast of the populace. Instead of governmental decisions resting on the ultimate sanction of the popular will, they would rest on a majority, a sufficiently legitimizing concept, but one that takes into account the fact that nearly half the people will consider the president to be politically fallible—and one that will prevail merely for the good and democratic reason that in a civilized community there must be some way other than violence to settle disputes. Control over the president derived from these propositions will be enhanced by the presence of the leader of the opposition and the alternative government that he heads. The tendency for the instincts, the whims, the idiosyncrasies, or the mind-sets of presidents to become manifest in dangerous initiatives should be greatly reduced. *Fourth*, the sovereign right of the majority to choose a government that, on balance, it considers more favorable to its interests would not be denied; but the emphasis would be placed, where it should be if the public is to have a practicable and active share in the awful responsibility of modern government, on the choice of who shall rule. *Fifth*, the divisions in the campaign should persist during the period of governance, subject, of course, to accretion and erosion of political parties "like a ball of sticky popcorn"; and this quality of persistence, along with previous characteristics of the new public, will further rationalize the relationship of the people to their goverment.

11. The new framework of government will increase the ability of politicians to bring bureaucracy as it has crystallized in America under control. And the balance of power between public government and private groups, which is unfortunately tipped toward private groups in the traditional polity of America, will be redressed.

12. Beyond these considerations looms the inability of the American system to replace a president who has become politically discredited. Impeachment is inadequate. The fault of impeachment for removing presidents lies essentially in its juridical character, its legal procedures, its indictments and its trial according to the rules of evidence, to ascertain the *individual's* criminal guilt or innocence. But emphasis on the *legal* criminality of *individuals* hides and even denies the *political* responsibility that must by *collective*. In the modern age the intricate and complex problems of government require a collegial approach (as the current political

argot recognizes—the White House team, the task forces, the national security council, the domestic council, the presidential game plan). Political adequacy is judged not by weighing individual guilt or innocence according to the rules of evidence but rather by political procedures for testing confidence in the prudence and judgment of government. Legal guilt by association is anathema; political liability by association is essential. The political process should be capable of registering the collective judgment of responsible politicians—who, in turn, are informed by their sense of public opinion—on the prudence and wisdom of governments. The legality of a president's acts may figure in such judgments, but more important are decisions on presidential prudence, grasp of events, will, wisdom, and self-control.

The reforms proposed will not in themselves provide a vote of confidence, but they will create the setting in which such votes should naturally evolve. For an essential assumption would be that a president needs a majority in the House of Representatives to govern. If he loses the majority he will be incapacitated, and it would be logical for him to resign. It will be argued that the experience of parliamentary regimes shows governments to be extremely durable: prime minsters no longer get ousted because they lose majorities. And yet prime ministers do resign because they have to retain the leadership at least of their own party; and there are ways short of defection in which party members can convey to the prime minister their loss of confidence.

13. Replacement of the president by an adverse vote of confidence—or by so obvious a disintegration in the loyalty of his supporters that he feels compelled to resign—should make way for another evolutionary step, namely, dissolving government and holding new elections. Once this step is taken, it is hoped, it will become the normal way that one government ends and another is chosen. When this happens, the endless nominating and electoral campaigns will be compressed into a few weeks. One benefit will be the reduction of the cost of campaigns and of the leverage of money in politics. Stringent laws on campaign financing will become enforceable.

14. Finally, there is the promise of more honest politics and less corruptible politicians. This result will come from the collegial responsibility of party government toward which all the reforms suggested above will work. The inherited American system puts all stress on the individual. He can keep himself clean, untainted by the sordid acts of the grafters who surround him, each of whom may profit individually from his crimes—but also may be

apprehended, convicted, and sentenced. In the new system members of a government will understand that, just as they govern collectively, so they will be judged collectively for the shortcomings of their colleagues. Party government will provide strong incentives for obedience to a code of political ethics.

Lloyd N. Cutler

2. To Form a Government (1980)

Lloyd Cutler, co-chair of the Committee on the Constitutional System, is an attorney in Washington. This article was published in Foreign Affairs *magazine while Cutler was serving in the White House as counsel to President Carter. Although it was severely criticized as an apologia for a weak presidency, it was welcomed by many experienced and thoughtful people as a cogent analysis of the structural weaknesses of American goverment and a bold call to reconsider the framers' design.*

[On May 10, 1940, Winston Churchill was summoned to Buckingham Palace.] His Majesty received me most graciously and bade me sit down. He looked at me searchingly and quizzically for some moments, and then said: "I suppose you don't know why I have sent for you?" Adopting his mood, I replied: "Sir, I simply couldn't imagine why." He laughed and said: "I want to ask you to form a government." I said I would certainly do so.

> Winston S. Churchill
> *The Gathering Storm* (1948)

Our society was one of the first to write a Constitution. This reflected the confident conviction of the Enlightenment that explicit written arrangements could be devised to structure a government that would be neither tyrannical nor impotent in its time, and to allow for future amendment as experience and change might require.

We are all children of this faith in a rational written arrangement for governing. Our faith should encourage us to consider changes in our Constitution—for which the framers explicitly allowed—that would assist us in adjusting to the changes in the world in which the Constitution must function. Yet we tend to resist suggestions that amendments to our existing constitutional framework are needed to govern our portion of the interdependent world society we have become, and to cope with the resulting problems that all contemporary governments must resolve.

A particular shortcoming in need of a remedy is the structural inability of our government to propose, legislate and administer a balanced program for governing. In parliamentary terms, one might say that under the U.S. Constitution it is not now feasible to "form a government." The separation of powers between the legislative and executive branches, whatever its merits in 1793, has become a structure that almost guarantees stalemate today. As we wonder why we are having such a difficult time making decisions we all know must be made, and projecting our power and leadership, we should reflect on whether this is one big reason.

We elect one presidential candidate over another on the basis of our judgment of the overall program he presents, his ability to carry it out, and his capacity to adapt his program to new developments as they arise. We elected President Carter, whose program included, as one of its most important elements, the successful completion of the SALT II negotiations that his two predecessors had been conducting since 1972. President Carter did complete and sign a SALT II Treaty, in June 1979, which he and his cabinet regarded as very much in the national security interests of the United States. Notwithstanding recent events, the president and his cabinet still hold that view—indeed they believe the mounting intensity of our confrontation with the Soviet Union makes it even more important for the two superpowers to adopt and abide by explicit rules as to the size and quality of each side's strategic nuclear arsenal, and as to how each side can verify what the other side is doing.

But because we do not "form a government," it has not been possible for President Carter to carry out this major part of his program.

Of course the constitutional requirement of Senate advice and consent to treaties presents a special situation. The case for the two-thirds rule was much stronger in 1793, when events abroad rarely affected this isolated continent, and when "entangling foreign alliances" were viewed with a skeptical eye. Whether it should be maintained in an age when most treaties deal with such subjects as taxation and trade is open to question. No parliamentary regime anywhere in the world has a similar provision. But in the American case—at least for major issues like SALT—there is merit to the view that treaties should indeed require the careful bipartisan consultation essential to win a two-thirds majority. This is the principle that Woodrow Wilson fatally neglected in 1919. But it has been carefully observed by recent presidents, including

President Carter for the Panama Canal treaties and the SALT II Treaty. In each of these cases there was a clear prior record of support by previous Republican administrations, and there would surely have been enough votes for fairly rapid ratification if the president could have counted on the total or near-total support of his own party—if, in short, he had truly formed a government, with a legislative majority which takes the responsibility for governing.

Treaties may indeed present special cases, and I do not argue here for any change in the historic two-thirds requirement. But our inability to "form a government" able to ratify SALT II is replicated regularly over the whole range of legislation required to carry out any president's overall program, foreign and domestic. Although the enactment of legislation takes only a simple majority of both houses, that majority is very difficult to achieve. Any part of the president's legislative record of any presidency may bear little resemblance to the overall program the president wanted to carry out. Energy and the budget provide two current and critical examples. Indeed SALT II itself could have been presented for approval by a simple majority of each house under existing arms control legislation, but the administration deemed this task even more difficult than achieving a two-thirds vote in the Senate. And this difficulty is of course compounded when the president's party does not even hold the majority of the seats in both houses, as was the case from 1946 to 1948, from 1954 to 1960 and from 1968 to 1976—or almost half the duration of the last seven administrations.

The Constitution does not require or even permit in such a case the holding of a new election, in which those who oppose the president can seek office to carry out their own overall program. Indeed, the opponents of each element of the president's overall program usually have a different makeup from one element to another. They would probably be unable to get together on any overall program of their own, or to obtain the congressional votes to carry it out. As a result the stalemate continues, and because we do not form a government, we have no overall program at all. We cannot fairly hold the president accountable for the success or failure of his overall program, because he lacks the constitutional power to put that program into effect.

Compare this with the structure of parliamentary governments. A parliamentary government may have no written constitution, as in the United Kingdom. Or it may have a written constitution, as in West Germany, Japan, and Ireland, that in other respects—such as an independent judiciary and an entrenched Bill of Rights—closely resembles our own. But while there may be a ceremonial president or, as in Japan, an emperor, the executive consists of those members of the legislature chosen by the elected legislative majority. The majority elects a premier or prime minister from among its number, and he selects other leading members of the majority as the members of his cabinet. The majority as a whole is responsible for forming and conducting the "government." If any key part of its overall program is rejected by the legislature, or if a vote of "no confidence" is carried, the "government" must resign and either a new "government" must be formed out of the existing legislature or a new legislative election must be held. If the program *is* legislated, the public can judge the results and can decide at the next regular election whether to reelect the majority or turn it out. At all times the voting public knows who is in charge, and whom to hold accountable for success or failure.

Operating under a parliamentary system, Chancellor Helmut Schmidt formed the present West German government with a majority of only four, but he has succeeded in carrying out his overall program these past five years. Last year Prime Minister Margaret Thatcher won a majority of some 30 to 40 in the British Parliament. She has a very radical program, one that can make fundamental changes in the economy, social fabric and foreign policy of the United Kingdom. There is room for legitimate doubt as to whether her overall program will achieve its objectives and, even if it does, whether it will prove popular enough to reelect her government at the next election. But there is not the slightest doubt that she will be able to legislate her entire program, including any modifications she makes to meet new problems. In a parliamentary system, it is the duty of each majority member of the legislature to vote for each element of the government's progam, and the government possesses the means to punish members if they do not. In a very real sense, each member's political and electoral future is tied to the fate of the government his majority has formed. Politically speaking, he lives or dies by whether that government lives or dies.

President Carter's party has a much larger majority percentage in both houses of Congress than Chancellor Schmidt or Prime Minister Thatcher. But this comfortable majority does not even begin to assure that President Carter or any other president can rely on that majority to vote for each element of his program. No member of that majority has the constitutional duty or the practical political need to vote for each element of the president's program. Neither the president nor the leaders of the legislative majority have the means to punish him if he does not. In the famous phrase of Joe Jacobs, the fight manager, "It's every man for theirself."

Let me cite one example. In the British House of Commons, just as in our own House, some of the majority leaders are called the whips. In the Commons, the whips do just what their title implies. If the government cares about the pending vote, they "whip" the fellow members of the majority into compliance, under pain of party discipline if a member disobeys. On the most important votes, the leaders invoke what is called a three-line whip, which must be obeyed on pain of resignation or expulsion from the party.

In our House, the majority whip, who happens to be one of our very best Democratic legislators, can himself feel free to leave his Democratic president and the rest of the House Democratic leadership on a crucial vote, if he believes it important to his constituency and his conscience to vote the other way. When he does so, he is not expected or required to resign his leadership post; indeed he is back a few hours later "whipping" his fellow members of the majority to vote with the president and the leadership on some other issue. But all other members are equally free to vote against the president and the leadership when they feel it important to do so. The president and the leaders have a few sticks and carrots they can use to punish or reward, but nothing even approaching the power that Prime Minister Thatcher's government or Chancellor Schmidt's government can wield against any errant member of the majority.

I am hardly the first to notice this fault. As Judge Carl McGowan has reminded us, the "young and rising academic star in the field of political science, Woodrow Wilson—happily unaware of what the future held for him in terms of successive domination of, and defeat by, the Congress—despaired in the late 19th century of weakness of the executive branch vis-a-vis the legislative, so much so that he concluded that a coalescence of the two in the style of English parliamentary government was the only hope."

As Wilson put it, "power and strict accountability for its use are the essential constituents of good government." Our separation of executive and legislative power fractions power and prevents accountability.

In drawing this comparison, I am not blind to the proven weaknesses of parliamentary government, or to the virtues which our forefathers saw in separating the executive from the legislature. In particular, the parliamentary system lacks the ability of a separate and vigilant legislature to investigate and curb the abuse of power by an arbitrary or corrupt executive. Our own recent history has underscored this virtue of separating these two branches.

Moreover, our division of executive from legislative responsibility also means that a great many more voters are represented in positions of power, rather than as mere members of a "loyal opposition." If I am a Democrat in a Republican district, my vote in the presidential election may still give me a proportional impact. And if my party elects a president, I do not feel—as almost half the voters in a parliamentary constituency like Oxford must feel—wholly unrepresented. One result of this division is a sort of a permanent centrism. While this means that no extreme or Thatcher-like program can be legislated, it means also that there are fewer wild swings in statutory policy.

This is also a virtue of the constitutional division of responsibility. It is perhaps what John Adams had in mind when, at the end of his life, he wrote to his old friend and adversary, Thomas Jefferson, that "checks and balances, Jefferson, . . . are our only security, for the progress of mind, as well as the security of body."

But these virtues of separation are not without their costs. I believe these costs have been mounting in the last half-century, and that it is time to examine whether we can reduce the costs of separation without losing its virtues.

During this century, other nations have adopted written constitutions, sometimes with our help, that blend the virtues of our system with those of the parliamentary system. The Irish Constitution contains a replica of our Bill of Rights, an independent Supreme Court that can declare acts of government unconstitutional, a figure-head president, and a parliamentary system. The postwar German and Japanese constitutions, which we helped draft, are essentially the same. While the Gaullist French Constitution contains a Bill of Rights somewhat weaker than ours, it provides for a strong president who can dismiss the legislature and call for new elections. But it also retains the parliamentary system and its blend of executive and legislative power achieved by forming a government out of the elected legislative majority. The president, however, appoints the premier or first minister.

* * *

We are not about to revise our own Constitution so as to incorporate a true parliamentary system. But we do need to find a way of coming closer to the parliamentary concept of "forming a government," under which the elected majority is able to carry out an overall program and is held accountable for its success or failure.

There are several reasons why it is far more important in 1980 than it was in 1940, 1900 or 1800 for our government to have the capability to formulate and carry out an overall program.

The first reason is that government is now constantly required to make a different kind of choice than usually in the past, a kind for which it is difficult to obtain a broad consensus. That kind of choice, which one may call "allocative," has become the fundamental challenge to government today. As a recent newspaper article put it:

> The domestic programs of the last two decades are no longer seen as broad campaigns to curb pollution or end poverty or improve health care. As these

programs have filtered down through an expanding network of regulation, they single out winners and losers. The losers may be workers who blame a lost promotion on equal employment programs; a chemical plant fighting a tough pollution control order; a contractor who bids unsuccessfully for a government contract, or a gas station owner who wants a larger fuel allotment.

This is a way of recognizing that, in giving government great responsibilities, we have forced a series of choices among these responsibilities.

During the second half of this century, our government has adopted a wide variety of national goals. Many of these goals—checking inflation, spurring economic growth, reducing unemployment, protecting our national security, assuring equal opportunity, increasing social security, cleaning up the environment, improving energy efficiency—conflict with one another, and all of them compete for the same resources. There may have been a time when we could simultaneously pursue all of these goals to the utmost. But even in a country as rich as this one, that time is now past. One of the central tasks of modern government is to make wise balancing choices among courses of action that pursue one or more of our many conflicting and competing objectives.

Furthermore, as new economic or social problems are recognized, a responsible government must *adjust* these priorities. In the case of energy policy, the need to accept realistic oil prices has had to be balanced against the immediate impact of drastic price increases on consumers and affected industries, and on the overall rate of inflation. And to cope with the energy crisis, earlier objectives of policy have had to be accommodated along the way. Reconciling one goal with another is a continuous process. A critical regulatory goal of 1965 (auto safety) had to be reconciled with an equally critical regulatory goal of 1970 (clean air) long before the auto safety goal had been achieved, just as both these critical goals had to be reconciled with 1975's key goal (closing the energy gap) long before either auto safety or clean air had lost their importance. Reconciliation was needed because many auto safety regulations had the effect of increasing vehicle size and weight and therefore increasing gasoline consumption and undesirable emissions, and also because auto emission control devices tend to increase gasoline consumption. Moreover, throughout this 15-year period, we have had to reconcile all three of these goals with another critical national objective—wage and price stability—when in pursuit of these other goals we make vehicles more costly to purchase and operate.

And now, in 1980, we find our auto industry at a serious competitive disadvantage vis-a-vis Japanese and European imports, making it necessary to limit those regulatory burdens which aggravate the extent of the disadvantage. A responsible government must be able to adapt its programs to achieve the best balance among its conflicting goals as each new development arises.

For balancing choices like these, a kind of political triage, it is almost impossible to achieve a broad consensus. Every group will be against some part of the balance. If the "losers" on each item are given a veto on that part of the balance, a sensible balance cannot be struck.

The second reason is that we live in an increasingly interdependent world. What happens in the distant places is now just as consequential for our security and our economy as what happens in Seattle or Miami. No one today would use the term "Afghanistanism," as the opposition benches did in the British Parliament a century ago, to deride the government's preoccupation with a war in that distant land. No one would say today, as President Wilson said in 1914, that general European war could not affect us and is no concern of ours. We are now an integral part of a closely interconnected world economic and political system. We have to respond as quickly and decisively to what happens abroad as to what happens within the portion of this world system that is governed under our Constitution.

New problems requiring new adjustments come up even more frequently over the foreign horizon than the domestic one. Consider the rapid succession of events and crises since President Carter took up the relay baton for his leg of the SALT II negotiations back in 1977: the signing of the Egyptian-Israeli peace treaty over Soviet and Arab opposition, the Soviet-Cuban assistance to guerrilla forces in Africa and the Arabian peninsula, the recognition of the People's Republic of China, the final agreement on the SALT II terms and the signing of the treaty in Vienna, the revolution in Iran and later seizure of our hostages, the military coup in Korea, the Soviet-supported Vietnamese invasion of Kampuchea, our growing dependence on foreign oil from politically undependable sources, the affair of the Soviet brigade in Cuba, the polarization of rightist and leftist elements in Central America, and finally (that is, until the next crisis a month or two from now) the Soviet invasion of Afghanistan and the added threat it poses to the states of Southwest Asia and to the vital oil supplies of Europe, Japan and the United States.

Each of these portentous events required a prompt reaction and response from our government, including in many cases a decision as to how it would affect our position on the SALT II treaty. The government has to be able to adapt its overall program to deal with each such event as it arises, and it has to be able to execute the adapted program with reasonable dispatch. Many of these adaptations—such as changes in the levels and direction of military and economic assistance—require joint action by the president and the Congress, something that is far from automatic under our system. And when Congress does act, it is prone to impose statutory conditions or prohibitions that fetter the president's policy discretion to negotiate an appropriate assistance package or to adapt it to fit even later developments. The congressional bans on military assistance to Turkey, any form of assistance to the contending forces in Angola, and any aid to Argentina if it did not meet our human rights criteria by a deadline now past, are typical examples.

Indeed, the doubt that Congress will approve a presidential foreign policy initiative has seriously compromised our ability to make binding agreements with nations that "form a government." Given the fate of SALT II and lesser treaties, and the frequent congressional vetoes of other foreign policy actions, other nations now realize that our executive branch commitments are not as binding as theirs, that Congress may block any agreement at all, and that at the very least they must hold something back for a subsequent round of bargaining with the Congress.

The third reason is the change in Congress and its relationship to the executive. When the Federalist and Democratic Republican parties held power, a Hamilton or a Gallatin would serve in the cabinet, but they continued to lead rather than report to their party colleagues in the houses of Congress. Even when the locus of congressional leadership shifted from the cabinet to the leaders of Congress itself, in the early nineteenth century, it was a congressional leadership capable of collaboration with the executive. This was true until very recently. The Johnson-Rayburn collaboration with Eisenhower a generation ago is an instructive example. But now Congress itself has changed.

There have been the well-intended democratic reforms of Congress, and the enormous growth of the professional legislative staff. The former ability of the president to sit down with ten or fifteen leaders in each house, and to agree on a program which those leaders could carry through Congress, has virtually disappeared. The committee chairmen and the leaders no longer have the instruments of power that once enabled them to lead. A Lyndon Johnson would have a much harder time getting his way as majority leader today than when he did hold and pull these strings of power in the 1950s. When Senator Mansfield became majority leader in 1961, he changed the practice of awarding committee chairmanships on the basis of seniority. He declared that all senators are created equal. He gave every Democratic senator a major committee assignment and then a subcommittee chairmanship, adding to the sharing of power by reducing the leadership's control.

In the House the seniority system was scrapped. Now the House majority caucus—not the leadership—picks the committee chairmen and the subcommittee chairmen as well. The House parliamentarian has lost the critical power to refer bills to a single committee selected by the speaker. Now bills like the energy bills go to several committees which then report conflicting versions back to the floor. Now mark-up sessions take place in public; indeed, even the House-Senate joint conference committees, at which differing versions of the same measure are reconciled, must meet and barter in public.

The recent conference committees on the Synthetic Fuels Corporation and the Energy Mobilization Board, for example, were so big and their procedures so cumbersome that they took six months to reach agreement, and then the agreement on the Board was rejected by the House. All this means that there are no longer a few leaders with power who *can* collaborate with the president. Power is further diffused by the growth of legislative staffs, sometimes making it difficult for the members even to collaborate with each other. In the past five years, the Senate alone has hired 700 additional staff members, an average of seven per member.

There is also the decline of party discipline and the decline of the political party itself. Presidential candidates are no longer selected, as Adlai Stevenson was selected, by the leaders or bosses of their party. Who are the party leaders today? There are no such people. The party is no longer the instrument that selects the candidate. Indeed, the party today, as a practical matter, is no more than a neutral open forum that holds the primary or caucus in which candidates for president and for Congress may compete for favor and be elected. The party does not dispense most of the money needed for campaigning, the way the European and Japanese parties do. The candidates raise most of their own money. To the extent that money influences legislative votes, it comes not from a party with a balanced program, but from a variety of single-interest groups.

We now have a great many diverse and highly organized interest groups—not just broad-based agriculture, labor, business and ethnic groups interested in a wide variety of issues affecting their members. We now have single-issue groups—environmental, consumer, abortion, right to life, pro- and anti-SALT, pro- and anti-nuclear—that stand ready to lobby for their single issue and to reward or punish legislators, both in cash and at the ballot box, according to how they respond on the single issue that is the group's raison d'etre. And on many specific foreign policy issues involving particular countries, there are exceptionally strong voting blocs in this wonderful melting pot of a nation that exert a great deal of influence on individual senators and congressmen.

*   *   *

It is useful to compare this modern failure of our governmental structure with its earlier classic successes. There can be no structural fault, it might be said, so long as an FDR could put through an entire anti-depression program in 100 days, or an LBJ could enact a broad program for social justice three decades later. These infrequent exceptions, however, confirm the general rule of stalemate.

If we look closely we will find that in this century the system has succeeded only on the rare occasions when there is an unusual event that brings us together and creates substantial consensus throughout the country on the need for a whole new program. FDR had such a consensus in the early days of the New Deal, and from Pearl Harbor to the end of World War II. But we tend to forget that in 1937 his court-packing plan was justifiably rejected by Congress—a good point for those who favor complete separation of the executive from the legislature—and that as late as August 1941, when President Roosevelt called on Congress to pass a renewal of the Selective Service Act, passage was gained by a single vote in the House. Lyndon Johnson had such a consensus for both his domestic and his Vietnam initiatives during the first three years after the shock of John Kennedy's assassination brought us together. But it was gone by 1968. Jimmy Carter has had it this past winter and spring for his responses to the events in Iran and Afghanistan and to the belated realization of our need for greater energy self-sufficiency, but he may not hold it for long. Yet the consensus on Afghanistan was marred by the long congressional delay in appropriating the small amounts needed to register 19- and 20-year olds under the Selective Service Act—a delay that at least blurred the intended impact of this signal to the world of our determination to oppose further Soviet aggression.

When the great crisis and the resulting large consensus are not there— when the country is divided somewhere between 55–45 and 45–55 on each of a wide set of issues, and when the makeup of the majority is different on every issue—it has not been possible for any modern president to "form a government" that could legislate and carry out his overall program.

Yet modern government has to respond promptly to a wide range of new challenges. Its responses cannot be limited to those for which there is a large consensus induced by some crisis. Modern government also has to work in every presidency, not just in one presidency out of four, when a Wilson, an FDR, or an LBJ comes along. It also has to work for the president's full time in office, as it did not even for Wilson and LBJ. When they needed congressional support for the most important issue of their presidencies, they could not get it.

When the president gets only "half a loaf" of his overall program, this half a loaf is not necessarily better than none, because it may lack the essential quality of balance. And half a loaf leaves both the president and the public in the worst of all possible worlds. The public—and the press—still expect the president to govern. But the president cannot achieve his overall program, and the public cannot fairly blame the president, because he does not have the power to legislate and execute his program. Nor can the public fairly blame the individual members of Congress, because the Constitution allows them to disclaim any responsibility for forming a government and hence any accountability for its failures.

Of course the presidency always has been and will continue to be what Theodore Roosevelt called "a bully pulpit"—not a place from which to "bully" in the sense of intimidating the Congress and the public, but in the idiom of TR's day a marvelous place from which to hort and lift up Congress and the public. All presidents have used the bully pulpit in this way, and this is one reason why the American people continue to revere the office and almost always revere its incumbent. Television has probably amplified the power of the bully pulpit, but it has also shortened the time span of power; few television performers can hold their audiences for four consecutive years. In any event, a bully pulpit, while a glorious thing to have and to employ, is not a government, and it has not been enough to enable any postwar president to "form a government" for his entire term.

Finally, the myth persists that the existing system can be made to work satisfactorily if only the president will take the trouble to consult closely with the Congress. If one looks back at the period between 1947 and 1965 there were indeed remarkable cases, at least in the field of foreign policy, where such consultation worked to great effect, even across party lines. The relationships between Senator Vandenberg and Secretaries Marshall and Acheson, and between Senator George and Secretary Dulles, come readily to mind. But these examples were in an era of strong leadership within the Congress, and of unusual national consensus on the overall objectives of foreign policy and the measures needed to carry it out.

Even when these elements have not been present, every president has indeed tried to work with the majority in Congress, and the majority in every Congress has tried to work with the president. Within this past year, when there has been a large consensus in response to the crises in Afghanistan and Iran, a notable achievement has been a daily private briefing of congressional leaders by the secretary of state, and weekly private briefings with all Senate and House members who want to attend—a step that has helped to keep that consensus in being.

Another achievement of recent times is the development of the congressional budget process, exemplified by the cooperation between the congressional leadership and the president in framing the 1981 budget.

But even on Iran, Afghanistan and the budget, the jury is still out on how long the large consensus will hold. And except on the rare issues where there is such a consensus, the structural problems usually prove too difficult to overcome. In each administration, it becomes progressively more difficult to make the present system work effectively on the range of issues, both domestic and foreign, that the United States must now manage even though there is no large consensus.

*   *   *

If we decide we want the capability of forming government, the only way to do so is to amend the Constitution. Amending the Constitution, of course, is extremely difficult. Since 1793, when the Bill of Rights was added, we have amended the Constitution only sixteen times. Some of these amendments were structural, such as the direct election of senators, votes for women and 18-year-olds, the two-term limit for presidents, and the selection of a successor vice-president. But none has touched the basic separation of executive and legislative powers.

The most one can hope for is a set of modest changes that would make our structure work somewhat more in the manner of a parliamentary system, with somewhat less separation between the executive and the legislature than now exists . . . . [Cutler here outlines several possible revisions of the Constitution, most of which appear in his Roberts Lecture (see page 93). He then concludes as follows:]

The point of this article is not to persuade the reader of the virtue of any particular amendment. I am far from persuaded myself. But I am convinced of these propositions:

- We need to do better than we have in "forming a government" for this country, and this need is becoming more acute.
- The structure of our Constitution prevents us from doing significantly better.
- It is time to start thinking and debating about whether and how to correct this structural fault.

C. *Douglas Dillon*

3. The Challenge of Modern Governance (1982)

C. Douglas Dillon, co-chair of the Committee on the Constitutional System, is an investment banker. He served as ambassador to France and undersecretary of state during the Eisenhower administration, and secretary of the treasury during the Kennedy administration. This address, which along with Cutler's article became a rallying-point for CCS, was delivered in May, 1982, at Tufts University, as Dillon received an honorary degree.

Today I want to share with you some thoughts on a subject that has concerned me ever since I left government service, seventeen years ago. It is our unique, American, constitutional system and its present and future ability to handle the increasingly complex problems that face our nation today and will face us in the years to come.

Before going any further, let us reflect a minute on what separates our system from other democratic systems. Where our Constitution differs fundamentally from the other major democracies is in the separation of executive and legislative power. When our founding fathers were drafting the Constitution they had just been through a war to overthrow the power of a ruler, who lived far away across the seas, to determine their destinies. The thirteen, newly independent colonies had many differences and treasured their individual freedom. As states in a new union they were not about to give authority to a distant central government to determine their fate. And in those days Washington, the new capital, was, indeed, far away. It took something like a full month to travel in unhurried fashion from Boston or Savannah to Washington— and at least a week for news to cover the same distance in the most rapid manner available.

Therefore our system of checks and balances between the executive authority and the legislative authority was devised. This system contrasts sharply with the parliamentary system as it developed in Europe, wherein

24

the legislative and executive authority are combined, with the government possessing both types of authority at the same time.

Our constitutional system worked as expected and served us well for over 150 years. It is only since World War II that serious strains began to appear. The basic reasons for these strains lie in the technological developments that make life, and in particular political life, quite different today from what it was only fifty years ago. These developments have annihilated time and distance. I refer to the airplane, in particular the jet airplane, and the development of television and inexpensive, instantaneous, communications networks that cover our entire nation and, indeed, the globe.

In earlier days members of Congress were elected and sent to Washington to represent their constituencies. Communication was slow and there was no way in which the congressman or senator could ascertain the views of his constituents on the many individual matters that would require decision while in Washington. Members of Congress were chosen because of their philosophic approach to government or more rarely because of their views on some one, dominating issue of the day. Because of this, political parties developed that had a certain cohesiveness and that gave the voters a relatively clear idea of where their members stood on the issues. Thus, party government in the first 150 years of our national existence was not too different from that in parliamentary governments. The power of the executive was held in check, but the basic programs of the president and his party were generally enacted. There were exceptions, of course, such as the rejection of the League of Nations after World War I. But these were exceptions, not the rule.

Things began to change after World War II. Because of faster means of travel, members of Congress spent more time at home, in their districts, and, because of the telephone and the news media, they were in constant touch with constituents who were informed on a day to day, if not an hour to hour, basis as to developments in Washington. Gradually but steadily there was an erosion in party loyalty. Political parties began to lose their ideological identities. We are all aware of the profound differences between the thinking of elected southern Democrats and their colleagues from the big cities of the North. And similar differences arose between Republicans elected to office in the east and those coming from the middle and far west.

So what do we have today? We have members of Congress who return to their districts regularly, when possible every week—members who are in close touch with the vocal elements in their districts and who, of necessity, put the expressed interests of such constituents ahead of any broader national or party interest. Only the president has a national constituency, but he has no authority to put his policies in place or to see that they are carried out. All he can do is to exhort and hope that this will bring pressure on the Congress to act.

An outgrowth of this situation has been the rise of single issue, special interest groups. Their number is legion. There is the gun lobby, the right to life lobby, the environmentalists, the anti-nuclear groups. Recently we have heard much of the power of these special interest groups. What we should realize is that their power and their existence is a natural outgrowth of our fractionated political system, where local pressures far outweigh any overall and necessarily abstruse national interest. One of the best characterizations of this situation has recently been given by Speaker Tip O'Neill, who is quoted as saying, "All politics is local politics."

Another characteristic of our system is the inability to place responsibility on any one person or group. The president is elected every four years on a program for which he feels that he has a mandate. But the Congress, be it controlled by his own party or the opposition, practically never implements these policies. We have to go back fifty years to Franklin Roosevelt and the New Deal, to find a time when the president has been able to develop a program and have it adopted by the Congress. President Reagan, by his success last year, came nearer than anyone to repeating the Roosevelt success story but now seems to be facing the same problem as his predecessors.

The result of all this is stalemate whenever important and difficult issues are involved. And no one can place the blame. The president blames the Congress, the Congress blames the president, and the public remains confused and disgusted with government in Washington. An interesting sidelight on this public perception of government is the extraordinarily low esteem in which the Congress is held. In various opinion polls only ten to fifteen percent of those polled feel that Congress is doing a good job. But at the very same time a majority usually give high marks to their own representative or senator. This clearly indicates that our governmental problems do not lie with the quality or character of our elected representatives, a substantial majority of whom are well meaning, hard working individuals of more than average ability. Rather they lie with a system which promotes divisiveness and makes it difficult, if not impossible, to develop truly national policies.

Another outgrowth of this situation is voter apathy. The public has come to realize that national political platforms are relatively meaningless. Even when a president has tried to carry out the promises in the platform after his election, he has, more often than not, been frustrated by congressional opposition. The success ratio has not been good. So it is natural for a feeling to grow that it makes little difference who is elected, and hence why bother to vote. This is certainly one of the chief reasons why the United States ranks at or near the bottom among the industrialized democracies in the percentage of citizens of voting age who actually go to the polls and exercise their franchise.

The problems of our present system have been and are vividly illustrated by the current difficulties with our national budget. Nothing could be more important to the health of our nation. The deficits that loom ahead are of incredible magnitude. Unless they are sharply reduced from the $250 billion level that we are facing only three years hence, there can be only two results, both of them very bad. One is continued high and probably ever higher interest rates, as federal government borrowing absorbs practically all private savings, leaving little or nothing for business or state and local use. Such a scenario would guarantee continuation of recession and high unemployment and could even lead to a depression comparable to that of the thirties. The only other possible result is financing the deficits through money hot off the printing presses, leading inevitably to roaring inflation of a type not seen in any industrialized country, in peace time, since the great German inflation of the inter-war period.

To handle the situation we clearly need increased tax revenues and reductions in spending in approximately equal proportions. Adequate spending reductions simply cannot be achieved without a reduction in the growth of the entitlement programs, including social security. There is no time to waste, but, in spite of the seriousness of the situation, there is every indication that we will have to wait until after the November election before any of the major issues will even be seriously discussed. All we have is more politics as usual, which comes close to fiddling as Rome burns. And this is not because of any lack of knowledge as to what needs to be done, which is perfectly clear. Rather it stems from the inability of our system to clearly place the responsibility for action in any one place.

Other illustrations of this sort are too numerous to list. One can point to the failure to take needed action on energy legislation in the mid-seventies, the failure to act on social security when everyone is aware that the system is rapidly going bankrupt and the failure to enact handgun control legislation, when all polls show that it is desired by at least three quarters of the electorate.

Another major problem area, which should be of special interest to you at the Fletcher School, is that of foreign relations. In an increasingly interdependent world, facing increasingly complex problems, it is essential for a nation with the economic, military and political power of the United States to be able to speak with one, clear voice.

In the turbulent world in which we live today there is no doubt that, as the years go by, our nation will be faced with recurring crises of types that cannot be foretold. Today, actions taken by others thousands of miles away can have the most serious impact on our economy and our way of life. We are no longer able to stand alone, but our fate is bound up with what happens elsewhere in the world. In such an era, our government must be able to act clearly and promptly in defense of our national interest, and, when it speaks, others should know that its policies will be carried out.

However, under our system of divided powers that is not now possible. There is no way in which the Congress can formulate or implement foreign policy, and there is no way for the president to have assurance that the Congress will support the executive branch in carrying out the policies formulated by it.

This situation is highly confusing to friend and foe alike and can lead foreign nations to miscalculations of our intentions that could easily have serious or even catastrophic consequences. In a recent interview, Sir Nicholas Henderson, the British ambassador in Washington, was asked his views of our government. His comments are most illuminating, and I will share them with you. He said, and I quote, "You don't have a system of government. You have a maze of government. In (other countries) if you want to persuade the government . . . or find out their point of view on something, it's quite clear where the power resides. It resides with the government.

"Here there's a whole maze of different corridors of power. There's the administration. There's the Congress. There are the staffers. There's the press. . . .

"Here, because of your Constitution, because you never wanted another George III, you made sure that the executive did not have ultimate power."

Then, finishing politely, the ambassador said, "That makes life in Washington for a foreigner very much more exciting, difficult and varied than anywhere else." Speaking more frankly he could have said, "That's what makes the life of a foreign diplomat in Washington so difficult, frustrating and dangerous."

This system was viable during the first 150 years of our history when we could and did exist in relative isolation. It continued to be viable in the immediate post-war era when our economic and military power dominated the world. But that is no longer the case. Today, possibly the most important longer range question facing us as a nation, a question transcending all immediate issues, is whether we can continue to afford the luxury of the separation of power in Washington between the executive and the legislative branches of our government.

You may ask, "What is the alternative?" The answer could well be some form of parliamentary democracy. Parliamentary systems vary from those where the chief of state is merely a protoclaire figurehead, to those such as France, where great power resides in the president. But all of them have one thing in common. Responsibility for policy and its execution lies clearly with the head of the government and his party, which stands or falls on its overall record. Legislators must follow the party line or face loss of party designation in the next election. As a result, individual issues tend to be submerged in the overall record of the government, which has far greater ability to act promptly and energetically in the face of a crisis, foreign or domestic, than is the case in Washington.

Such a significant shift in our Constitution is unlikely to come about except as a result of a crisis that is very grave indeed, one that I hope we never have to face. But we cannot be complacent, and, if such a crisis does come upon us, we should be as prepared as possible. That requires extensive thought and debate, led in the first instance by our academic community. There are many leading scholars today, interested in studying our constitutional system with a view to improving the operations of government. The bulk of these studies are aimed at relatively modest changes, designed to make our present system work better. I refer to such things as a single, six-year term for the president, four-year terms for members of the House of Representatives or government financing of congressional as well as presidential elections.

Some or all of these changes may be helpful, and studies of this sort are important and well worth pursuing. However, they do not address the much more serious problem of the inability to place responsibility for events on any one party or person. That can only be remedied by a truly significant shift—a change to some form of parliamentary government that would eliminate or sharply reduce the present division of authority between the executive and legislative arms of government. Ten years ago you could count on one hand the number of scholars who were prepared to tackle this subject. Today, I am glad to say, this has changed and there are many who are beginning to think in these terms.

This is all to the good. For unless our scholars and those who have had experience in government explore, carefully and fully, the various parliamentary alternatives, we may some day find ourselves unprepared in the face of a major crisis. I recognize that this presents a difficult challenge, largely because it is hard to foresee the circumstances that would lead to such a drastic change in our Constitution. But it is a challenge that must be taken up if we, as a nation, are to be ready for whatever the future may have in store.

Nancy Landon Kassebaum

---

4. Statement on Campaign Finance (1985)

Nancy Landon Kassebaum, who became co-chair of the Committee on the Constitutional System in 1984, has been a Republican senator from Kansas since 1978. She was re-elected in 1984. She serves on the Senate Budget and Foreign Relations committees, and chairs the subcommittee on African affairs.

One of the ongoing changes in our political life that deeply concerns me is the inordinate—and increasing—importance of money. What concerns me most is that the steady increase in the amount of money spent in political campaigns has been accompanied by a steady decline in the quality of our public dialogue. I suspect there is a connection in these two trends.

To me, that connection can be found in the fact that our mass media—newspapers, magazines, radio and especially television—have become the primary means of communication between private citizens and public officials. Television is an extremely expensive way to communicate, and that places a premium on short, simple messages. As each election seems to confirm, the line between simple and simple-minded is a thin one, and very easy to cross in a thirty-second TV spot.

Washington, Jefferson, Franklin and Madison would be appalled by the enormous sums spent on campaigns today. And those men, who valued clear thinking and plain speaking, probably would be equally appalled by what the money buys. What should appall all of us is the fact that there is no consensus on what can, or should, be done about this. In fact, there is no consensus on whether this is even a problem.

I don't have an instant solution for this predicament, but none of us should be complacent about the fact that a House campaign often costs $1 million and a Senate race can run up bills totalling more than $20 million. I know that we spend far larger sums advertising dog food or perfume, but it's one thing to sell merchandise. It's a far different matter to turn public office into merchandise. We seem to be exchanging Madison's view of representative democracy for Madison Avenue's view of successful marketing.

This produces two serious problems in the functioning of our democracy. First, the extraordinary importance of money forces elected officials to place a high priority on raising money. Second, the enormous amount of money being spent not only in election campaigns but in single-issue mass mailings and other "grassroots" efforts to influence Congress has tended to shrink, rather than expand, our political debates.

Fund raising is one of the most deadening and demeaning requirements of public office today. But it clearly is a requirement for anyone who wants to be reelected. Money cannot yet buy happiness—or an election—but it can improve the possibilities, and a lack of adequate funding can be a severe handicap in today's high-cost campaigns. While this is troubling for individual members of Congress, the real price of our present system of campaign finance, I think, is a loss of clarity and an increased questioning of motives.

When a member of Congress receives a large campaign contribution, it may not affect a specific vote, but it inevitably affects his or her relationship with the giver. As money becomes more important, major contributors loom larger on the political landscape. Voters know this, and they wonder why all of these groups are giving all of this money to someone who is supposed to represent them.

Our methods of campaign finance may not subvert the processes of democracy, but they can erode the confidence and trust that are the foundation of democracy.

This problem is further aggravated by the ways we spend all of the money that is raised. The major way we do that is by buying dozens of television spots that discuss the weighty issues of the day in thirty seconds. There is much to be said for simple, direct arguments. Unfortunately, little of it can be said about the kinds of TV ads that dominate our political campaigns. After our over-long and over-expensive campaigns are finally over, most voters enter the polls with a vague impression of the candidates based on catch words, buzz phrases, slogans and snazzy tunes.

The unhappy fact is that in any campaign at almost any level of government, image is often more important than reality, symbols frequently outweigh substance, and the cute quip regularly receives more prominence than the careful analysis. This set of values pervades our public life so that the outlandish claim, the fervent war-cry and the clash of confrontation are routinely preferred to thoughtful debate, the careful compromise and the molding of consensus.

While spending large amounts of money for an election may not itself be a bad thing, the way we spend that money can be very debilitating in a society that depends on shaping consensus from a diverse people with diverse and often competing needs. By playing to the demands of our mass media, we overlook the demands of democracy and undermine our ability both to govern and to be governed.

Any effort to correct this predicament quickly runs into an immovable barrier: our constitutional guarantee of freedom of speech. Nearly every proposal advanced to limit campaign funding or spending faces a severe constitutional test. We are strongly, and properly, wary of any step that smacks of an abridgement of the fundamental right to speak out on public issues.

I do not know how to resolve the current impasse. I for one have serious problems with the idea of public financing of all federal campaigns. But I also know we must never allow financial muscle to become an increasingly direct factor in political muscle.

If government becomes the captive pawn of the well-heeled moneyman and the sharp media adviser, it will no longer be the champion of the average citizen. At that point, average citizens will have a lot to say about this matter, and they won't require large sums of money to deliver their message.

Lester Thurow

5. The Moral Equivalent of Defeat (1981)

Lester Thurow is professor of economics and management at MIT. This article was published in Foreign Policy *magazine. It argues that our political system must be changed if we are to reverse the decline in our relative productivity.*

The United States has fallen to tenth among all nations in per capita gross national product (GNP). It ranks behind almost every country in northern Europe except the United Kingdom. A year ago, the United States was fifth. Productivity is falling in the United States; almost everywhere else it is rising. Extend current economic trends twenty years into the future, and, regardless of missiles or diplomats, present U.S. alliances and foreign policies will be in shambles.

Does anyone imagine that the American voter will be willing to pay for the defense of those wealthier than he? Sooner or later, someone will point out that it is much cheaper to defend North America than it is to defend U.S. allies abroad. Does anyone imagine that West Germany and Japan can act as senior partners in the Western alliance, making basic military decisions? Both countries lie on the periphery of the Soviet empire and are relatively small geographically. Both have histories that would make it difficult for them to exercise military leadership among other allies.

When Great Britain was no longer economically able to play its traditional foreign policy role, there was a larger, more economically powerful and more geographically defensible country—the United States—ready to take its place. The changes are not apt to be so easy when the United States declines to the point that it cannot or will not play a leadership role. Obviously, a new set of alliances and foreign policies

will emerge in a world where America is economically weak. But at
the very best, the transition will create risks and uncertainties. Those
who worry about Soviet adventurism in the window of relative U.S.
military weakness in the mid-1980s ought to have nightmares about
Soviet adventurism in the window of relative American economic weakness in the 1990s. If adventure is what the Soviet Union wants, it will
then have even more opportunities given the likely disarray in Western
alliances. In short, the major American foreign policy problems lie at
home. Unless those domestic economic problems are cured, there is no
panacea to be found abroad in projecting military power or displaying
diplomatic skill.

Consider the British at the turn of the century. They had just yielded
first place to the United States in the per capita GNP race and were
shortly to begin writing articles about re-vitalizing their economy. But
in any given year, the difference between one percent British growth
and three percent U.S. growth was small. No particular year was a
crisis. But this state of affairs continued for eighty years, giving Britain
a per capita GNP half that of the United States.

Other countries have also passed Britain, whose performance is now
below that of East Germany; yet to this day no progress has been made
in accelerating Britain's economic growth. Obviously, there is nothing
wrong with the British character. When Britain faced a military crisis
in 1939, it pulled together as few societies ever have. The British, and
now the Americans, face the most difficult problem any society ever
faces—slow economic rot. Americans must change their traditional ways
of doing things without the spur of defeat to force them to act. . . .

An autopsy report on the death of U.S. productivity—up three percent
a year before 1965; down one percent a year after mid-1977—would
conclude that death was caused by a thousand cuts. No one overriding
factor led to the present disaster. Many different factors explain a small
fraction of the end result. They range from geological blows—less oil
found per hour spent drilling wells—to social blows—several hundred
thousand private security guards added to hours of work, protecting
old output but generating no new output and hence no productivity.

The problem with death by a thousands cuts is that the cure consists
of a thousand Band-Aids. But someone benefits by each one of those
thousand cuts. When it comes time to bandage any particular cut,
someone points out that the patient could survive quite well with the
cut and that society therefore should repair the other 999 cuts and leave
his cut alone. But with each cut defended, every cut goes uncured, and
the patient dies.

Inadequate investment is an especially unkind cut, accounting for one
quarter of the observed decline in productivity. But the investment

problem is not what it is usually reported to be in the press. When productivity growth was running at a three percent rate in the 1950s, Americans invested 9.5 percent of the GNP. As productivity growth fell into the negative range, investment rose to 10.3 percent of the GNP. And after correcting for inflation, the stock of plant and equipment rose faster in the 1970s than in the 1950s and early 1960s. Why did productivity fail to rise? Basically, Americans failed to live up to an implicit promise that they made twenty years ago. If the United States has a baby boom, it promises that over the next twenty years it will cut its consumption enough to equip each of its grown children with an average of $50,000 in plant and equipment. The labor force expanded because of the baby boom, but investment did not rise fast enough to provide it with sufficient productive capacity.

What has happened was illustrated in 1978. Americans invested 10.8 per cent of the GNP, and after correcting for inflation, the capital stock rose 3.4 percent. However, capital per worker fell 1.4 percent while hours of work rose 4.8 percent. With less equipment to perform more work, it is not surprising that productivity fell.

If U.S. workers were to acquire new equipment as fast as their Japanese competitors, America would have to invest almost thirty percent of its GNP. But raising investment from ten to thirty percent of the GNP creates another problem. Until the factories come into production in ten years, consumption must fall.

Americans have begun to talk about stimulating savings and investment, but such talk should not be taken seriously until they also begin to talk about cutting consumption. Until the average U.S. citizen believes that the consequences of doing nothing are more painful than the consequences of cutting consumption, U.S. economic decline will continue, and foreign policy makers will have to anticipate disarray, if not chaos, in U.S. alliances.

True supply-side economics would involve tax cuts, but would focus primarily on tax increases. Taxes on investment and work effort would be cut, and taxes on consumption would be raised. The problem with the proposed Kemp-Roth tax cut, now before Congress, is simple. The average American family saves five percent of its income. Given another $100, the average family will save or invest $5, but it will consume $95. Taxes have been cut across the board several times since 1965; nevertheless, the American savings rate has fallen continuously. (Only increasing corporate and government savings rates have enabled overall investment to increase slightly.)

There are many ways to raise the savings rate. Higher taxes, such as a value-added tax, could be levied on consumption. Consumer credit could be abolished, forcing consumers to save in order to buy what they want. Policies could be adopted to cut corporate dividends and increase corporate saving. Governments could run large surpluses in their budgets. Each measure would reduce someone's spending power. Once again, the country must face the problem of allocating and imposing losses.

It is a mistake though to look solely at what government must do. The problems extend far beyond those cured by reforms in taxation or regulation. Up and down the chain of economic activity, major changes are needed.

Consider education. College achievement test scores have been falling for more than a decade. At every grade level, Japanese children outscore U.S. children in mathematics. Among graduates of big-city school systems, functional illiteracy is so common it is not clear where tomorrow's work force will come from. A scientific defeat—Sputnik—led to the last U.S. campaign to improve educational quality. A less dramatic but more important economic defeat makes urgent another educational effort in the 1980s. If big-city public school systems cannot deliver, then the time has come to try something different, such as educational vouchers, not because free enterprise vouchers are ideologically better, but because public education has failed, and society cannot afford to live with the failure.

Major changes will be necessary in the world of work. Productivity depends not on the work ethic, but on the willingness to accept technical change. Think of a Japanese worker and an American worker facing a new machine. To the Japanese worker with his guaranteed job, his bonus, and a wage rate that does not depend upon the particular task he performs, the new machine represents an opportunity to increase his pay. To the U.S. worker, the new machine is a real threat. It may eliminate the need for his job skills and lower his wages. Or it may lead to unemployment. If new technology hurts workers, labor unions will fight it even if the technology helps society as a whole. The United States will have to adopt Japan's techniques or invent new ways of making technological improvements consistent with worker self-interest.

Many foreign observers, particularly the Japanese, believe that U.S. corporate time horizons have become much too short. American firms with their 3–5 year time horizons cannot compete with foreign firms using their 10–15 year time horizons. There is no mystery about why this is true.

American investors buy into and sell out of firms daily, without any interest in the long run. Top corporate management earns bonuses based on current profits. Middle management is promoted or demoted based on current profits. Business school students are taught that only the short-run bottom line matters. Given this incentive system, anything but a short time horizon would be astounding. New corporate incentive structures will be needed to correct the problem. Bonuses and promotions will have to be given on the basis of expected long-run performance rather than on the easier measures of short-run profitability. Antitrust laws need to be repealed to allow the kind of intimate cooperation between industry and banking that now exists in West Germany.

Major changes are needed in the adversary legal system. Although the U.S. economy is not over-regulated, it has the most cumbersome adversary regulatory process in the world. The economy can function with almost any set of standards as long as those standards are quickly and consistently applied. It cannot function when no one knows what standards—environmental or otherwise—are required, when nothing is decided in less than eight years, and when no one knows what future rule will be retroactively applied.

The gap between the six years it takes to build a nuclear power plant in Japan and the twelve years it takes in the United States is caused almost exclusively by legal delays. Although investment was up as a fraction of GNP in the 1970s, the building of major new industrial facilities was down. Bolting new equipment in old factories works for only a short time. The United States must regain the ability to construct major facilities quickly. To do so, the legal system will have to be rebuilt. The United States should consider wider use of conflict settlement techniques—mediation and binding arbitration—that are now used in labor relations disputes to diminish these delays.

Higher productivity growth will mean policies to stimulate new investments, but will also require actions to speed up disinvestment. Instead of protecting dying low-productivity industries, the United States must discard them faster. Recent proposals to speed the movement of workers from the frost belt to the sun belt are precisely the kinds of measures needed, no matter what the outrage of northern big-city mayors. Real costs, such as energy costs, demand a substantial relocation of economic activity. When a New Yorker moves to a better job in Texas, the country has benefited, not suffered, economically. Slowing down this process strangles the country economically and dooms it internationally. The British experience shows how propping up dying industries and regions retards progress.

Fundamentally, America must alter its structure of government. The men of 1776 may have designed a set of checks and balances that succeeded for the nation's first 200 years, but they did not anticipate the dilemmas of the 1980s. Every group has the ability to veto anything it does not like; no group or even coalition of groups has the ability to act positively.

To regain our economic vigor, the society—not just the economy—is going to have to undergo major structural change. Former President Carter was fond of referring to America's economic problems as the "moral equivalent of war." He was wrong. They are the moral equivalent of defeat. The United States has been defeated economically. Americans have to change their ways of doing things—not as they did during World War II, but as the Japanese and West Germans were forced to do after that war. The challenge is not "us versus them" but "us versus us."

At the same time, it is well to remember that it is impossible to regain the comfort of the immediate postwar era when America was economically pre-eminent in the world. That was a peculiar period created by the military destruction of America's competitors and allies alike. The United States did not lead in every economic category prior to World War II, and it will not lead in every category again. The United States has now joined the rest of the world in depending on international trade. Since World War II imports have risen from less than four percent of the GNP to more than thirteen percent. Never again will Americans as a nation feel so economically self-sufficient and indestructible as they did from 1945 to 1965.

This does not mean that the United States cannot act as the leader of the Western alliance. The emergence of serious economic competition undermines the United States only if the U.S. economy is unable to compete. Should the United States become a poor cousin in the wealthy Western family, it will lose the ability to unite and lead its allies. The bracing measures required to restore U.S. economic performance will not be as painful as dealing with the fragmentation of the Western alliance. There is nothing to be gained and much to be lost if the United States does not begin to act soon.

Don K. Price

6. Words of Caution About Structural Change (1983)

Don K. Price is professor emeritus and former dean of the John F. Kennedy School of Government at Harvard University. He has served in the Bureau of the Budget and at the Defense Department, and directed studies of the presidency for the first Hoover Commission (1947–1948) and for the National Academy of Public Administration (1979–1980). The following material is excerpted from America's Unwritten Constitution, *in which he argues that the need for more coherence in government can best be pursued through measures other than constitutional reform.*

The lesson that the United States might well learn from the United Kingdom . . . is not to imitate the parliamentary system by formal amendment of the Constitution, but to imitate its essence—at least to some extent—by changes in our unwritten constitution. It is hard to imagine Congress deciding by informal political agreement to subject the executive to only a single big test of accountability, such as a parliamentary vote of no confidence, rather than the multitude of little checks that now destroy the coherence of national policy. But it is even harder to imagine that it would permit an amendment to the written Constitution that would make such a change.

The Need for Delegation

But it is possible to imagine—and we may well consider—how Congress might move to insure a somewhat higher degree of executive accountability by changes in the unwritten constitution, and then ask how far in that direction it ought to go.

As for how it might do so, it would only need to continue the process by which, for nearly a century, it has delegated to the president the measure of administrative authority that he now enjoys. If it does so, it should surely take steps to strengthen substantially its ability, as a whole, to hold him accountable.

The first step in the right direction would be to quit talking about the constitutional separation of powers. The Constitution sets up no such thing as an executive branch. We should acknowledge that in all major issues of management and policy the Congress and the president are jointly involved in the direction and control of the departments and agencies. There are frequent conflicts involved in the control of the departments between the Congress and the president, or more frequently, between some committee of the Congress and the president. But it is not a zero-sum game, in which one side gains to the extent the other loses: the Congress as a whole may gain more effective control over the government not by weakening the president, but only by delegating authority, with proper measure of accountability, to him and his executive officers.

The proper extent of delegation from the Congress will determine the way in which the president too delegates to his department heads, and even to the staff in his executive office. The Congress may delegate either formally by statute, or tacitly by refraining from interference. If it is to do so, it must develop a greater concentration of leaderships and responsibility within each house, backed by more effective political discipline, so that it will have a stronger position in bargaining and negotiating with the president.

More coherent and effective leadership within each house of Congress, with stronger party discipline, would let the Congress as a whole (even if the two houses were not controlled by the president's party) bargain on equal or more than equal terms with the president on issues of sufficient importance to warrant the attention of the voters. Without it, as at present, the party rivalry turns on special issues generated by subcommittee oversight of particular bureaus or departments, and there is no way for the president to know on what policies the Congress as a whole will support him, or for the public to be clear on what issues the next election should turn.

If such effective political leadership could be developed in the Congress as a whole, it might then be possible to focus responsibility on the executive side clearly on the department heads, to whom Congress by statute appropriates funds and grants the powers that operate directly on private citizens. That responsibility is now confused because of the growth in the size and glamour of the executive office. That growth has been far beyond the genuine interests of either the president or of the Congress as a whole; it has come about because special interests in both executive agencies and in congressional committees, many of them good in purpose, have sought to establish footholds at higher levels in the political hierarchy.

There is no question that the president needs a strong executive office. His legal authority over the departments is guaranteed by his constitutional power to dismiss their heads. But such authority is meaningless if it is not supported by staff resources, and even more if it is not freed from undue statutory procedural constraints. The executive office was set up to provide the staff; if Congress is to be asked to leave it free from statutory constraints, and at the president's discretion with respect to its organization and control, the president will need to live up to the tacit bargain on which the office was founded—that it not become a rival of the executive departments in the exercise of direct authority. For, unlike members of the executive office, the department head is not only directly responsible to the president, who may fire him, but he is also accountable to both the courts and the Congress, which may control the powers and the funds that are granted to him.

Various presidents have come into office promising to make more effective use of their department heads—to strengthen "cabinet government" in the American sense of the term—and have drifted back to relying more on executive office staff, especially those in the White House office. They have been tempted to do so because their department heads have been under congressional pressure less from the overall leadership, to which they could respond with some degree of unity as the principal members of the president's political team, than from the subcommittees and their staffs, which usually press them in the direction of their several special interests.

If there were some such effective congressional leadership it might be possible to raise the level of negotiation with the president from the details that have preoccupied committees and their staffs to more general questions of broad policy. Thomas Jefferson remarked that under the Articles of Confederation, "executive details" put us in the position "as if we had no federal head, by diverting the attention of that head from great to small subjects." If there were more effective and disciplined leadership in the Congress, the bargaining between the leadership of the Congress and the president might be elevated to large subjects rather than the comparatively petty issues that dominate when the bargaining is between a congressional committee or its staff and a bureau chief.

There is no political force which can make such a change take place except a consensus based on the understanding and conviction of political leaders generally. The Congress . . . amended the unwritten constitution during the mid-nineteenth century by taking away from the president the controls over the tools of administration—personnel, financial management, and organization—that had been conceded to him during the Federalist period. Then, with the Civil Service Act of 1883, the Budget and Accounting Act of 1921, and the Reorganization Act of 1939, it delegated these responsibilities back to the president—in limited ways and subject to careful checks. It can continue the process, if it and the public understand the importance of doing so. It will not do to give up in impatience: it took nearly a half century to get a federal budget system after it was first discussed in congressional circles in the 1880's, and another half century for the Civil Service Reform Act of 1978 to be enacted after personnel reformers began to discuss the need for a higher civil service based on more general standards of competence and commitment.

The Limits to Delegation

When Congress delegated these responsibilities to the president, it had in mind that it was furthering efficiency in management, rather than granting authority over the substance of policy. It is harder to delegate further to the president when the purpose is not efficiency in carrying out policies determined by legislation, but the development of a more coherent policy.

Greater coherence is the ideal of those who would like to imitate the British parliamentary system, and to move toward a single big check on the tenure of the executive. The parliamentary model, however, was never as persuasive with American public opinion as the model of the business corporation. If politics could be eliminated and government made to run like a business, with the president as general manager, the criterion of efficiency could guide public administration in the best utilitarian tradition. New intellectual support for the efficiency criterion has come from the applied social sciences: with cost-benefit analysis we should be able to calculate the choices involved in achieving the greatest good for the greatest number. But either the calculation of aggregate costs and benefits, or the choice between the programs of two disciplined parties, may ignore two crucial political values.

The first is the value of justice, with respect both to fundamental rights, and to the distribution of benefits and costs among the various regions and groups of the population. The Congress and the president will not want the secretary of defense, for example, to be able in his calculation of our military needs to ignore the civil rights of minority groups, or even to allocate contracts without regard to the impact on various regions or segments of the economy. Nor will they want to let the administrator responsible for the protection of the environment ignore the special impact of particular regulations on particular industries, or on employment opportunities.

The second is the value of freedom from arbitrary political power: a free people will prefer less bread and fewer circuses if the sacrifice will let them maintain more popular control over their own affairs.

Especially in a larger federal system, with a diverse population, it is inevitable that the electorate will want to draw back from the idea of a tightly unified system, in which the only check on the power that it delegates is by its choice between two political parties. It is not only inevitable but desirable, in recognition of what history may teach us of the temptation of any political elite or any tightly organized bureaucracy to distort its perception of national policy in order to maintain its own profit and power. In a unitary state in an era of restricted governmental functions, a tightly unified and disciplined parliamentary system produced an admirably coherent policy. But it did so on a completely unscientific basis. In order to bring various groups together in teamwork, there is no way to calculate precisely, on a systematic utilitarian basis, just what choices will most fairly distribute benefits among them. A somewhat looser system, in which parts of the majority may open issues up for public debate and independent voting in the legislature, may have its advantages.

Those advantages seem especially compelling since, in an era of government control over the economy and its technological development, it is hard for the political leader to be sure that his view of policy is based on a realistic comprehension of the scientific alternatives. He may be badly served if his own subordinates, either in political or career positions, do not fully comprehend what the technological options are, or if they deliberately ignore some alternatives in order to push their own prejudiced views on policy. The possibility that better alternative choices may emerge from free-wheeling debate in an undisciplined legislature, with free access to private scientific advice, may be worth preserving even if it is less tidy than the classic parliamentary system of responsible government.

While it is important to have a government that can deal effectively with the great issues of the day, it is equally important to make sure that it does so in ways that take into account the essential moral and political values of justice and freedom. It is obviously essential to cope with the threat of war, or of our loss of command of the sources of energy for our industrial system, or of the deterioration of our environment. But these are special manifestations of a broader problem, namely, how can our political system insure that our ends are not corrupted by our means, that is to say, that our moral and political values control our technological and managerial skills, and not *vice versa.* To this end, we must pay at least as much attention to insuring the accountability of our executive institutions as to improving their efficiency and economy. Indeed, we need to give prior attention to accountability, for it is the fear of irresponsible power that leads us to hobble our executives and destroy their effectiveness. Only by insuring their accountability will we be willing to grant them enough authority to act. . . .

Most of the important issues on which the American system of accountability is constantly being revised are adjusted by informal consensus or procedural rules; few require statutory change, and none needs amendment of the written Constitution. A few examples may illustrate the point.

Number of legislative checks. For purposes of enforcing accountability, how many legislative check points are most effective? Under the classic parliamentary system the legislature has only one big check—to vote the government out of office. Under the congressional system, the legislature runs several simultaneous checks on each agency or program: legislative authorizations, appropriations, personnel ceilings, and a wide variety of oversight procedures—audits, reporting requirements, legislative vetoes, and scientific standards. How many different checks provide the optimum in accountability? The number of checks now provided is probably so great as to be counterproductive, and serves no purpose except to enhance the influence of specific members or staff members of Congress. Indeed, the Congress, by having an authorizing committee, for example, seek to build up a program, and then an appropriations subcommittee cut it down, and another committee control its organization or personnel, and a budget committee go over the whole sequence again, involves itself in levels of administrative detail that add nothing to its ability as a whole to control, or to educate the public on, major policy issues. But this issue is one of degree and proportion; just as Congress by creating the Congressional Budget Office not only put some restraint on the competing powers of various appropriations and budget and finance committees, but also increased the effective accountability of the executive, so it might do more to cut down on the multiplicity and detail of its controls over the executive and consolidate its own effective power.

Legal or political checks. Are checks more effective when expressed in formal statutory terms or in less formal political understandings? Congressional committees, in their present relationship with executive bureaus, sometimes have enough confidence in the continuity of their relationships with career officers to be willing to define controlling decisions not in rigid statutory terms, but in the legislative history as informal agreements. Presidents often object to this practice because it prevents them from coordinating policies. But if the less legalistic understandings were to be made between general congressional leadership, supported by political discipline, and the president, supported by a stronger career staff, the effect might be quite different. It would allow for greater executive discretion, but subject it to more immediate political control.

Procedures for initiative. Can procedures be devised to leave more flexible initiative in the hands of the president without weakening congressional control? The type of legislative veto that was originally devised to apply to reorganization plans seemed such a device. But there were constitutional objections even to it, and they became stronger when the veto came to be exercised on detailed regulations and by a single house or committee of Congress. In the other direction, would something like an item veto for the president be desirable? Both approaches are worth exploring, provided that congressional action be taken by the political leadership of Congress as a whole.

Distinction between discussion and determination of policy. At what stage in the formulation and presentation of a new policy should accountability be exercised? If freedom of information is an absolute value or as it is often exercised by leaks to the press, it may be impossible for a policy to be developed into mature form for congressional consideration, since special interests may more easily block its development by one political tactic or another.

This issue is especially significant if the president is to be encouraged to involve department heads more intimately in the formulation of policy through cabinet committees. Is accountability furthered by leaving the membership and agenda of such committees at the discretion of the president, as the first Hoover Commission recommended in 1949, or by subjecting them to public scrutiny and congressional control? Presidents are often reluctant to involve department heads in committee deliberation on major policy issues because it is difficult to keep such discussion confidential. They fear with some reason that Congress will undertake to decide what cabinet committees should exist, who should serve on them, and how they should operate. This fear may have justified the president in relying more on executive office staff, and excluding department heads from the more important and confidential policy discussions.

It would make the entire process more responsible if Congress should act on what the president actually decides and recommends publicly, and leave to the discretionary management of the president the processes and procedures of preliminary thought within the executive office, the cabinet, and other interdepartmental committees.

Political and career staff. If accountability should be defined not in terms of compliance with statutes or strict rules, but conformity to general policy leadership and the broad intentions of the leadership, is such responsiveness more to be expected from political appointees or from career officers, or by what kind of mix of both? The answer to this question will depend in part on the type of training and incentive system by which the higher civil service is developed. Will the new senior executive service make a difference, both by producing superior generalists, and by making it easier for a president or a departmental head to bring to a particular position an officer responsive or congenial to his policies?

The rigidities of the old personnel system led political executives to want larger numbers of political appointees at the head of their agencies. Yet, especially in the executive office, this approach had its limits. Political appointees (except for a few intimate friends) were usually less loyal to the president than to some special interest or faction that had promoted their appointment. As the executive office grew larger, so that most of its staff had no personal contact with the president, the partisan loyalty of political appointments often proved less reliable than the professional loyalty of the career officer. As a matter of proportion, the executive office could well do with a much smaller number of political appointees, as it did during its early years.

Size of the Executive Office. If the questions above can be answered, what do they imply for the size of the executive office? If the focus of accountability is to be on the executive departments, the executive office staff—even the institutional staffs—must be small enough so that its members can be close enough to the president so that they know his views intimately and can speak for him. On the other hand, that would call for a staff far too small to help the president respond to initiatives or questions from congressional staff now something like ten times as large as his own. A very large proportion—my guess is three-quarters to nine-tenths—of the time of the executive office staff and of congressional staff is spent in defensive maneuvers against each other, with no benefit either to the substance of policy or to accountability. If the original principles of the executive office are worth trying to reestablish, it might be necessary at the same time to reduce the size of the congressional as well as the executive office staffs, so as to focus public and legislative attention on the major policy issues confronting the departments, rather than on a mass of administrative details, especially those involved in services to constituents. We have learned that deregulation may improve the efficiency of private business; is it not possible that the executive departments could be made more efficient, with no loss of essential accountability in broad policy terms, if freed from some of the detailed regulation by the executive office and congressional staffs alike?

Adjustment Without Amendment

Those who drafted the Constitution of 1789 could not have foreseen some of these questions, but they would surely have been prudent enough not to try to answer them for all time in rigid legalistic terms. Their Constitution was more adaptable than the state constitutions of the preceding decade, when legislative supremacy was the ideal, or than those adopted during the mid-nineteenth century, when the direct popular election of minor officers left both legislatures and governors incapable of dealing with the aggressive power of the great private corporations. The written Constitution of 1789 has been flexible enough to permit, within its formal framework, a higher degree of delegation by the electorate to the Congress, and on in turn to the president. And such delegation has made possible the evolution of a richly varied unwritten constitution that can be adapted by political bargaining to new needs and circumstances.

Even though the United States abandoned the theory of sovereignty that Edmund Burke and other English traditionalists affirmed, in political practice Americans followed Burke in making their main adjustments in their unwritten constitution on the basis of Burke's "computing principle"—the unquantifiable process of working out "balances between differences of good; in compromises between good and evil, and sometimes between evil and evil. Political reason," he went on to say, "is a computing principle; adding, subtracting, multiplying, and dividing, morally, and not metaphysically or mathematically, true moral denominations." Once we Americans lost our innocence about sovereignty—the kind of innocence that, as Walter Bagehot argued, made the parliamentary system possible by letting most people know only the "dignified" parts of the constitution while practical politicians in the cabinet controlled its "efficient" parts—the only way to reestablish a workable authority was by delegation on the computing principle.

In this approach, the Americans and the British were closer to each other than to continental Europe. Both came to believe in the most fundamental kind of separation of powers in their political systems, namely, the separation of the institutions that wielded political power from those concerned with the search for truth, whether on a religious or a scientific basis.

This separation originated in fundamental beliefs, but effectively depended on institutional habits. The fundamental belief of the Puritan dissenters in the depravity of mankind made it hard to maintain an institutional structure with absolute political authority. This was not because they were consistent in applying their beliefs; in the seventeenth century John Milton was already attacking the Puritans for trying to be as authoritarian as the Papists: in his words, "New *Presbyter* is but old *Priest* writ large." But without either a traditional establishment or a theology that justified hierarchical authority, the Puritan commonwealths collapsed—rejected in England by the Stuart restoration, and in New England by the competition of other dissenting denominations. From that time on, the English-speaking world—having been, so to speak, politically inoculated—was comparatively immune to the virus of a tyranny based on confidence either in the old priesthood or in the new kind based on faith in science. Comte and Marx and their followers were never able to exercise the influence on the evolution of political ideas that they had on the continent, especially in Eastern Europe. But in Britain the persistence of an establishment—not only the established churches of England and Scotland, but the civil service establishment and the tight unity of policy that it maintained in support of a conservative class structure—gave the doctrines of Marx a chance to gain a modest foothold in the Labour Party, although never to the extent of making a proletarian dictatorship in the slightest degree plausible.

Britain and America were rather more vulnerable to the rival doctrine of perfectibility—the belief of Herbert Spencer and William Graham Sumner that the advancement of science would lead to general happiness and prosperity if only government would avoid interfering with the economy. This belief may have been useful as an insurance against undue concentration of power: if the sciences had not been established and supported on the institutional patterns set by the religious dissenters, there might have been some danger of the development of the new scientific priesthood that Comte hoped for, and Spencer and Huxley feared.

The Spencer-Sumner doctrine, however, had its costs, especially in the United States where it was taken more seriously than in Britain. It was a belief that ignored the need of modern technological society for some authority to reconcile conflicting class interests and assure justice to the poor. This belief was taken as an excuse for the lack of a tradition of public service in the wealthier class of American citizens. And it made very difficult the development of an administrative service that could maintain the supremacy of general political values over the competing scientific specialties and thus provide the basis for a more effective system of political accountability.

To establish the kind of accountability that is necessary in the constitutional system of the United States today, it is essential to avoid a legalistic worship of the ancient text, and to look at the more important political issues of the unwritten constitution. If we fix our attention on that aspect of our problem, we may still learn useful lessons from those who drafted the Constitution of 1789. For the general attitude they brought to the constitutional convention was one that is still appropriate: political responsibility depends on the recognition that the duties of political leadership and public administration are the most important obligations of the citizen and call for the dedication of the highest talents in society. And the specific insight that they had learned from painful experience with the Articles of Confederation may still be useful: a republican policy without a monarchical or bureaucratic establishment to give it stability will do well to have a chief executive and a legislative body with fixed and independent tenures.

The relationship that such an arrangement encourages is a partial protection not only against the disintegration of the executive by the distracting loyalties of legislators to their local constituents, but also against the corruption of Congress by presidential pressure or patronage. Even more important, it serves a purpose that the United Kingdom may need less than the United States, where we maintain a more naive and literal faith in the direct application of religion or science to public policy: it helps to define the boundary between government and the established institutions of education and research, as well as those of religion. And along this line of mutual defense, it is sometimes the politicians who are more in need of protection from aggression.

Arthur M. Schlesinger, Jr.

7. Leave the Constitution Alone (1982)

Arthur Schlesinger, who served as a special assistant to Presidents Kennedy and Johnson, taught for many years at Harvard and has been Schweitzer professor of humanities at the City University of New York since 1966. He has written studies of the presidencies of Andrew Jackson and Franklin D. Roosevelt, and The Imperial Presidency *(1973). This article was originally published in* The Wall Street Journal.

There is a revival of interest in fundamental constitutional change. I am not referring to special-interest amendments—proposals, for example, to permit school prayer or to forbid abortion or to require an annually balanced budget. I have in mind rather the rising feeling that we must take a hard fresh look at our government and determine whether its basic structure is adequate to the challenges of the future.

Those calling for such reexamination aren't just academic theoreticians. They include distinguished public servants, persons with long and honorable government experience, like Douglas Dillon and Lloyd Cutler. Without prejudging conclusions, they raise searching questions. In particular, they ask whether the separation of powers hasn't become a crippling disability. The separation, they suggest, leads to legislative stalemate, increases voter frustration and apathy, invites the meddling of single interest groups and makes it impossible for any party or person to be held accountable for policy. The "question transcending all immediate issues," Mr. Dillon writes, "is whether we can continue to afford the luxury of the separation of power in Washington" and whether we shouldn't consider "a change to some form of parliamentary government that would eliminate or sharply reduce the present division of authority between the executive and legislative arms of government."

These are certainly interesting questions. One wishes the new bicentennial Committee on the Constitutional System all luck in exploring them. They aren't new questions. In the 1880's, for example, Sen. George Pendleton and Prof. Woodrow Wilson argued for movement toward a parliamentary system. After World War II Thomas K. Finletter in his closely reasoned book, *Can Representative Government Do the Job?*—still perhaps the best book on the subject—and Congressman Estes Kefauver proposed modifications of the Constitution in the parliamentary direction.

A Function of Weakness

The parliamentary system is to be defined by a fusion rather than by a separation of powers. The executive is drawn from the legislative majority and can count on automatic enactment of its program. No one doubts where responsibility lies for success or failure. But while the parliamentary system formally assumes legislative supremacy, in fact it assures the almost unassailable dominance of the executive over the legislature.

Parliament's superiority over Congress in delivering whatever the executive requests is a function of weakness, not of strength. The no-confidence vote is so drastic an alternative that in Britain, for example, it succeeds in forcing a new general election only two or three times a century.

Churchill made the point to Roosevelt in a wartime conversation. "You, Mr. President," Churchill said, "are concerned to what extent you can act without the approval of Congress. You don't worry about your cabinet. On the other hand, I never worry about Parliament, but I continuously have to consult and have the support of my cabinet."

Thus the prime minister appoints people to office without worrying about parliamentary confirmation, concludes treaties without worrying about parliamentary ratification, declares war without worrying about parliamentary authorization, withholds information without worrying about parliamentary subpoenas, is relatively safe from parliamentary investigation and in many respects has inherited the authority that once belonged to absolute monarchy. As Lloyd George told a select committee in 1931, "Parliament has really no control over the executive; it is a pure fiction." The situation has not improved in the half century since. Only the other day the *Economist* spoke of "Whitehall's continuing contempt for Parliament."

Congress is far more independent of the executive, far more responsive to a diversity of ideas, far better staffed, far more able to check, balance, challenge and investigate the executive government. Take Watergate as

an example. The best judgment is that such executive malfeasance would
not have been exposed under the British system. "Don't think a Watergate
couldn't happen here," writes Woodrow Wyatt, a former British MP.
"You just wouldn't hear about it."

In a recent issue of the British magazine *Encounter*, Edward Pearce
of the *London Daily Telegraph* agrees:

> If only Mr. Nixon had had the blessing of the British system. . . . Woodward
> and Bernstein would have been drowned in the usual channels, a D-Notice
> would have been erected over their evidence, and a properly briefed judge,
> a figure of outstanding integrity, would have found the essential parts of the
> tapes to be either not relevant or prejudicial to national security or both.
> The British system of protecting the authorities is almost part of the con-
> stitution.

While American constitutional reformers muse about the virtues of
a fusion of powers, British reformers yearn for separation. They want
to set Parliament free. They want to increase executive accountability.
They want a written Bill of Rights. They have finally achieved standing
parliamentary committees and want to increase the professional staffs
and extend the powers of investigation and oversight. They want the
right to examine witnesses in committee during the consideration of
pending legislation. They want a select committee to monitor the
intelligence services. And the government, the *Economist* recently reported, "is faced with an all-party parliamentary coup aimed at seizing
from the treasury the appointment and functions of the comptroller and
auditor general, and restoring to the House of Commons power over
many aspects of government spending."

A former prime minister spoke to me a few months ago with envy
about our mid-term elections. "The only means we have between general
elections of bringing national opinion to bear on national policies," he
said, "is through by-elections, and this depends on a sufficiency of MPs
resigning or dying. Luck has been with Mrs. Thatcher, and she has had
far less than the average number of by-elections. How much better to
give the whole country a chance to express itself every two years!"

Before succumbing to romantic myths of the parliamentary advantage,
Americans would be well advised to listen to those who must live with
the realities of the parliamentary order. But fortunately, given the nature
of the American political tradition, the parliamentary system is an unreal
alternative. The thought that in this era of conspicuous and probably
irreversible party decay we can make our parties more commanding
and cohesive than they have ever been is surely fantasy. Centralized
and rigidly disciplined parties, the abolition of primaries, the intolerance

of mavericks, the absence of free voting—all such things are against the looser genius of American politics.

One must raise a deeper question: Is the difficulty we encounter these days in meeting our problems really the consequence of defects in the structure of our government? After all, we have had the separation of powers from the beginning of the republic. This has not prevented competent presidents from acting with decision and dispatch. The separation of powers did not notably disable Jefferson or Jackson or Lincoln or Wilson or the Roosevelts. The most powerful plea of this century for a strong national authority—Herbert Croly's *The Promise of American Life*—didn't see the separation of powers as an obstacle to effective government. Why are things presumed to be so much worse today?

It cannot be that, nuclear weapons apart, we face tougher problems than our forefathers. Tougher problems than slavery? the Civil War? the Great Depression? World War II? Let us take care to avoid the fallacy of self-pity that leads every generation to suppose that it is peculiarly persecuted by history.

The real difference is that the presidents who operated the system successfully *knew what they thought should be done*—and were able to persuade Congress and the nation to give their remedies a try.

That possibility remains as open today as it ever was. In his first year as president, Mr. Reagan, who knew what he thought should be done, pushed a comprehensive economic program through Congress—and did so with triumphant success in spite of the fact that the program was manifestly incapable of achieving its contradictory objectives. He is in trouble now, not because of a failure of governmental structure, but because of the failure of the remedy. If his program had worked, he would be irresistible.

Our problem is not at all that we know what to do and are impeded from doing it by some structural logjam in the system. Our problem— let us face it—is that we do not know what to do. We are as analytically impotent before the problem of inflation, for example, as we were half a century ago before the problem of depression. Our leadership has failed to convince a durable majority that one or another course will do the job.

Majority Is Not Strong Enough

If we don't know what ought to be done, efficient enactment of a poor program is a dubious accomplishment—as the experience of 1981 demonstrates. What is the great advantage of acting with decision and dispatch when you don't know what you are doing?

The issues aren't new. A century ago foreign visitors leveled the same criticism against our governmental structure. Lord Bryce in his great work, *The American Commonwealth*, reported the British view that the separation of powers, party indiscipline and the absence of party accountability made it almost impossible for the American political system to settle major national questions. He also reported the response to this criticism by American political leaders. Congress, they said, had not settled major national questions not because of defects in structure "but because the division of opinion in the country regarding them has been faithfully reflected in Congress. The majority has not been strong enough to get its way; and this has happened, not only because abundant opportunites for resistance arise from the methods of doing business, but still more because no distinct impulse of mandate towards any particular settlement of these questions has been received from the country. It is not for Congress to go faster than the people. When the country knows and speaks its mind, Congress will not fail to act."

When the country is not sure what ought to be done, it may be that delay, debate and further consideration are not a bad idea. And if our leadership is sure what to do, it must in our democracy educate the rest—and that is not a bad idea either. An effective leader with a sensible policy, or even (as in the recent Reagan case) with a less than sensible policy, has the resources under the present Constitution to get his way.

I believe that in the main our Constitution has worked pretty well. It has ensured discussion when we have lacked consensus and has permitted action when a majority can be convinced that the action is right. It allowed Franklin Roosevelt, for example, to enact the New Deal but blocked him when he tried to pack the Supreme Court. The court bill couldn't have failed if we had had a parliamentary system in 1937. In short, when the executive has a persuasive remedy, you don't need basic constitutional change. When the executive remedy is not persuasive, you don't want constitutional change.

My concern is that this agitation about constitutional reform is a form of escapism. Constitution-tinkering is a flight from the hard question, which is the search for remedy. Structure is an alibi for analytical failure. As Bryce wisely reminds us, "The student of institutions, as well as the lawyer, is apt to overrate the effect of mechanical contrivances in politics."

Fascinating as constitutional-tinkering may be, like the Rubik cube, let it not divert us from the real task of statecraft. Let us never forget that politics is the high and serious art of solving substantive problems.

Lloyd N. Cutler and C. Douglas Dillon

8. A Rebuttal to Arthur Schlesinger, Jr. (1983)

Cutler and Dillon, co-chairs of CCS (see pages 11 and 24), replied to the preceding article with the following piece, also published by The Wall Street Journal.

In a recent article on this page titled "Time for Constitutional Change?" Arthur Schlesinger Jr. answers no. And he refers to our Committee on the Constitutional System and its hypothesis that the better answer may be yes.

Mr. Schlesinger concludes there is no need for any change in our government structure, only a need for more capable presidents with sounder policies. In his view, when presidents propose sound policies, the public and therefore Congress will go along.

Of course there have been times in our history, as there undoubtedly will be again, when a crisis is so serious and a president so gifted that he can persuade the public and the Congress to adopt policies that do indeed resolve the crisis. But these are rare occasions. Most of the time the crisis is not that deep and the president is not that gifted. Yet every president must face the formidable task of "forming a government" with a majority of Congress that can legislate and execute an agreed set of policies over his term. It is our hypothesis that under our present constitutional structure, this task has become too difficult for any but the most unusual president under any but the most unusual circumstances.

The central anomaly of our structure is apparent from Mr. Schlesinger's article. He recognizes that the separation of powers between the executive and legislative branches requires them to agree on a policy in order to legislate and execute it. If they fail to agree, we have a stalemate in which the sum of government policies become a contradictory hodgepodge which neither the president nor the legislators support, and for which none of them accepts responsibility. When this happens—as it has repeatedly since World War II—we usually blame the president more the legislators. All of us expect modern presidents to formulate policy and to lead the Congress into supporting it. When Congress does not, we blame the president for bad policies or bad leadership or both.

For half the time since World War II, we have placed control of the White House in the hands of one party and control of one or both houses of Congress in the hands of the other party. In five of the last eight presidential elections we have shifted control of the White House from one party to the other, but we have shifted control of the Senate only twice (1952 and 1980) and control of the House only once (1952). In 1980, when the voters rejected President Carter's bid for reelection by a wide margin, they reelected 231 out of 268 Democratic senators and congressmen, even though President Carter lost a majority of the states and districts these same legislators carried. The same phenomenon occurred in the four preceding presidential elections in which party control of the White House changed hands:

Year:	Senators and congressmen reelected despite their party's loss of White House
1952 (D)	187 out of 208
1960 (R)	142 out of 145
1968 (D)	246 out of 257
1976 (R)	125 out of 134

In 1984, we may see the same phenomenon on the Republican side. [*We did not; President Reagan was reelected.—Ed.*] Because we do not blame a party's legislators when we blame that party's president, we allow most of these legislators to escape the president's electoral fate.

This is an important structural reason why presidents find it so difficult to form a government with a majority of Congress. Even when they are members of the same party, the president and the legislators do not feel committed to work together on a common policy for which they will jointly take credit and blame. Benjamin Franklin's maxim, "We must all hang together, or assuredly we shall all hang separately," does not apply to the individual members of Congress.

The weakness of these ties between a party's legislators and its president is fostered by our constitutional structure. The Constitution not only separates the Congress from the president; it separates Congress from itself. Congress has two separate houses that have every incentive to differ with one another except when they join to differ with the president. With two-year terms for representatives, six-year terms for senators, and four-year terms for presidents, incumbent legislators need to run only half their reelection campaigns in years when a president is also being elected.

As a result, we do not even have a congressional set of policies that stand opposed to the president's set of policies. There is no such thing as a congressional set of policies, or even a congressional opposition party set of policies. Congress makes policy one issue at a time, and forms a variety of shifting cross-party coalitions to enact or defeat each measure.

As Mr. Schlesinger points out, the incentives under a parliamentary system run in the opposite direction. The party or parties that hold a legislative majority choose some of their number to "form a government" led by a premier or prime minister; the "government" adopts what it considers to be an appropriate set of policies, and the majority votes together to legislate and execute those policies. If the majority splits on a major measure, the "government" falls, and a new majority must be found to form a new government or a new election must be held. Because the majority usually does not like to fall, it normally hangs together to legislate the policies of its leaders and to stand jointly accountable for the results.

Our Constitution rejects the parliamentary system, and it is far too late to re-argue that proposition. We agree with Mr. Schlesinger that, in its pure British form, the parliamentary system has important weaknesses different from our own. But the parliamentary system has elements that we might well adapt to our advantage, just as the basically parliamentary systems of France, West Germany, Japan, Canada, Italy and Ireland have adopted parts of our system.

For example, without changing our basic separation of powers in any fundamental way, we might provide greater incentives for presidents and legislators of the same party to cooperate in "forming a government" (1) by allowing incumbent leaders of Congress to serve in the president's cabinet, or (2) by establishing simultaneous four- or six-year terms for presidents and legislators alike, or (3) by requiring voters to cast a single ballot not only for a party's presidential and vice-presidential candidates as an indivisible bloc, as we now do, but for the party's House and Senate candidates as well. We could also make it possible for governments to "fall" by authorizing the president or Congress or both to call for new elections when a stalemate becomes intolerable.

The Committee on the Constitutional System is not committed to all, some, or any of these possibilities for change. Each may present more problems than it solves. Other ideas may prove better, including some that do not require changing the Constitution at all.

In the end, the Committee might even come out where Mr. Schlesinger has already arrived. But the Committee is being formed because of our shared belief that our national government isn't coping adequately with our national or international problems, and that the fault lies less in the quality of our leaders or the soundness of their policies than in the structure we require them to operate within.

If the framers of our Constitution could return on its bicentenary to examine the results of their remarkable work, they might or might not agree with our hypothesis, or on the desirability of any particular change. But as men who adapted their structure of government twice in their own lifetimes, and believed with Jefferson that every future generation should be free to do the same, they would certainly agree that these issues are worthy of the fullest examination. That is the task the Committee has set for itself as its contribution to the bicentenary celebration the framers so richly deserve.

James M. Burns

9. Why Think About Constitutional Reform? (1982)

James M. Burns is Woodrow Wilson professor of political science at Williams College. He is the author of many books on Congress, the presidency and the party system, including a prize-winning biography of FDR. In 1958, he was the Democratic nominee for the congressional seat from western Massachusetts. He is past president of the American Political Science Association and co-director of Project '87, an interdisciplinary study of the Constitution during the bicentennial era. He made the following remarks during testimony before the Joint Economic Committee's hearings on political economy under the Constitution.

I personally am dubious about the possibility in this country of sweeping constitutional change, such as the adopting of the parliamentary system. But I think, for two reasons, it's vitally important that we think hard about that alternative.

First, because there may well be—in the tumultuous century that undoubtedly lies ahead of us, there undoubtedly will be—a series of national and worldwide crises in which the capacity of our system will be so sorely tested that many Americans—perhaps rather suddenly—will feel an urgent need for a change. It's very important, if we come to a point of great debate in this country over alternative systems, that we have done our homework, that we have in our intellectual bank the kinds of ideas, the kind of analysis, the kind of daring, imaginative posing of alternatives that I think will come out of these hearings.

Reprinted from Joint Economic Committee, Hearings: "Political Economy and Constitutional Reform," 97th Cong., 2d Sess. (November–December, 1982).

And second, we have had to learn in this century that it's almost always the impossible and the unpredictable that do happen. We, you and I, in our early years, could not possibly, I think, have imagined the kinds of incredible developments, both benign and malign, that have taken place in the past fifty years.

So again, it seems to me that to consider the systemic changes is a matter of hard-headed practicality and not simply a kind of dreamy investigation.

Neal R. Pierce

10. A Remedy for Defects in the Federal System (1984)

Several members of CCS have been particularly concerned about the awkwardness of the federal system in adapting to modern conditions. In the following selection, taken from an address to the Advisory Commission on Intergovernmental Affairs, Neal Pierce notes these concerns and outlines a proposal developed by members of CCS. Pierce is a journalist and author of The People's President *(1966), a critical analysis of the electoral college.*

The Advisory Commission on Intergovernmental Relations has described itself as "the first official" 'federal' body created since the constitutional convention itself. With its regular representation of states, and perhaps most particularly the role it accords local government, the commission represents an historical advance in bringing hitherto unheard voices into the circles of national policy debate.

But think for a moment about the Constitution of the United States. Nowhere in that great document or its amendments do the words "federalism," "country," "city," "town" or "municipality" appear as much as once. Local government is a total non-being within the Constitution. Even in an urban age, Justice William Brennan could write— as he did in the Boulder cable television case—"ours is a 'dual system of government' which has no place for sovereign cities."

Since 1982, there has been a privately constituted Committee on the Constitutional System, looking towards 1987 and considering needed constitutional amendments. In one of that group's subcommittees, chaired by former Congressman Henry Reuss of Wisconsin, an amendment of potentially great interest to you has been written. Its chief author is Benjamin Read, former president of the German Marshall Fund of the U.S. The text is quite short; let me read it to you:

Article _____. Section 1. Every decade the president shall convene a convocation to make recommendations to achieve a more cooperative, responsive, equitable, accountable, and efficient federal system.

Section 2. Such decennial convocations shall consist of citizens knowledgeable about intergovernmental relations who are selected in equal numbers by federal, state and local governments under procedures established by act of Congress.

Section 3. When a convocation so requests, its recommendations for legislation shall be considered and voted upon promptly by the Congress and the state legislatures.

For this audience, it's scarcely necessary to underscore the import of such an amendment. Local governments would be constitutionally recognized for the first time in American history, a fitting development at a time when, in matters ranging from foreign trade to technological innovation, their efforts and success or failure are of substantive importance to the entire nation. The state and local and intergovernmental agenda would be raised to a level of concentrated national attention it has rarely received in American life. The president and Congress would be obliged, at least once in a decade, to join with state and local officials in examining those vital questions that the ACIR has dealt with for a quarter century: How well is the system functioning? What are the new and evolving systemic problems, as separate from economics and health and defense and a thousand and one discrete policy areas that normally preoccupy us? Which level of government should be responsible for what? And how to steer our course on judicial federalism?

We continue to face the problem of a tenth amendment which provides the courts with only the vaguest outlines for the intergovernmental division of powers and responsibilities. A convocation could and should set down guidelines for the benefit of the judiciary.

A decennial convocation might also dramatize to the nation oft-hidden issues of federalism: gross inequalities between our rich and poor states and the case for a representative tax system; state neglect of beleaguered inner cities; the dilemmas of governing metropolitan areas that sprawl across state lines; proliferations of special districts that undermine budgeting causes for the states and localities. The media would unquestionably devote much more serious attention than could ever be hoped from regular ACIR meetings. And with the requirement of congressional and state legislative votes on recommendations, the decisions of the convocation would be well publicized to the nation.

Yet it goes without saying, I should hope, that Congress would make ACIR the staff agency for these decennial convocations. I can imagine the ongoing research agenda of this Commission oriented to preparation for those meetings. Some of the friends of ACIR—city and country and state officials—would, I should imagine, see substantive promise for their levels of government in the proposed amendment and constitute a built-in constituency to press for its passage. And if they decided to do that, they might just succeed, for it is hard to see why anyone's blood would race hot in opposition.

As with any constitutional proposal, a myriad of questions arise. What is this new animal called a convocation—not a constitutional convention, not a legislative body, not a court—yet still constitutionally mandated? And how would delegate selection be accomplished? The president might well designate federal executive branch representatives, majority and minority congressional leaders might choose persons from their ranks, the chief justice delegates from the federal judiciary. But how would state representatives be picked?—by groups such as the National Governors Association and the National Conference of State Legislatures and chief justices of the state supreme courts? Perhaps. But what of local government—the National League of Cities, U.S. Conference of Mayors, National Association of Counties? But how about those who don't represent general purpose elected governments—the International City Management Association, or school board officials, or local bar associations?

And then the size of the convocation. The amendment's text leaves the question open; one possibility is eighteen persons from each level of government, plus a chair appointed by the president or elected by the convocation. That would add up to the rather neat total of fifty-five, the same number which attended the Philadelphia convention of 1787. And of course there would be questions about the duration of the convocation, partisan balance, and of course how the recommendations might emerge, whether as general principles and guidelines, or more precise structural or procedural changes, and how Congress and the legislatures could practicably vote on them.

All those questions, I would say, are resolvable detail. The essential point would be to write the requirement for the decennial convocations into the Constitution and *not* settle for statute alone. And for very clear reasons:

- The constitutional path would avoid the various legal challenges that could be raised against a convocation created by statute alone.
- A constitutional amendment would dignify each level of our intergovernmental system.
- Most importantly, it would pledge the people of the United States to regular and far more serious effort, as their history rolls on, to mold their system of governance, from White House to town hall, to the changing exigencies of the time.

Do we owe our system of government any less? I think not. Every person in this room, I am sure, has heard Woodrow Wilson's words: "The question of the relations of the states to the federal government is the cardinal question of our constitutional system. At every turn of our national history we have been brought face to face with it, and no definition of either statesmen or of judges has ever quieted or decided it. It cannot, indeed, be settled by the opinion of any one generation because it is a question of growth, and every successive stage of our political and economic development gives it a new aspect, makes it a new question."

I would submit that Wilson's admonition of openness to growth, of imperative of adaptability within the parameters of our wondrously flexible American federalism, will be relevant, and as important as a spur to progress, as long as the system itself shall endure.

Elmer Staats

11. Priorities in Governmental Reform (1984)

From time to time, members of CCS have set down in correspondence their personal reactions to items on the group's agenda. We include here, as representative of these contributions, a letter by Elmer Staats, who served from 1966 to 1981 as comptroller general of the United States.

I decided to drop you a note to give you a few reactions which may or may not be helpful. First, I somehow am not too happy with the choice of the term "deadlock" as being the happiest term to describe our objective. I see it rather as an objective of making the separation of powers between the Congress and the White House more effective and improving the collaboration between the two branches of government which has eroded badly in recent years. I believe this point was articulated several times during the meeting, but "deadlock" strikes me as being too rigid in its connotation as to what has really taken place.

Second, while I do not oppose the idea of a constitutional amendment per se, I believe that we should focus also on actions that can be taken to improve the present system, recognizing that a constitutional amendment is hard to come by. . . .

Let me list a few areas which might bear further staff work, although I hasten to say that I have not dug into any of them deeply enough to determine whether they might be taken administratively or by legislation. I think, however, that they could be accomplished without constitutional amendment.

1. Provide that the president submit a balanced budget as an alternative to the one which he recommends for approval by the Congress. This would give the Congress a much better idea as to how the president assesses priorities and would develop a realistic picture of what would be required to bring the budget into balance.

2. Provide for a biennial budget phased in over a five-year period, to provide not only less hassling between the two branches but also to give the Congress more time for oversight during the year following the budget year. . . .
3. Merge the appropriations and authorizing committees of Congress which would speed up congressional action and more clearly fix responsibility within the Congress.
4. As an alternative to the legislative veto, provide for delayed implementation on major new legislation to provide an opportunity for Congress to hold hearings on implementation plans by the executive branch. . . .
5. Provide for a question period in each house of Congress to give an opportunity to the executive branch to appear and respond to questions. . . .
6. Give former presidents the right to floor debate without vote. I don't believe this would require a constitutional amendment. It could be provided by concurrent resolution.
7. Institutionalize meetings between the president and congressional leaders by providing through legislation a formalization of congressional-White House legislative liaison meetings in much the same way that the Congress enacted legislation establishing the National Security Council. The arrangement could provide for staff officers from both branches who would be designated to prepare agenda, schedule meetings, and provide secretarial services generally.
8. One of the suggestions included in the materials distributed in advance of the meeting provided for campaign financing through political party organizations. I like this idea and hope that we can pursue it further.
9. Experimentation could be made with nonbinding referenda on major issues by the Congress or the president, to be financed with federal funds and limited to a small number of cases in any given session of Congress. Preferably, the wording of the questions would be worked out between the Congress and the White House. I have had serious reservations about the validity of the opinion polls which have been conducted as lacking in objectivity and appropriate coverage.
10. Extension of television coverage in both houses of Congress would be helpful. . . .

Finally, with respect to the proposed constitutional change in the terms of office of Congress and the president, I would personally favor a three-year term for members of the House, continue the six-year term for members of the Senate with half being selected every three years, and, finally, a six-year term for the president who would be limited to one term of office. I am well aware of the argument that people should have the right to reelect a successful president, but what concerns me far more is what happens toward the end of a presidential term, namely, holding all controversial issues over until after the presidential election and concern as to whether actions taken during the course of the campaign are designated for serious purposes or purely for political purposes. To be sure, any president would like to have his party succeed, but that is a far different question than the desire of a president and his immediate advisors to vindicate themselves personally at the polls. Witness the current situation, where there has been general agreement that action should be taken early with respect to the federal deficit, but nearly everybody also agrees that nothing can be done until after the election. I doubt whether this problem would be nearly as great if the president was not desiring to vindicate his administration through his reelection. . . .

12. A Statement of the Problem (1983)

The following statement, drafted for CCS by a group headed by James Sundquist (see page 89), summarizes the outlook that has guided the Committee's deliberations.

In the last *Federalist* paper, Alexander Hamilton urged ratification of the Constitution despite its imperfections, on the ground that its defects could be corrected by later amendment. The founding fathers regarded the national government they had organized as an experiment, and they hoped that succeeding generations would correct the mistakes that time and experience revealed. Indeed, Thomas Jefferson suggested that the constitution-drafting process should be repeated by each generation of Americans.

Yet after two hundred years, the basic constitutional structure bequeathed to the country by the eighteenth century remains intact. This is partly because the process of constitutional amendment is long and arduous, requiring a level of national consensus so high as to be rarely attainable. But it is mainly because, until this century, each generation has been generally satisfied that the system of government it inherited was serving the nation well.

Today's world, however, is far more complex than that of 1787—or even 1887. Technology has transformed the early agrarian economy, modern transportation and communications have made scattered settlements into a single national community. American prosperity has become enmeshed with world prosperity, and nuclear weaponry has put the country and the globe in constant peril.

And these profound changes have caused an explosion of demands upon the nation's government. The presidency, once a leisurely part-time job, is now the center of grueling pressure for fast decisions on a range of subjects inconceivable two hundred years ago. A Congress that customarily met for only a few weeks each year now sits almost continuously—and still reaches the end of its term with urgent business unattended.

Citizens, seeing their government besieged by seemingly uncontrollable events, have lost confidence in their leadership and institutions. Some trends have been positive. (Improved civil protection, accountability, and public participation are examples.) But the picture as a whole suggests a society unable to cope with current events. Polls reveal that the traditionally buoyant, optimistic American has become fearful of the future and doubtful of the competence of politicians to prevent disaster.

To some extent this loss of faith reflects the performance of particular elected leaders. But the quality of leadership is itself the product of the constitutional processes by which these leaders are chosen. And the basic question is whether *any* set of leaders, however wise and public-spirited, can make the present constitutional structure function to restore public confidence in government.

One feature of that structure is unique among the mature democratic nations, creating difficulties faced only in the United States. This is the separation and balance of powers between the executive and legislative branches. In order for the government to act, three independent centers of power must be brought into agreement. But these centers—the presidency, Senate, and House of Representatives—are elected at different times and responsible to different constituencies. And each center is structured to prevent any "faction"—such as a political party—from establishing control over the machinery as a whole.

This scheme was deliberately designed in the aftermath of the revolt against George III to protect the young republic against a new despotism. It has unquestionably served that purpose well. Yet a governmental structure crafted to frustrate would-be tyrants must also, inevitably, frustrate democratic leaders exercising these powers for worthy ends.

That is the dilemma of the American constitutional system. The checks and balances inspired by the experience of the eighteenth century have led repeatedly, in the twentieth century, to governmental stalemate and deadlock, to indecision and inaction in the face of urgent problems. For the most part, rash and arbitrary actions have been deterred. But this benefit has been gained at a growing cost. Except in times of great crisis, the government is now unable to act in a timely manner—or at all.

And even when policies are produced, after arduous delays, they are often a contradictory hodge-podge that no one supports as a whole. Neither the president nor any legislator wants a budget $200 billion in deficit; but none of them feels responsible for legislating such a result;

and none of them can be held accountable for it. The president blames the Congress; members of Congress blame the president and one another; and amid this recrimination, people lose confidence in government itself.

The consequences have been most severe in international affairs. The president has the constitutional responsibility for conducting foreign relations, but the Congress has virtually unlimited means to intervene in any aspect at any time. If the president pursues one policy and the Senate or House (or even a committee or a key leader) presses another, the result is no policy at all. The president negotiates with other governments without anyone being confident that he is, in fact, speaking for the United States. And when it turns out that he is not, friendly governments are confounded and hostile governments confused. The nation's thrusts for peace are blunted and the dangers of war increased.

Similar difficulties arise in domestic matters. Controlling inflation, recession, budget deficits and other economic threats calls for firm and consistent governmental policy. Yet again, if the president pursues one policy and either house of Congress supports another, the result is weakness and incoherence. On sensitive political issues—budget deficits and immigration as current examples—the three power centers are often unable to agree on necessary national decisions even when matters reach the crisis stage.

In sum, the confusion in this nation's policy-making process reflects the diffusion of policy-making responsibility. (A symptom of this diffusion can be seen in the recent recourse to *ad hoc* high-profile commissions to build consensus on key issues such as social security, nuclear armaments, and Latin American relations.)

On earlier occasions, the political party brought a semblance of unity to the scattered elements of the government. When the president was a strong party leader and his party had majorities in both houses— something that occurred mainly during major wars and depressions— the harmony needed to adopt and execute effective policies was sometimes attainable.

But contributing to the present malaise has been the progressive disintegration of political parties throughout this century. Legislative candidates get elected and re-elected essentially on their own, without much help from a party organization, and they place their personal survival above party policy and leadership. They have no major role, furthermore, in selecting their party's presidential candidate.

Since they do not share the same political fate, the party's congressional and presidential candidates have little incentive to cooperate in creating and conducting a coordinated program—and frequently fail to do so. *Ad hoc* legislative decisions are made by shifting cross-party coalitions and often implemented without conviction. The sum of the outcomes lacks coherence and political accountability.

When conflict between the branches renders government ineffective, the people usually blame the president. They expect modern presidents to formulate policy and to lead the Congress to support it. But under our present constitutional structure, this task may have become too difficult for even the most gifted president under any but the most critical conditions. When the Congress does not go along, the president is charged with bad policies or bad leadership, or both. Yet voters do not hold their members of Congress equally responsible. So when they express their displeasure by turning the incumbent out of the White House, they do not usually vote for a parallel change in the Congress; legislative incumbents generally manage to win reelection even when their party's presidential candidate is defeated. (In the last five presidential elections where a party lost control over the White House, 92% of that party's legislative incumbents who ran for reelection were victorious anyway.)

And as the legislators escape the president's electoral fate, the result is often divided government. During eighteen of the last thirty years, for instance, one party controlled the executive branch and the other organized one or both houses of the Congress. At such times, the healthy party competition that is essential to democratic government erupts into bitter confrontation between the branches. The tendency toward stalemate and deadlock is accentuated—often to the point of paralysis.

* * *

To state the problem is, of course, only the beginning. To find a solution is a challenge comparable to that which faced the Founding Fathers. Much can be learned from examining the structure and practices of other countries—where legislative and executive powers are blended rather than balanced. But any constitutional and related changes that might now be proposed for this country must accord with our own history and traditions. The aim must be to build upon the American experience, to preserve the great strengths of our constitutional structure but correct the growing weaknesses, to achieve a government that is decisive but not oppressive.

To prescribe such changes is a task as exacting—but also as compelling—as the one undertaken in Philadelphia in the summer of 1787.

Part 2

Reforms of the Electoral System

Elections are fundamental to a constitutional democracy. They are the process by which "government of the people, by the people, and for the people" renews itself. They draw the nation into a debate about its purposes and policies, and they confer legitimacy on those who win.

Thus, the conduct of elections is crucial to the health of a democracy. It is not enough just to invite the people to cast ballots. Dictatorships do that. Democracies must be sure that elections are competitive, and that the competition is free and fair. Citizens must have ample opportunity to participate in the campaign. Winners must be put in position to deliver on their campaign promises. Unless these conditions are met, the appearance of popular sovereignty is fraudulent.

Do elections in America meet these standards?

Certainly they are competitive. In almost every election, voters have choices to make. But campaigns are also appallingly expensive, which severely limits the range of choice. Most candidates for the House of Representatives must now spend hundreds of thousands of dollars on their campaigns. Some candidates for the Senate spend many millions of dollars. And campaigns for the presidency are estimated to cost over $100 million.

Obviously this level of expenditure means that most Americans cannot even consider running for a national political office, and only a few wealthy individuals, or those who have skills in raising large sums of money, can hope to have influence over the recruitment of candidates. In America, there are lots of ways to raise political money—from political action committees, wealthy individuals, solicitations by mass mailings, fund-raising events. Money is available for both liberals and conservatives. But enormous sums of money must be raised, and every candidate must do it for him- or herself. Candidates must be individual entrepreneurs.

Despite the huge amounts of money that are spent in campaigns, many Americans do not participate in political life at all, not even to the point of voting. There are many reasons for this failure to participate. Registration laws discourage some people from voting. Some potential voters feel no enthusiasm for the candidates. But one major obstacle is that citizens are skeptical about the effectiveness of their vote. Experience has made them cynical. They doubt that candidates will be able to carry out their promises.

All of these problems—the need for individual candidates to raise vast sums of money, the tendency for candidates to approach campaigns as individual entrepreneurs, the inability of winners to carry out their promises, the cynicism of voters—reflect the weakness of political parties in our electoral process. If parties had clear and relatively distinct platforms, if they were able to recruit candidates committed to these programs, if they had sufficient resources to conduct appealing campaigns, and if they could induce their candidates, once in office, to work together for the achievement of the promises the party had made during the campaign, then elections might more closely realize the promise of popular sovereignty.

The Constitution is partly responsible for the difficulties that parties face in our system. The framers saw "factions" as a threat to republican government. They knew that wherever men were free to organize in pursuit of selfish interests, factions would arise. But they also believed that the Constitution could be arranged so as to diminish the risk that factions would subvert liberty.

In the first place, the nation would be large enough that no single interest (manufacturers, bankers, tradesmen, plantation-owners) would constitute a majority by itself. Thus, while majorities ruled, no faction pursuing a single interest would be able to gain control over the government. Furthermore, the separation of powers would discourage factional control. In other governments, a faction that controlled the legislature also dominated the executive; it could write the laws and control their execution. This led to "tyranny." Under the Constitution, the legislature and the executive would be separately chosen, and the legislature would be divided into co-equal, separately chosen chambers. The framers were satisfied that it would be virtually impossible for any single interest to take control over such a complicated structure of government.

As soon as the new system was inaugurated, political leaders—including some of the leading framers—began to organize followings to enact and implement their policies. These groups emerged first in Congress and were soon active in congressional and presidential campaigns. But the parties that developed were not "factions" in the earlier sense. They were not committed to a single interest. In order to command majorities in Congress and in the race for the presidency, they had to embrace a broad coalition of interests. The work of party building forced political leaders to seek common ground, rather than to press for the satisfaction of the limited goals of any particular interest. The tremendous variety of the nation made the tyranny of any particular interest impossible.

Nevertheless, the Constitutional system continued to discourage the effort of party building. The campaign for the presidency induced politicians to pull together into national coalitions, but the campaigns for seats in the House and Senate led them to cater to local interests. Staggered elections strengthened the centrifugal forces. Only very rarely were political leaders (Jefferson, Jackson, Lincoln, McKinley, Franklin D. Roosevelt), by a combination of great political skills and circumstances that forced a single issue to the head of the nation's political agenda, able to achieve any semblance of party government. Even in these rare cases, the Constitutional system operated to discourage party discipline. To achieve great purposes (the purchase of Louisiana, the revision of the banking system, the preservation of the union, coping with the Great Depression and waging a world war), presidents were often forced to act alone.

In short, the framers' design has worked to discourage party government. It does not matter that parties do not fit the framers' definition of "faction." The system that was designed to frustrate factions has also worked to discourage party government.

Given the difficulty of amending the Constitution, it is reasonable to begin our inquiry into reform by asking whether anything can be done to strengthen parties within the constraints of the existing Constitutional system.

The materials in this section accept as given the Constitutional separation of powers, including the provision for staggered, locally oriented elections for Congress. Within this framework, they explore the possibility of strengthening the major parties, in order to make them more effective instruments of popular government: internally more cohesive, standing before the electorate as organizations capable of seeking a mandate and forming a government.

Alexander Heard

13. 'Tis Done—But 'Tis Never Done (1983)

Alexander Heard, a political scientist and author of seminal books on Southern politics and campaign finance, was chancellor of Vanderbilt University from 1963 to 1982. He is currently directing a major study of the presidential nominating process. The following address was delivered at the University of Virginia. It surveys the changes that have altered, and repeatedly re-altered, the way in which Americans choose their presidents and outlines principles that should guide any attempts at further reform.

On July 9, 1788, Benjamin Rush of Pennsylvania wrote: "Tis done. We have become a nation. . . . [A]mple restitution has at last been made to human nature by our new Constitution for all the injuries she has sustained in the old world from arbitrary government . . . ." In ten months enough states had ratified the Constitution for the new nation to begin the task of creating itself. Two centuries later we are still at it.

The avenues to the American presidency have been altered more than any other Constitutionally prescribed aspect of our political system. Constitutional amendments have changed the fundamental procedures for choosing presidents and vice presidents, including the guarantees of who may take part. Also radically modified have been the extralegal, informal and private processes that are part of presidential selection. Taken altogether, changes affecting presidential selection have, in fact, been more frequent and more extensive than changes in any other major part of our governmental structure.

The Presidential Nominating Process: The George Gund Lectures, Vol. III, Kenneth W. Thompson, ed., pp. 3–19. Copyright 1984 by University Press of America, Inc. Reprinted by permission of the publisher.

Adoption of the Constitution by the states in 1787 and 1788 was no easy passage. Lord Bryce concluded ninety-five years ago that had the decision lain with the electorate in each state voting on the same day, instead of with conventions deliberating over an extended period, "the voice of the people would probably have pronounced against the Constitution." That thought is sobering. In 1787, a small group of fifty-five tested, influential leaders worked by explicit policy in secret. Unobserved by others, they went boldly beyond their instructions to recommend revisions in the Articles of Confederation and created a new kind of Constitution for a new kind of nation, and then saw it approved.

Our nation's Constitutional functioning two centuries later is increasingly strained by fundamental, elemental changes in the nation's life. Now, in contrast to 1787, our political values, popular expectations, and often legal stipulations require exposed deliberations and a consequent popular influence on Constitutional adjustments.

*   *   *

The new Constitution proved remarkably adaptable to changing expectations and circumstances. Enduring values were articulated and protected, notably by the first ten amendments. But in a sensitive, central matter, the way the president would be chosen, one that the framers dealt with haltingly and by a special process for compromise, the Constitution has been mercifully both restrained and malleable. The changes in law and practice have extended across the whole life of the nation, which in fact carries a special irony. Despite the disputatious deliberations that led to the way of choosing presidents that was finally prescribed in the Constitution, Alexander Hamilton opened the sixty-eighth *Federalist* paper with his much noted observation that: "The mode of appointment of the Chief Magistrate of the United States is almost the only part of the system, of any consequence, which has escaped without severe censure or which has received the slightest mark of approbation from its opponents."

Modification since the eighteenth century in the way American presidents are chosen have stemmed from many sources.

The potential for deadlock, or alternatively for manipulation, was considerable under a system in which each elector in the electoral college voted for two persons without specifying one for president and the other for vice president, as provided originally in Article II. The anomaly became evident early. A president's chief rival would become his vice president and hence his possible successor. As the linking of political interests developed into factions with a degree of continuity and cohesion, the arrangement was clearly unsatisfactory. The twelfth amendment to the Constitution, adopted in 1804, provided for the separate election of the president and vice-president in the electoral college, thus making factional and later party slates possible, or inevitable.

It is emphasis misplaced, however, to stress—as sometimes is done—that only once since ratification of the Constitution has an amendment been adopted, referring to the twelfth amendment, that substantially altered the method of electing the president. The substance of presidential selection processes has been directly affected by nine amendments subsequent to the twelfth.

The fourteenth amendment invalidated the three-fifths compromise of Article I by apportioning United States Representatives among the states on the basis of a population that included former slaves (but excluding, still, those untaxed Indians). That amendment therefore altered representation in the electoral college as well as providing, among many other fecund provisions, that no state should abridge the privileges or immunities of citizens of the United States, the pertinent intended ones here being black.

The fifteenth amendment bore directly on the electoral process by declaring that the right to vote shall not be denied on account of race, color, or previous enslavement.

Women's suffrage was guaranteed by the nineteenth amendment.

The twentieth amendment deals extensively with presidential succession under special circumstances. The twenty-second declares that no person may be elected president more than twice, or under a certain condition more than once. The twenty-third gave the District of Columbia the right to participate in presidential elections. The twenty-fourth said no person could by prevented from voting for president or vice-president in any primary or other election for failure to pay a tax. The twenty-fifth amendment treats extensively and importantly presidential disability and succession, and the twenty-sixth protects persons who are eighteen years of age or older from being denied the right to vote because of age. These ten amendments—and Constitutional interpretations by courts—have altered in consequential ways our selection of presidents.

Congressional enactments have also addressed presidential selection. Procedures for selection of a president by the House of Representatives were adopted in 1825. An important statute was adopted in 1887 as a belated aftermath of the Hayes-Tilden controversy of 1876. It regulated the counting of electoral votes in the Congress. Congress has also enacted three presidential succession laws—in 1792, 1886, and 1947.

The first, passed by the 2nd Congress on March 1, 1792, provided for succession (after the vice-president) of the president pro tempore of the Senate, then of the speaker of the House; if those offices were vacant states were to send electors to Washington to choose a new president.

Moreover, if a presidential vacancy or disability occurred at a time when there was no vice-president and when more than six months of the presidential term remained, the contingent successor would act as president only until a new president and vice-president could be chosen in a special election conducted under the electoral college method used for regular elections. The maximum period a contingent successor could serve was seventeen months.

Almost a century later, passage of the Presidential Succession Act of January 10, 1886, changed the line of succession to run from the vice-president to the secretary of state, secretary of the treasury and so on through the cabinet department heads, in the order in which their departments had been created. The 1886 law excluded the two congressional posts from the line of succession and appeared to give Congress discretionary authority to decide whether to call a special presidential election, and, if so, when.

That law stood until Congress enacted the third presidential succession law on July 18, 1947. It is still in force. It placed the speaker of the House and the president pro tempore of the Senate (reversing their order in the 1792 law) ahead of cabinet officers in succession after the vice-president. In this Act, Congress rejected the idea of a special election in the event of a double vacancy in the presidency and the vice-presidency. For the first time, a contingent successor was directed to serve "until the expiration of the then current presidential term," and the speaker (or the president pro tempore) was required to resign both his legislative leadership post and his seat in the chamber as a condition of assuming the presidency.

State governmental regulation has significantly shaped presidential and vice presidential selection. So has action by the political parties at both state and national levels. Especially conspicuous has been the enactment of diverse state presidential primary laws, beginning in Florida in 1901. Their use has expanded, contracted, and expanded again in irregular patterns during the eight decades since. The composition and conduct of national nominating conventions and their decisiveness in choosing candidates have seen much change, too. And, of course, campaigning has altered with technology, especially with changes in transportation, communication, opinion polling, and the ability to manipulate data. Political technology radically affects costs. The price in constant dollars per voter long was generally stable, but has risen startlingly during the last two decades. Sources of money have altered with the new impacts of government on a society of growing interdependence increasingly subjected to public regulation. The ultimate significance of the dramatic innovation of federal campaign subsidies is uncertain. The undesirability of the several thousand newly developed political action committees, mostly active in Congressional elections, however, seems certain.

These are far from all the modifications of law and practice that have been made affecting presidential selection processes since 1788. They are enough, however, to back the contention that the ways and context of presidential and vice-presidential selection have evolved steadily, importantly, and with diversity throughout our history and continue to do so.

*   *   *

Many of these changes during the first two centuries of our government's life can be attributed directly to the flawed nature of the original plan. Those who under pressure of time wrote the procedures for electing the president that were embodied in the Constitution of 1787 thought segmentally. They framed provisions to keep the president and Congress independent of each other in certain ways. They sought to insulate the way of choosing the president from the threat of faction or manipulation. They devised a plan that struck an acceptable balance between the interests of the large and small states. And they conceived of a presidency filled by a wise leader possessed of lofty insight into the requirements of a nation that had certain, albeit limited, common interests. The prospect of George Washington as the first president, acknowledged or not, pervaded conceptions of the office. But the system established for choosing a president did not satisfy the needs of the system established for governing the country. It addressed only part of the equation. Consequently, the presidential selection system was modified early and has been adapted continuously to the evolving values, circumstances, and political expectations of the nation. Changes in the national environment of presidential selection have stimulated modifications well beyond those readily attributable to flaws on the original selection plan.

The impulse to continue in that reform tradition persists today. Expressions of dissatisfaction with the observable, external characteristics of the process are frequent and widespread. They focus on the declining rate of voting among Americans; on the growing length of presidential campaigns; on increasing campaign costs; on the apparent superficiality of television-centered electioneering; and on the lessened cohesion and functions of the political parties. Some lament, while others applaud, that presidential and vice-presidential nominees are no longer named by deliberative, negotiating processes within the national conventions. And a few applaud, while most deplore, the increasingly personal political campaigns of candidates conducted independently of the political parties.

Michael Barone wrote in the *Washington Post* last February 27, "The Democratic candidates for president are starting—actually, they started some time ago—on the longest obstacle course in quest of the leadership of a nation since George IV waited 23 years for his father, King George III, to be declared mad. . . . Many of the things they have to do to win the Democratic nomination will work against them in the general election. Many of the things they do in the campaign will work against them if they become president. . . ."

David Broder had written on June 5, 1980 in the *Washington Post*: "There is a sense that something has gone terribly wrong."

Underlying this kind of discontent with the process are deeper anxieties over the state of the nation's governance. The long-established two-party system decreasingly performs its traditional mediating functions. The proliferation of highly organized, well-financed special interest groups disrupts the representative functions of representative government. Government's ability to deal successfully with the nation's problems is not seen to be keeping pace with the mounting numbers and varieties of problems it is expected to address. Since 1932, the role of the national government has expanded qualitatively as well as quantitatively. It has undertaken new functions.

Presidents especially are weighted down by the new burdens. The presidency has become the converging point for those increased governmental responsibilities. It is also the place to which the public's dissatisfaction with their discharge is directed. Presidents, feeling unable to satisfy all the expectations centered on them, engage in what Sidney Blumenthal calls the "permanent campaign." Presidents now routinely use the political consultant's tools, especially sophisticated polling. They take what they learn of the public's perceptions of them to shape carefully crafted television and radio presentations, to launch direct-mail efforts, and otherwise to seek mass support for themselves and their programs— not just for purposes of the next election, but as a method of governing.

When public support wanes, presidential effectiveness declines. We have one-term presidents because it is authentically difficult for a president to satisfy the hopes of a sufficiently large number of voters to get reelected. Defeated presidents leave office enjoying low public esteem. Presidents don't look like the giants our early political socialization led us to think they should.

We thus have twin discontents: with the process of presidential selection and with perceived shortcomings in governmental performance. We are easily tempted to seek improvements in the latter by changing the former. The cry is heard, "If only we had a process that gave us presidents who are more knowledgeable, more experienced, more stable, politically better armed to lead. . . ." As part of the syndrome, enhancing presidential effectiveness is seen as an avenue to increasing general success in governing. It clearly is not enough, however, in the struggle toward that goal, to ask only how our methods of producing presidents can be improved. More is required than "getting better presidents," however defined. And it may even be that the presidential selection process cannot be engineered to produce reliably whatever we might agree "better presidents" to be.

*   *   *

Yet, effectiveness in government is a requisite for citizens of a democratic republic. Hamilton wrote in the seventieth *Federalist* paper that "a government ill executed, whatever it may be in theory, must be, in practice, a bad government." While we expect effectiveness, it is the essence of constitutional democracy to limit the means available to government for achieving effectiveness. In the twilight years of the eighteenth century, the framers believed it possible to have effective government that would concurrently preserve our liberty and maintain republican bearings. These aspirations could be conceptualized as antagonistic to each other. They could be accommodated successfully in a system of government only if appropriate institutional arrangements could be devised.

The basic skeletal structure of the institutions they settled upon for combining these unfriendly objectives remain essentially as it was. Probably we should not be surprised that the effectiveness of government in mastering the problems it has taken unto itself over the subsequent two centuries is more and more criticized in many quarters of American society. Have the problems with which American constitutional institutions must deal so changed that the basic institutional design initiated in the Constitution is no longer able to accommodate both effectiveness and liberty, and the changing notions of what each of those concepts embraces? Is it possible that cumulative changes occurring within the basic structure have diminished the capacity of the system to perform effectively? Is it possible for any set of institutions, however arrayed, to continue to combine liberty and effectiveness in our increasingly interdependent yet, ironically, increasingly fragmented world?

On the front of the current issue of *The Center Magazine* appears a quotation from the interpreter of the American frontier, Frederick Jackson Turner. Turner said: "Other nations have been rich and prosperous and powerful. But the United States has believed that it had an original contribution to make to the history of society by the production of a self-determining, self-restrained, intelligent democracy."

In the forbidding context of the late twentieth century, however, the challenge to achieve both effectiveness and liberty looms ominously. Yet the problem is as old as constitutional government. Frederick Watkins, in a 1940 essay called "The Problem of Constitutional Dictatorship," posed the dilemma in its sharpest terms. He placed it in the context of crisis—a clear and present danger to a society's survival.

Crisis has historically been the exceptional condition for the United States. We have survived those we have known, retaining or regaining our liberties and moving ahead. Even in today's dangerous world, a sense of crisis is not constant. If it were, liberal society would likely perish. As Watkins argues, "Where the conditions of survival are persistently severe, absolutism generally tends to become the normal form of government." The government of permanent crisis depicted by George Orwell in 1984 provides a graphic literary illustration of Watkin's analytical point. The challenges posed to free society by the crisis are instructive in thinking about more commonplace tensions between liberty and effectiveness in government. Watkins writes:

> Legal restraints are bound at some time or other to stand in the way of effective political action. Other things being equal, it is clear, therefore, that absolutism will always tend to be more efficient than constitutional government.

But he then quickly goes on to caution that, "of all political fallacies none is more deceptive . . . than the . . . tendency to confuse absolutism with omnipotence. . . ." All the same, Watkins acknowledges that effectiveness and liberty cannot always be joined to good result, the most apparent case being in time of crisis.

> When a man is trying to save himself from falling off a stepladder, he is not likely to give much thought to the dangers of over-exertion. When a social group is faced with an immediate threat to its existence it also cannot afford to calculate in terms of a very distant future. . . . There is no point in worrying about the future unless you are sure that you have a future to worry about.

Fortunately, the United States still has a future to worry about and a plausible chance to sustain a political system that combines basic liberty with adequate governmental effectiveness. But this need not always be so.

We cannot wisely ignore perceptions that government is ineffective in dealing with large problems of our time, whatever the source of those perceptions. Political change can often be more easily accomplished in a crisis, but political change is needed in quieter times to avoid crisis.

How can the United States improve the effectiveness of its political system while retaining and enhancing its democratic values, its liberty? The question has been continuously with us in its modern form for half a century. It is being raised currently with new undertones of urgency and by disparate voices. Many of these voices speak of their hope for help through changing how we bring the nation's chief executive to office. Doing that forces the issues in presidential selection beyond the process itself.

Much said and written assumes that proper modifications in the way we choose presidents can help repair deficiencies in presidential leadership. But we would not necessarily get adequate presidencies by choosing better presidents. Presidents discharge their duties and pursue our dreams through a system of government and politics. The institutions of government and circumstances of politics as well as the means of presidential selection determine the effectiveness of presidents. We cannot assume that by periodic adaptation in the selection process we can sustain the democratic values we cherish, ignoring the governing system whose principal leader it chooses and whose policies it affects.

To give perspective to those of us who would have committed ourselves to the importance of presidential selection, and therefore of the presidency, I quote from Don K. Price's new book, *America's Unwritten Constitution— Science, Religion, and Political Responsibility.* Professor Price writes:

> Through its committees, Congress had long since taken over a major part of the control of administration: its legislation determined the missions of executive departments and the pattern of organization and personnel systems, its appropriations systems controlled the details of expenditure, and its agent, the General Accounting Office, settled the accounts.
>
> On the other hand, such administrative authority as the president had (or now has) is the result of action taken by the Congress to delegate to him, especially through its enactment of the civil service system, the budget system, and other procedures for planning and management. If the president has control over administrative matters it is not the result of the written Constitution but of delegation from Congress, either by enacting explicit statutes or by refraining from interference. . . .

It is the glory of the American Constitution that it has extended fundamental liberties that it sought in 1787 to guarantee. The magnitude of the transformation of our national life that would come with the two centuries following 1787 could not have been envisioned, yet the Constitution has proved to be hallowed with remarkable realism and to be capable of amendment with remarkable success. So far it has embodied a magic mixture of flexibility and constancy that has kept it viable.

The constitutional arrangements that evolved after 1787 did not prevent the Civil War three-quarters of a century later. Possibly no constitutional system could have assured a peaceful solution to the problems of slavery and their related economic and political issues. That is a reminder that nations have lives far deeper than their political structures and procedures and than their constitutions, written or unwritten. The resort to arms in 1861 demonstrated that the capacity of the constitutional system to force, or accommodate, social reform was limited. We do not now face the kind of divisive issue that brought violence then. But that experience is instructive. It demonstrated that evolving values deeply held and a radically altered social context could impose strains on the then existing American constitutional arrangement beyond its capacity to cope.

We have no way of calibrating finely the ability of our political system to accommodate stress. We do not know with certainty the limits to its capacity to make procedural, structural, philosophical adjustments to new burdens while sustaining old values. We do know, however, three things.

First, our democracy will not survive through an automatic process of adaptation. The hard work of creative intelligence diligently applied is needed in the twentieth century as it was in the eighteenth.

Changes in a political system, large and small, flow from competitive pressures. The incentives of some influential participants are always narrowly self-serving. Others will be moved by more general and less parochial incentives, by a concern for a large welfare over a longer run. Self-interest is always present, but the capacity for insight and the impulses of statesmanship are latent in many, perhaps most people. They can enlarge an outlook, letting it identify personal with national purposes. Watkins states the case pointedly:

Nothing is more intensely human than a desire to have a cake and eat it too. In some cases where the connection between having and eating is fairly indirect, the demand can even be made to sound quite plausible and humane. . . . Even though immediate concerns may tend to carry unusual weight, the fact remains that most individuals have a very real interest in the welfare of the larger community in which they live. In many cases it will be found to have a stronger emotional appeal than the particular interests with which it comes in conflict. Under these circumstances all that is needed to achieve unified national action is to make the issue between having and eating wholly clear and definite. This is one of the major tasks of contemporary statesmanship.

We ought not to rely passively on existing constitutional practices for future success. Nor should we depend solely on incentives for personal political advantage to spur adequate adaptations to our radically altered governing requirements. A larger vision of the American destiny is needed to animate what is to be done.

Second, we face a new order of challenge to American processes of self government. The challenge is not provoked by a single intractable danger that must be addressed successfully or the nation will perish. It derives not from even so potent a new thing as nuclear weaponry, or so potent an old thing as the impact of technological innovation on the job market. Nor is the new order of challenge the consequence of a sudden, apocalyptic recognition by many of a life-threatening condition previously recognized by a few—like depletion of the underground water supplies on which our industries, our agriculture, and we ourselves are dependent.

We are confronted by a complex of interrelated phenomena that sum up to a gestalt, and it is that gestalt that is the new national condition. It is new in the multiplicity and interconnectedness of its origins, in its defiant complexity, and in its potential for worldwide societal disruption.

We have been moving toward this intensity of interdependence for at least four decades—or, more realistically, since the fifteenth century, or more realistically still, since the Garden of Eden.

It means that the presidency, and selection for it, has a new order of relationship to what happens outside the sphere of present politics and public policy, a new order of relationship to what happens far beyond American control among other peoples, in other nations, in other parts of the world.

Third, the critical question then becomes, put too narrowly, whether our evolving way of choosing presidents can produce presidents with attributes adequate to the evolving context of the office. The basic question is whether the process can produce *presidencies* adequate to our nation's needs.

The issue is fundamental. The overarching concern of the Constitutional Convention was the totality of the national government it would create. The failure of the founding fathers to devise a presidential selection system fully compatible with the structure and values of the new democracy led not to crisis or disaster but to early change. Americans need now to assess their presidential selection process in the perspective of the American constitutional system as a whole and that system's capability.

*   *   *

James L. Sundquist in 1980 described our condition compactly. He wrote:

> For in the last decade or two, the political scene has changed profoundly, and the changes all militate against governmental effectiveness. Four of the trends, all interrelated, affect the government's ability to formulate policy: the disintegration of political parties, the popularization of presidential nominations, the rejection by Congress of presidential leadership, and fragmentation of authority in Congress that prevents its development as an alternative source of policy integration and leadership. A fifth trend is the gradual deterioration of administrative capability.

Although how we nominate and elect presidents surely cannot be expected to carry the full burden of our federal life, much can be asked of it.

But it is essential to remember that services to be rendered or functions to be performed by a system for choosing presidents do not match neatly features of structure or process so that by altering the latter, one can in predictable ways modify the former. Institutional changes have cross-cutting effects, and processes and functions have multiple origins. That is one reason for the unintended consequences often precipitated by procedural and other formal changes in nomination and election procedures.

The ideal mode of institutional development is to define the values desired, hypothesize means to achieve them, adopt those means as policy, administer them as intended, and modify them in light of experience. But experience has taught that the process is more tangled than that. From the original provisions in Article II for choosing the chief magistrate through changes in party rules and statutes of the past decade, including the Federal Election Campaign Act Amendments of 1974 as interpreted, the difficulty of regulating electoral processes to achieve specified goals has proved mammoth.

It is not hard to articulate ambitions for our political system. We want effectiveness in coping with the problems thrown up by the changing conditions of the nation's life. We want to preserve democratic-republican values of participation in the political system as ends in themselves—but also, we insist, as instrumental in gaining greater governmental effectiveness over a longer run. We envision a presidency that is one part of a Madisonian web of government functioning not in opposition to, but in concert with, other political institutions, especially the Congress.

Our polity does not function, however, in generalities. Written constitutional provisions, Congressional enactments, state statutes, and party rules are shaped and twisted by judicial interpretation and administrative application. Competitive urges and ingenious initiatives both within the law and rules and in unregulated spheres contribute to unpredicted results. Powerful subliminal forces have shaped presidential selection from the very beginning, progressively converting it into an operation radically contrary to the founders' concepts. While the processes of exploration and adaptation proceed as they always have, anxiety mounts as the danger and difficulty of the country's conditions increase. Can we still govern ourselves?

We are concerned to select the wisest, ablest leaders from those who present themselves for office. But we hold that all the individuals elected to office, plus all they call to help them, will not have the wisdom and information possessed by a whole society of individuals. That society turns to government for decisions, but it can provide information, intelligence, and creativity that may at times complicate decisionmaking but will in the end enhance the quality of the decisions. We hold that concept to be true. That fact itself helps to make it true.

A presidential selection process that encourages robust participation in politics, that facilitates exchange of information and opinion among the governed and their governors, that educates the electorate to the nature and possibilities of government, that contributes to national unity in the presence of diversity, that strengthens commitment to our democratic political life, can increase the likelihood that we will enjoy a government of both liberty and power.

It cannot guarantee effective governance. It cannot shield the United States from a world of threat and hazard. It cannot by itself settle the intractable substantive problems that beset us. It cannot guarantee prosperity or safety in an interdependent world of independent actors. But the process can contribute to our most important collective responsibility—governing ourselves well.

Good governments, self-governments, are never established once and for all time. In the sweep of human experiences they are ephemeral creations. Their self-governing mechanisms often function differently than intended. That is a durable, vexing characteristic of democratic government. If good governments are to endure, their creation must be seen as done, but yet never fully done.

James L. Sundquist

14. Reversing the Decay of Party (1982)

James Sundquist, senior fellow in governmental studies at The Brookings Institution since 1965, served earlier in the Bureau of the Budget and the Department of Agriculture, and as an aide to the Democratic National Committee, the governor of New York and a United States senator. He has written books on the development of public policy, federalism, and the evolution of the party system. The following is an excerpt from his essay, "Party Decay and the Capacity to Govern."

Directions of Reform

The ills of the American political party system are deeply rooted in the traditions of political behavior in this country, entrenched public attitudes, and even the Constitution itself. The remedies will come—if they come at all—not through any sudden and sweeping reform measures but through the gradual development and adoption of new doctrine by the elite cadre of political activists and, through them, by the public at large, which will lead to incremental changes in institutions and behavior. With a sense of direction, those who would strengthen political parties can be alert to the opportunities that arise to shape those incremental changes and, in doing so, give birth and force to what may someday become a new set of dominant traditions.

A set of approaches intended to improve the cohesion of the government in Washington must encompass the party structure outside as well as within that government. On that basis, my own list of directions in

Excerpted from "Party Decay and the Capacity to Govern," published in *The Future of American Political Parties: The Challenge of Governance*, edited by Joel L. Fleishman. Copyrighted 1982 by the American Assembly, Columbia University; published by Prentice-Hall, Inc.

which reformers should try to nudge the party system include the following half dozen.

1. *Strengthen the national parties vis-à-vis the state parties.* Lack of cohesion within the governing party in Washington is traceable in large measure to the fact that the national parties have been federations of largely autonomous state organizations, which are free to nominate candidates for the House and the Senate who may be in total disagreement on major issues with the national party as a whole. It is difficult to envision any system whereby congressional nominees of American parties would have to be approved by the national headquarters, as is commonly the case with European parties. Yet in recent years, both the Democrat and Republican parties have established a greater degree of control from the center, and this trend should be encouraged. The Democrat's centralization has been expressed mainly through rules governing the presidential selection process, the Republican's principally through the use of substantial resources at the disposal of the national party committees whose policies the party leaders can influence. The success of the Republican effort is perhaps evidenced, as Huckshorn and Bibby suggest, in the remarkable degree of unity of Republican senators and representatives behind President Reagan's economic program in 1981.

2. *Strengthen the party organizations vis-à-vis presidential candidates and presidents.* Again the Republicans have shown the way, in using their resources not merely to promote the party's candidates for president and vice-president but also to finance institutional advertising for the party as a whole and financial and technical assistance to candidates at all levels, down to and including those running for state legislative seats. Since such activity depends wholly on the availability of resources to the national party headquarters—as distinct from resources in the hands of candidates—a direct way to strengthen the national parties would be to provide public funds to sustain party activities between presidential campaigns. The same logic that justifies the appropriation of public money to finance the campaigns themselves would appear to justify public support of other party activities as well, but it would be subject to the same hazards of discrimination against new and minor parties.

3. *Strengthen the party leaders vis-à-vis the party membership.* This recommendation, in particular, runs against the grain of the progressive tradition and the concept of democracy it embodies. Yet while in any democracy the electorate at large must choose among

party nominees in a general election, there is nothing in democratic theory that requires it to make the judgment on the capacity for national leadership of candidates who offer themselves in primary competition—and much to suggest that that is a task for which the rank and file of voters is ill-equipped. Before the vast proliferation of primaries in the 1970's, the presidential selection system had an admirable balance. The relatively few primaries enabled candidates to demonstrate their popular appeal, but the national political leadership—senators, representatives, governors, mayors, and other party leaders—could exercise a peer review and, when necessary, a veto. That balance needs to be restored. Reduction in the number of primaries should be encouraged, but even if that occurs, the caucuses that take their place will be—and should be—open to the widest possible participation. The solution therefore appears to lie in the reservation of a proportion of convention seats for uncommitted officeholders and party leaders, along the lines of the proposal the Hunt commission has advanced for the Democratic party. . . .

4. *Strengthen the party bonds between the legislative and executive branches.* Proposals for new institutional devices for this purpose appear impracticable for reasons discussed earlier. But the informal relationships that have evolved instead depend for their success on a sense of collective party responsibility among those participating. Presidents have to admit the congressional party into genuine participation in policy formulation—as distinct from pronouncing party policy on their own and then attributing narrow, parochial, or corrupt motives to members of Congress who disagree. Presidents have to refrain from unilateral announcements of legislative strategy, priorities, and timing from the White House. In return, congressional leaders have to see to it that the committee chairmen to whom legislative action on presidential proposals is entrusted are not in fact narrow, parochial, corrupt, or otherwise unresponsive to the will of the party as a whole. This leads directly to the next suggestion.

5. *Strengthen the party apparatus within the Congress.* This means the development of the influence of the party leadership, the party policy and steering committees, and particularly the party caucuses, as discussed earlier. The caucus should become steadily more assertive in informing committee chairmen and members of the will of the party membership and relieving of their committee assignments those who are unresponsive to it. This would require great innovative skill on the part of the speaker of the House—and, in the Senate, the majority leader—especially in creating and

utilizing a structure of party committees to develop policy positions that the caucus could endorse. Such a procedure would add new complications to an already cumbersome and overloaded legislative process, but there are promising precedents for its use. In any case, it appears to be the route toward obtaining cohesion and order in a Congress that has become fragmented and—except insofar as it abdicates to presidential dictate—anarchical.

6. *Discourage the split-ticket voting that leads to divided government.* Any measures that strengthen the unity and homogeneity of the national parties, as suggested in the first three points, will tend to discourage split-ticket voting. But the evils of divided government are so severe that creative thinking is needed to devise other measures also. Constitutional amendment to require voters to vote for party slates of candidates for president, vice-president, and House (and perhaps Senate also) is one effective solution, though hardly a feasible one in the short run. Short of amending the Constitution, much can be done through modifying election laws and the design of ballots and voting machine layouts to discourage rather than encourage split-ticket voting for national offices.

For all these purposes, the first requirement is to recognize the profound truth in V.O. Key's metaphor: the party truly *is* the web.

Lloyd N. Cutler

15. Party Government Under the Constitution (1985)

Lloyd Cutler (see page 11) delivered the following lecture at the Law School of the University of Pennsylvania in honor of Supreme Court Justice Owen Roberts. It provides a rationale and summary of proposals under active consideration by the Committee which Cutler co-chairs.

When Owen Roberts left the Supreme Court, he chose not to retire but to resign. He made this financial sacrifice to work for a federal union of the world's democracies, to be built on the fundamental lines of the American Constitution. He and his colleagues, who included Clarence Streit, George Marshall and John Foster Dulles, urged the creation and popular election of a transnational congress. They also proposed a transnational executive to be elected either by the congress or by the people of the member states. They expected that transnational political parties would arise and that party government would be the organizing principle of the new federal union.

During Owen Roberts' time in public life, party government was the organizing principle of American national politics. By party government, of course, I mean a government in which the same party holds the White House and a majority in both houses of Congress. From the time Justice Roberts took his first public job as assistant district attorney to 1945 when he left the Supreme Court, party government prevailed during 20 out of 23 congresses, all but the last Congresses of the Taft, Wilson and Hoover administrations. During that period no president was elected without carrying a majority for his party in both houses of Congress.

Since 1945, party government in America has been the exception rather than the rule. In the twenty Congresses elected after 1945, party government has prevailed during only nine. In the nine Congresses elected from 1968 to date, party government has prevailed during only two. In the five presidential campaigns from 1968 to date, only one presidential victor carried a majority for his party in both houses of Congress.

This remarkable decline in the frequency of party government has been accompanied by a parallel decline in party loyalty among voters and among each party's members of Congress. Indeed, the evidence suggests that this decline in party loyalty is closely related to the decline in party government.

At the turn of the century, when Owen Roberts was teaching at this law school, party loyalty was habitual among voters and members of Congress. From 1900 to 1908, only four percent of the nation's congressional districts split their tickets to give a majority to one party's candidate for president and to the other party's candidate for the House of Representatives. Ticket-splitting increased gradually during the first half of this century. After World War II, it exploded. In the 1984 election, fully 45 percent of all congressional districts voted in favor of President Reagan's reelection and the election of a Democratic congressman. Polling data show that about one-third of all voters now identify themselves as independent rather than as members or supporters of any party, and that more than half of all voters now split their presidential and congressional ballots. When Presidents Eisenhower, Nixon, and Reagan were reelected by majorities as huge as 16 to 23 percent, the same voters returned Democratic party majorities to the House all three times and to the Senate twice.

In Congress, the decline in party loyalty has been almost as dramatic. *Congressional Quarterly* computes the annual percentage of House and Senate ballots in which a majority of one party's members were on one side of the issue and a majority of the other party's members were on the other side. In 1900 the figure was 70 percent. It is only 40 percent today. As between the president and his fellow party members in the House and Senate, the loyalty percentage on presidentially-supported measures has averaged below 75 percent since World War II. This means that whether or not the president's party has a majority in both houses, he usually needs to form a coalition with a sizeable bloc of the opposite party in order to enact most elements of his party's program.

You may well ask whether these parallel declines in party government and party loyalty are of more than historical interest. I submit they are of enormous current importance, and that they go far to explain the national disappointment in the ineffectiveness of Congress and of the national government as a whole.

That disappointment, confirmed by all polling data, centers in the evident inability of the president and Congress to get together on a coherent program for governing and to stand accountable to the voters for the results of that program. With divided government and the lack of cohesion among each party's members of Congress, national policy has to be made one issue at a time. Each issue is decided by a cross-party coalition whose makeup shifts from one issue to the next. The result is a hodge-podge of ad hoc policy decisions that are usually inconsistent with one another, and in a sum of outcomes that most voters condemn. Neither the president nor any legislator defends this sum of conflicting outcomes or accepts responsibility for bringing it about.

There are many current examples over the nine most recent Congresses, seven of them periods of divided government. Time and space allow mention of only two: the shape of the budget, the most important domestic issue that any modern government has to decide; and the making of agreements with other governments, a *sine qua non* of foreign policy and security and even of economic policy as the world becomes ever more interdependent.

Budget Deficit. The federal government now spends more than five dollars for every four it takes in, even in a period of high economic growth. This condition arises out of a series of ad hoc decisions, each made by a different cross-party coalition, on the levels of particular taxes and expenditures. The longer this condition continues, the harder it will be to correct. Net interest payments already consume 3.5 percent of GNP and fourteen percent of the total 1985 budget, double the percentage of the much smaller 1970 budget. According to the Congressional Budget Office, interest payments will reach 4.1 percent of GNP and seventeen percent of the much larger 1990 budgets. The 1985 deficit alone will be larger than the total of all government expenditures in 1971. Most economists warn that while continuing large deficits stimulate the economy in the short run, the long term impact on interest rates, exchange rates, trade balances and inflation will be disastrous. All elected politicians, from the president to the most junior congressman, agree that this growing cancer must be removed, and they each have a plan to do so. Each of these plans would reduce the annual deficit by 25 to 50 percent per year over the next several years, but they would do so in differing and inconsistent ways. Any of these plans would be better than letting the deficits continue to accumulate at their present annual rate. But those we elect cannot form a consensus about which plan to adopt, and the cancer continues to grow.

Treaty Making. Many of our most important agreements with other nations take the form of treaties. The Constitution requires that, to become effective, treaties signed by the president must win the consent of two-thirds of the Senate. This means that thirty-four senators can upset a treaty the president has negotiated with another nation or nations. Even during periods of party government, this minority pre-rogative is frequently exercised, sometimes by the minority party voting as a bloc, but more often by an ad hoc, cross-party coalition. When the president's party does not have majority control of the Senate, treaty approval faces even higher odds. Over forty treaties submitted to the Senate since World War II have either been rejected or have never come to a vote. Among the important treaties that have never been ratified are SALT II, the 1974 and 1976 treaties with the Soviet Union on underground nuclear tests and explosions, the maritime boundary treaties with Mexico and Cuba, the Genocide Convention, a number of UN and OAS human rights conventions, the Vienna Convention on the Inter-pretation and Enforcement of Treaties, and a wide variety of bilateral trade, tax and environmental treaties.

With the decline in party government and party cohesion, neither the president nor any member of Congress need accept the blame for this hodgepodge of national policies, and none of them does so. Each of them can fairly say that he or she did have a coherent program, but that the others blocked its adoption. Their success in shifting the blame has been truly remarkable. Seven incumbent presidents have run to succeed themselves since World War II, and five of them—Truman, Eisenhower, Johnson, Nixon and Reagan—have won another term. That is a success rate of over seventy percent. Four of the five, all but Johnson, were victorious while presiding over a divided government. Since World War II, ninety percent of the Senate and House incumbents of both parties who ran for another term were successful, whether their own party won or lost the presidential elections. That was true even for the incumbents of the losing party in the landslide presidential elections of 1956, 1964, 1972 and 1984. In 1984, the reelection success rate of House incumbents of both parties was a whopping 96 percent. Polls show that the Congress as an institution has a very low approval rating among voters, but almost without fail the voters reelect their own individual members of Congress. In contrast, when the Canadian Liberal Party fell from power in the 1984 election, the percentage of incumbents who ran and won reelection was a mere 61 percent, and for Liberal Party incumbents, it was only 26 percent.

With reelection success rates like these, each party's incumbent legislators have no need to follow Benjamin Franklin's famous maxim, "We must indeed all hang together, or most assuredly we shall all hang

separately." Indeed, their preferred path to survival is to take the advice
of the Damon Runyon character who said, "It's every man for theirself."

Does the presence or absence of party government and party loyalty
really matter to the effectiveness and accountability of government?
Listen to Woodrow Wilson, speaking at a time when party government
was the rule and divided government was the exception. In 1912 Wilson
ran for president during the first divided government of the twentieth
century. He had the benefit of a Democratic majority in the House of
Representatives and a Republican rift that put both the incumbent,
President Taft, and his predecessor, Theodore Roosevelt, into the race
for the presidency. One of Wilson's campaign themes was the danger
of divided government. In a speech in this city [Philadelphia], at the
Academy of Music, before an audience including many progressive
Republicans, he said:

> The most interesting thing about the government of the United States is that
> under its constitutional balances it postpones everything. You can capture
> your House of Representatives in any second-year period, but you cannot
> capture your Senate in two years; and it may be that at the time you capture
> your House you haven't a chance to capture your presidency. The present
> House of Representatives is Democratic because the Republican party broke
> its promises. But even with the assistance of the independent Republicans
> in the Senate of the United States, it wasn't possible to put the program for
> which the country had been waiting past the veto of the president. So that
> you have an arrested government. You have a government that is not
> responding to the wishes of the people. You have a government that is not
> functioning, a government whose very energies are stayed and postponed.
> If you want to release the force of the American people, you have got to
> get possession of the Senate and the presidency as well as the House.

Wilson won the presidency and a good majority for the Democrats
in both the Senate and the House. His first term carried out the party
program by laying the legislative foundations of the New Freedom,
generally regarded as the most productive period of national government
between the abolition of slavery and the New Deal. The principal means
adopted to legislate the Wilson program was the binding party caucus,
a Democratic reform that filled the power vacuum left by the progressive
movement's successful attack on the arbitrary power of Speaker Joe
Cannon. It was used so effectively that it won the epithet "King Caucus,"
and soon fell victim itself to the progressive drive to remove all party
constraints on the individual conscience of each legislator. By the time
of Wilson's last Congress, divided government had returned, "King
Caucus" had fallen apart, and Wilson failed to achieve approval of his
most important initiative, joining the League of Nations.

A comparison of presidential success rates under party government and divided government bears Wilson out. Even under divided government, newly elected presidents enjoy a brief "honeymoon" with Congress, but it rarely lasts more than six months to a year. By that time incumbents of both parties become too concerned about the next House or Senate election to vote with the president at the risk of losing the support of an important interest group. Wilson's first two years and FDR's first term are the only peacetime examples of longer honeymoons in this century, and both occurred during periods of party government. Over the full term, the president's position has succeeded under party government on about eighty percent of all major congressional votes since World War II; under divided government the rate has been about 66 percent. The notable exception, of course, was president Reagan's success rate of 81 percent in 1981. But after this honeymoon, his rate quickly reverted to divided government form, and he appears unlikely to match his 1981 success during his second honeymoon in 1985.

In the parliamentary systems of Western Europe and Japan, of course, the prime minister's success rate is very close to one hundred percent. Efficiency is not the only measure of a system of government. But if we were to measure the efficiency of democratic governments by the ability of the elected leader to legislate his party's program, the American system today is only four-fifths as efficient as the parliamentary systems when we achieve party government, and only two-thirds as efficient when we have divided government. Even these figures overstate the president's actual success, since the bills finally adopted contain substantial modifications of the president's initial proposals, which he accepts to salvage at least half a loaf.

But there are many thoughtful citizens who think that our present condition of divided government and the resulting hodgepodge of national policies is preferable to the consequences of a return to party government and party cohesion. They accept the hodgepodge as the best available consensus that can be achieved among the diverse interest groups that make up so huge and variegated a nation. They see the consensus as conceding enough to each group to avoid the degree of divisiveness that would impair the national unity. They fear that party government and party cohesion would give an administration too much power to work its will, and lead to the kind of extreme swings in national policy that have occurred since World War II in the United Kingdom, along with the bitterness that has grown among Britain's competing interest groups. They also note that only a decade ago divided government helped to expose the excesses of an arbitrary and corrupt president and force his resignation. They read the results of the 1984 election, with its wide degree of ticket-splitting, as showing that many who voted for

President Reagan affirmatively wanted the insurance policy of a Democratic majority in the House. They would interpret the reelection of the president and more than ninety percent of the congressional incumbents of both parties in 1984 as a public endorsement of divided government and loose party ties.

This benign view of divided government was also shared by at least some of the framers. The Constitution makes no mention of party. It was drafted when political parties were first emerging in the British Parliament. They were feared the way we fear "special interest" groups today. They did not fit the Madisonian ideal of the president and Congress as men who would rise above the pressures of "faction" (Madison's euphemism for "party") and decide every issue in the national interest as each of them individually saw it. A majority of the framers did not want any individual to hold enough power to have his way completely, nor did they want any party to hold that much power. That is why they decided to share all major governmental powers among the branches and, in the legislative branch, between two co-equal chambers. That is why they arranged for the president and each House to be elected by different constituencies and for different periods of time.

Nevertheless, party government grew rapidly, because it proved essential in practice to make the new Constitution work. John Adams, Jefferson, Madison and Monroe were among its most successful practitioners. In the seven consecutive administrations of these four presidents, divided government never occurred. In their presidencies, each was the de facto leader of his party in the Congress. Although Adams and Jefferson were more activist vis-à-vis Congress, while Madison and Monroe were more deferential, all four maintained a high degree of party cohesion. Adams and Jefferson never had to cast a single veto, Madison did so only seven times, and Monroe only once. Since World War II, most presidents have cast vetoes by the dozens.

Over our history power has tended to shift between the presidential and the congressional wings of each party's axis. But party government prevailed more than 75 percent of the time between 1796 and 1945, compared to less than fifty percent of the time since 1945 and less than thirty percent of the time since 1968. There has been a parallel decline in party loyalty among voters and legislators. Two deductions seem warranted. One is that whatever the intent of the framers, the constitutional barriers did not keep party government and party loyalty from predominating for a century and a half. The second is that other factors, in addition to the constitutional barriers, must account for their decline over the last four decades.

Those factors have been widely identified as popular primaries, the explosion of campaign financing costs, the rise of well-financed, single-issue pressure groups, the arrival of television as our primary method of conveying and receiving political information, and the reforms of congressional procedure that have lessened the authority and power of legislative party leaders and of the legislative party caucus.

The party today has become a passive mechanism which individual candidates utilize to win nomination and election. The party's "leaders" no longer select the candidates. They no longer raise or control the allocation of most campaign funds. The presidential and congressional candidates win nomination with little or no help from one another or from the party organization. In the general election, they all stress their own personal qualifications and play down those elements of the party program that disturb important voting groups, and they persuade half of all voters to split their tickets. Those who reach Congress are more independent of party selection, support and discipline today than at any previous time in our history. That does not mean that they are more independent in the Madisonian sense of being free to vote on every issue in the national interest as each of them sees it. Their former dependence on the party for campaign funds and career advancement has been replaced by dependence on the many single-issue interest groups to whom they must turn to raise the constantly increasing amount of money needed to win and hold their seats. They now owe loyalty not to a party with a reasonably coherent view of the right mix of national policy, but to a variety of narrowly focused pressure groups with disparate and conflicting views.

If you accept this analysis, you will be asking a number of questions. Are these present conditions of loose party ties and a high frequency of divided government merely unintended and unavoidable consequences of the progressive reforms in party and congressional procedures over the last two generations, or are they necessary, evolutionary responses in the party system as the social and technological environment has changed? Should we try to rebuild party cohesion and party government? Or do the present conditions offer a better way of running this vast and diverse nation as it faces the growing complexities of modern life?

There are no empirical answers to these questions. But I would submit these reasons why the present conditions are not inevitable and why we should make the effort to rebuild.

- Party government and party cohesion are not anachronisms in modern democratic societies. They exist in most of the other industrial democracies and in many of our own states. The fact that they flourish in these other democracies and in our own state governments is strong evidence that their recent decline in our national government is neither inevitable nor irreversible.

- Our national government today has many more major decisions to make today than ever before. The competing interests involved in each decision are far more complex. We hold government responsible today not merely for the goals set forth in the preamble of the Constitution—to establish justice, insure domestic tranquility and provide for the national defense—but also for the macro-management of the national and world economy and the defense of the entire free world. Even conservative incumbents now accept this broad mandate.

- Because of the growing interdependence between our national economy, national security and domestic tranquility and the economy, security and tranquility of other nations, many of the decisions our government must make involve reaching and keeping agreements with other governments.

- Without party cohesion and party government, it is extraordinarily difficult to make major domestic decisions and agreements with other governments, because each decision depends on forming a different cross-party coalition.

- Without party cohesion and party government, both parties and their elected officials usually condemn the resulting hodgepodge of outcomes, yet manage to avoid being held accountable for them. As we have seen, the ability of incumbents of both parties to shift the blame and win reelection has been phenomenal.

- If we can succeed in rebuilding a modicum of party government and party cohesion, there is little risk that we will veer from one extreme policy to its opposite, or that significant interest groups will become severely disaffected. We had party government for most of the time before World War II, and putting the split over the constitutional entrenchment of slavery to one side, neither of these grievous consequences befell us. And in contrast to the United Kingdom, the constitutional role of the Supreme Court limits the extremes to which party government and party cohesion can take us. Justice Roberts' own career is a reminder that the Court will not permit party government to legislate beyond its constitutional rights. In part because of our diversity and size, but primarily because of the constitutional barriers, party government in America has never been efficient enough to achieve extreme and divisive results.

- Party government does not assure creative and effective government, but divided government comes close to assuring stagnant and ineffective government. All of the great presidents—Jefferson, Lincoln, Theodore Roosevelt, Wilson and Franklin Roosevelt—presided over party governments. It is hard to think of a single major change of legislative policy in this century—with the exception of the Reagan 1981 tax cuts—that was adopted during a period of divided government, and that change occurred in the brief honeymoon period during the first year of President Reagan's term.

- A return to party government would not impair the congressional power to oversee executive performance and curb executive excesses. Nor would it restore the arbitrary power of party bosses and legislative leaders. Popular primaries and the democratization of congressional procedures are here to stay. These reforms, together with the penetrating surveillance of the investigative press, are sufficient guarantees that the basic constitutional checks and balances will continue to function. They do not depend on divided government to work. Teapot Dome, for example, was exposed during a time of party government, with Owen Roberts playing the same prosecutor's role that Archibald Cox was to fill in the Watergate scandal half a century later.

If the case for rebuilding party unity and reducing the frequency of divided government is accepted, the easier place to begin is with changes in party and congressional rules and the election laws, rather than with the far more difficult task of adopting constitutional amendments. As we have noted, party government did predominate until after World War II despite the constitutional barriers. If the recent developments that have led to divided government could be offset by changing these rules and election laws, this would appear to be the place to start.

Six such ideas seem to me worthy of special mention.

1. Amending party rules so as to provide that in the presidential nominating conventions, the winners of the party nominations for the House and Senate, plus the holdover senators, would be entitled to seats as voting delegates. These 500 or so additional delegates could have an important influence on the selection of the presidential nominee. This in turn would tend to build greater interdependence and closer party cohesion between the presidential and congressional wings of each party, and identify them more closely together in the voter's mind.[1]

2. Amending campaign financing laws to create a Congressional Campaign Broadcast Fund, similar to the existing Presidential Campaign Fund.[2] This fund would be available to each party and its congressional candidates in the general election for broadcast expenses, on condition that they not expend any other funds on campaign broadcasts.[3] Half or more of each party's share would go to the party itself, which could place its bets among its candidates

so as to maximize its chances to win a majority.[4] This should help to build party cohesion by making candidates depend on the party for a large part of their campaign funds and by reducing their dependence on raising funds from single-issue interest groups.

3. Providing by federal statute that the presidential elections be conducted two-to-four weeks before the congressional elections.[5] This would tend to reduce divided government by enabling voters to know which party has been entrusted with the White House before they vote for members of the House and Senate. While voter participation in a later congressional election might be lower than in the presidential election,[6] a two-stage election would maximize the new president's chances, in the honeymoon of his own election, to win a majority for his party in the Senate and House and thus improve the party's chances of carrying out its program. This is what happened in the two-stage French election of 1981.[7]

4. Providing by federal statute that every state must include on its ballot for all federal elections an additional line or lever by which a voter may (but need not) cast his vote for all the candidates of one party for the open federal offices.[8] Connecticut has such a ballot, and in 1984 President Reagan's coattails in Connecticut were more effective than in many other states.[9]

5. Providing by party legislative rule that by a sixty percent vote, the party caucus in each house could bind all party members to vote the party position on up to a stated number of particular bills (e.g. fifty) per session. Such a rule would be enforced by automatic loss of any chairmanship or other party office held by a member who votes against the caucus position more than a stated number of times (e.g. five) per session. This would be a more moderate version of the binding party caucus so effectively employed in Wilson's first Congress and briefly revived during FDR's first term. It would greatly enhance party legislative loyalty while leaving reasonable scope for party members to make occasional departures on principle from the party caucus position.

6. Changing party and legislative rules to create a "shadow cabinet" for the party not holding the White House. The shadow cabinet would consist of the party's highest ranking member in the House and Senate and on each of from six to ten major House and Senate committees. The House and Senate leaders would alternate annually as leader of the shadow cabinet. The shadow cabinet would meet regularly to formulate party positions, and its members would serve as party spokesmen on particular issues. If the House and Senate leaders could be persuaded to form such a cabinet and to

make it work, this would go far to build party consciousness in the minds of voters and greater cohesion among the party's legislative members.

These are all rather modest proposals. None of them would shake the foundations of the republic. Singly or in combination, they would not alter the basic political system. But they would somewhat improve the chances of tightening party cohesion and achieving party government.

To improve these chances even more, it would be necessary to lower some of the barriers raised by the Constitution. To amend the Constitution, a two-thirds vote of the House and Senate or the calling of a constitutional convention by two-thirds of the states is required, plus the approval of any specific amendment by the legislatures of three-fourths of the states. For proposals that would strengthen party cohesion, and thus reduce the individual power of incumbent legislators and interest groups, that is a very heavy burden indeed.

That is why the most effective constitutional amendment for restoring party government—the team ticket—is unlikely to get off the ground. Under the team ticket plan, in presidential election years each party would be required to present a slate in each congressional district for all federal offices (president, vice-president, House member and any open Senate seat), and voters would be required to vote for the entire team of the party of their choice. It seems unlikely that either congressional incumbents or state legislatures would approve depriving voters of the right to split their tickets.

But there are a few more popular amendment ideas that do not threaten incumbent legislators or curtail voter freedom, and that would further strengthen party cohesion and the prospect of party government, or at least provide a means of breaking the deadlocks that occur under divided government.

1. Providing for four-year terms for House members, running simultaneously with the presidential term. In the version I prefer, the Senate term would also be extended from six to eight years. There would be two classes of senators instead of the present three. One class would be elected in each presidential election. Simultaneous elections for all federal offices once every four years would increase the potential for party government by eliminating the mid-term elections in which the president's party almost always loses House and Senate seats. With four years between elections, incumbents would have more time to discharge their legislative duties. Their time horizon to the next election would be lengthened to the same four years as the president's, thereby improving the

chances of party cohesion and extending the president's "honeymoon" period. Congressional incumbents with at least four years before the next election would be more likely to support programs calculated to impose short-term sacrifices in order to achieve longer term benefits. President Johnson proposed the four-year congressional term,[10] and President Reagan is expected to do so during his second term.

2. Granting the president discretion to include sitting members of Congress in his cabinet without requiring them to give up their seats, something the Constitution now forbids. Chief Justice Story and President Wilson were among the first to propose this step as a way of building party cohesion between the president and the legislators of his own party.

3. A package amendment that would (a) reinstate the constitutionality of a legislative veto of certain presidential and agency actions, subject to presidential veto of the legislative veto and in turn to an override by two-thirds of both houses,[11] and (b) reduce the requirement for treaty ratification from two-thirds of the Senate to sixty percent or to a simple majority of both houses.[12] This mutual exchange of powers would encourage broader delegation of discretionary authority to the executive and greatly facilitate the government's ability to make and perform agreements with other nations.

4. This package could be enlarged to include an amendment authorizing the president to make a "line-item" veto of any bill appropriating expenditures, subject to override by majority vote of both houses, rather than the two-thirds override for general vetos.[13] A line-item veto now exists in most of the states, and it would be of at least some assistance in breaking deadlocks on how to reduce deficits.[14] President Reagan has recommended it in his last two inaugural addresses.

There is another pair of amendment proposals that would improve the chances of avoiding or breaking deadlocks, but would work a more fundamental change in our present constitutional structure. One such proposal would create a simultaneous five-year term for president and for members of the Senate and House (or a six-year presidential term combined with a three-year House term and a six-year, two-class Senate term).[15] The most widely advocated proposal of this type would limit the president to a single six-year term.[16] The second proposal would build on the first. It would compensate for the longer terms by allowing a majority of both houses, or the president plus a majority of one house, to call at any time for new national elections for the presidency and

Congress for new full terms. Its supporters urge that by adopting in modified form this basic feature of most parliamentary systems, the president and Congress would be given an added incentive to avoid deadlocks and a means of breaking them when necessary. They also urge that in addition to its salutary effect on deadlocks, it would provide a way to turn a weak but non-impeachable president out of office.[17]

All of these ideas, and others, are now being studied by the Committee on the Constitutional System. The Committee's two hundred members include many present and former legislators, cabinet members, White House staffers, governors and mayors of both parties (including the governor of this commonwealth and the mayor of this city), and a wide cross-section of academic, business, labor, political and interest group leaders. It is chaired by Senator Nancy Kassebaum, Douglas Dillon and your speaker this evening. It is proceeding on the theory that a constructive way to commemorate the bicentenary of our constitutional system is to analyze its few weaknesses along with its many strengths, and to consider how those weaknesses might be corrected.

As the committee proceeds with its analysis, some of the measures I have listed may be judged not potent enough to help restore party cohesion and undivided government or to prevent deadlock. Others may have overriding, adverse side effects. Some which pass both these tests, especially the constitutional amendments, may not yet be politically viable. But further analysis may also produce a set of possible changes that are relatively free of such defects and would help to correct the weaknesses we see today. In any event, we will do better by pursuing this analysis than by merely deploring how television and other modern phenomena have changed our political process, or by continuing to blame what are really the faults of the structure on the individuals we elect to run it. And if the pending call for a constitutional convention to propose a "balance the budget" amendment is joined by the two additional states needed to provide the triggering two-thirds—an outcome we do not favor—our committee may be ready with some better ideas.[18]

What would Owen Roberts have thought about the need for restoring party government and party cohesion and of the various proposals I have described? He despised junk amendments to the Constitution such as prohibition, and he probably would feel the same way about the current amendment proposals to balance the budget and to prohibit abortion. But as I noted at the beginning, he was also a fervent advocate of Atlantic union, and therefore a man who was not afraid to consider adapting our political structure, even the Constitution itself, to accommodate the complexity and interdependence of modern life.

In 1949, Justice Roberts was a co-author of *The New Federalist*, which expounded the case for an international convention to draft a constitution creating a federal union of the world's major democracies. *The New Federalist* recognized the importance of political parties and accountable party government. It envisioned that a transnational party or parties would win a majority of the federal union congress, and that a member of the majority would be selected as the premier. Indeed, it went so far toward insuring accountability as to propose that the premier would have to resign if he lost a congressional vote of confidence, and that new elections could be called if a deadlock occurred. Implicitly, it recognized that, to accommodate the transfer of sovereignty to the new federal union, our own Constitution would have to be modified in ways more fundamental than any I have mentioned.

We cannot know whether Justice Roberts would have agreed with what I have said tonight about the need to adapt our national political structure so as to encourage party government and party cohesion. In his time, the problem was not a serious one. But I venture to suggest that if he had witnessed the last forty years, he would have been interested enough to become an active member of our committee, and that if he accepted our analysis of the problem, he would not have drawn back from advocating the structural changes needed to solve it.

Notes

1. Another version of this idea would create a bicameral nominating convention. *See page 114.*

2. Under this statute, each major party nominee is entitled to receive an equal amount for the presidential campaign, on condition that a nominee accepting federal funds agree not to receive or expend any other funds. Minor party nominees are entitled to proportionately lower amounts based on the party's record in the last election, but may receive and expend privately raised funds up to the major party ceiling. The Supreme Court upheld the constitutionality of this fund, including its limits on other contributions and expenditures, in *Buckley v. Valeo*, 424 U.S. 1 (1976).

3. Broadcast expenses now account for a high percentage of all campaign costs. Ceilings on broadcast expenditures would be the virtual equivalent of ceilings on all expenditures. The proposed statute could be structured to limit use of the federal funds to live or taped personal appearances by the candidate, in order to bar its use for "canned" political commercials. It might also bar the use of private funds for such commercials by any candidate accepting the public funds. As in the case of the Presidential Campaign Fund, however, the statute could not reach expenditures by contribution-supported "independent" committees. (See *Federal Election Commission v. National Conservative Political Action Committee*, No. 83–1082, decided March 18, 1985.)

4. One possible method might be to allocate fifty percent of the public funds directly to each party nominee on a population-based formula and to allocate

the other fifty percent to each national party organization or its congressional campaign committee. The designated party body could then allocate its share among nominees in the same way it now allocates privately raised funds. With greater difficulty, the proposed statute's objective might also be achieved by allocating blocks of broadcast time to the candidates and required stations, as a condition of their license, to provide the time without charge. But the practical problems of allocating time are considerably greater than in the case of money, and the opposition of broadcasters would be severe.

5. Under Article I, section 4, and Article II, section 1, Congress has clear power to fix the time of elections to federal office and is free to fix different dates for elections to different offices.

6. Voter turnout in "mid-term" congressional elections is usually lower than in the years of presidential elections. Voter turnout in two-stage, state primary elections is also usually lower in the run-off phase, unless the race is expected to be a close one.

7. Under the Constitution of the Fifth Republic, the election for the seven-year presidential term is out of phase with the election for the five-year Assembly term. However, the president has the power to dissolve Parliament and call for new parliamentary elections. When Francois Mitterand was elected president in 1981 as the candidate of the Socialist Party-Communist Party coalition, he promptly dissolved Parliament and called for new elections a month after the presidential election. In the parliamentary election, the Socialists won a decisive majority by themselves and did not need the support of the Communist deputies to govern.

8. Such a statute would clearly be within the authority of Congress to regulate the time, place, and "manner" of elections to federal office.

9. Although the Republicans lost ten House seats and one Senate seat nationwide as compared to the 1980 elections, they gained one House seat and reelected the incumbent Republican Senator in Connecticut.

10. To satisfy possible concerns about the utility of the mid-term election as a "referendum" to resolve deadlocks between the president and the opposition party in Congress, the amendment could authorize a mid-term election for the balance of the Senate and House terms by action of a majority of both houses or of the president and a majority of one house.

11. For the Court's opinion invalidating the legislative veto, see pages 241–243. A two-house veto provision subject to presidential approval or veto and in turn to override of his veto by two-thirds of both houses—in other words, a statute—would of course comply with the presentment clause and would not require a constitutional amendment.

12. The SALT I agreements consisted of an interim freeze on offensive weapons and a ban on anti-ballistic missile systems. When these were presented to Congress, the Senate insisted on treating the ABM agreement as a treaty, but allowed the interim freeze to be approved by a majority of both houses. At the same time, Congress passed a statute providing that future nuclear arms control agreements required approval by a majority vote of both houses. However, when the SALT II agreement was signed in 1979, the Senate insisted that it be presented to the Senate alone as a treaty.

13. With President Reagan's support, Senator Mattingly (R., Ga.) has recently introduced a bill that would authorize line-item vetoes by statute. It provides that every numbered section and separate paragraph of every subsequent appropriations bill passed by Congress shall automatically be enrolled and presented to the president as a separate bill. The constitutionality of such a statute appears open to considerable doubt. In any event, congressional draftsmen could easily frustrate its purposes by writing future appropriation bills without numbered sections or separate paragraphs.

14. Forty-two states now have line-item vetoes.

15. A simultaneous five-year term for all elected federal officials would come closest to a parliamentary system. It is noteworthy, however, that the present French constitution, which combines a parliamentary system with even greater powers for the president than the American Constitution, does not provide for simultaneous terms. It does, however, authorize the president to dissolve parliament and call for new elections. A six-year presidential term with a three-year House term and a six-year, two-class Senate term would have the disadvantage that half the Senate would always be elected in a presidential election while the other half would always be elected in a non-presidential year.

16. Presidents Eisenhower, Johnson and Carter have all favored the single six-year term. A Committee for the Single Six-Year Presidential Term, co-chaired by Milton Eisenhower, William Simon, Cyrus Vance and Griffin Bell, is now urging a constitutional amendment to bring it about. For further analysis, see pages 167–174.

17. Unless the present method of nominating candidates and conducting general elections were sharply revised, elections following dissolutions would face enormous practical difficulties. Some advocates of a dissolution procedure, noting the high cost and extended length of current campaigns, regard the necessary foreshortening of a post-dissolution election as one of the idea's positive virtues.

18. Under the proposed amendment, except during a declared war, a sixty percent vote of both houses would be required to approve a budget with greater expenditures than receipts, or to increase the federal tax share of the gross national product. However, the amendment provides no enforcement procedures and does not even call for a transition period during which current deficits (exceeding twenty percent of current expenditures) could gradually be reduced.

16. The Impact of Television (1985)

Newton Minow, a lawyer, has been chairman of the Federal Communications Commission and chairman of the board of governors of the Public Broadcasting Service. He was special assistant to Adlai Stevenson in the presidential campaigns of 1952 and 1956 and co-chairman of the League of Women Voters committee that staged the presidential debates of 1976 and 1980. The following remarks are from an address he gave to CCS in March, 1985.

When we look in the books to read the Constitution, we learn that the Constitution is subject to amendment only through specific, prescribed procedures. I suggest to you that sometimes the law and the Constitution are amended without any of us realizing it. Sometimes, as in the case of the electoral college, this happens through the evolution of political practices, and sometimes, this happens when the Constitution is amended by technology. Then it happens silently and instantly.

For example, consider the relevance of political jurisdictions. When the technology of television developed, the television and advertising industries quickly saw that television signals did not correspond with political boundaries. A television signal spreads through the air in a circle with a radius of about sixty miles. Viewers of a signal broadcast from my hometown of Chicago live in the city of Chicago, the Cook County suburbs, the other five counties in the metropolitan area of Chicago, and in other parts of Illinois, Wisconsin, Indiana and Michigan. The same situation exists throughout the United States, and across our national boundaries into Canada and Mexico.

When this became apparent, the broadcasting and television industries quickly acted. They drew their own map, ignoring city, county, state and national boundary lines, and divided the country into 211 ADI's— areas of dominant influence. They didn't call for a Constitutional convention or persuade Congress to change any laws. They simply threw away the official governmental maps and boundaries and adapted to the new technology, by defining their business in terms of ADI's, instead of cities, counties, states, and the nation.

In government, however, we haven't acted, or reacted, to the new technology.

For example, government failed to act and react while television fundamentally altered the balance between our three branches of government. Only one branch, the executive, has access to television on its own terms, essentially at the discretion of the president. Congress now knows that television fundamentally altered legislative debates. The other day, Senator Howard Baker observed that senators do not need to participate much in Senate debates these days because "if no one listens, the senators don't care because they go outside the Senate floor and someone will listen to them with a television camera. . . ."

Watching television is how most Americans spend most of their time—close to eight hours a day in the average home. Most Americans now receive most of their information through broadcasting. As Professor Benjamin Barber observes:

> The community of citizens governing themselves face-to-face has given way to the mass society, and live talk has been replaced by telecommunications. Once a nation of talkers, we have turned into a nation of watchers—once doers, we have become viewers—and the effect on our democracy has been profound.

Yes, the effect on political process has been more profound than any other technological change since the printing press. And its effect on the democratic process, its effect on law, its effect on government, and its effect on politics all are a set of questions which call for more attention from the best legal minds in America.

Television does enlighten citizens and does advance the democratic process in ways far beyond the capacity of any other medium. Television's coverage of the Watergate hearings and the impeachment hearings gave the American people more than a civics lesson; it also gave them front row seats in the hearing room and a sense of unparalleled participation. The presidential debates, with all their faults, do bring the candidates into millions of homes and offer citizens a first-hand chance to evaluate the candidates.

But, with all the advances through this powerful medium, there are also setbacks to the democratic process. Theodore White, the best historian-journalist in our time, said it best when he wrote last year that the flood of money that gushes into politics to buy television time is the pollution of democracy.

I propose that citizens address, analyze, and reflect on this question: what is the best way to harness this great gift of television to improve and advance the electoral process? We have the expertise, analytical skills, and vision to find ways—constitutional ways, consistent with First Amendment freedoms—to achieve four goals:

- To promote rational political discussion in presidential campaigns.
- To reduce the amount of money required to run for political office, especially to buy television time.
- To shorten campaigns.
- To assure basic access to television for all significant candidates for president and vice-president.

Let us examine each goal.

First, to promote rational political discussion in presidential campaigns. Sophisticated campaign strategists and political consultants now create commercials and spots which dominate the airwaves at a cost of many millions of dollars. In my own state of Illinois, in the recent Senate election, our major candidates, Paul Simon and Chuck Percy, found our Illinois situation even worse that usual. A California businessman, unauthorized by Simon, spent more than $1.1 million of his own money to "help" Simon by buying radio and television commercials that attacked Percy. Although Simon disavowed the ads, he could not stop them. A law, which I think could be drafted to satisfy constitutional tests, is needed to stop not only this form of assault on the democratic process, but to stop all political commercials. John O'Toole, chairman of one of the nation's leading advertising agencies, put the issue in plain English: "The time has come to stop trivializing the electoral process by equating a candidate and a public office with an antiperspirant and an armpit. It is time to stop selling television spots to political candidates."

Second, to reduce the amount of money required to run for political office, especially to buy television time. Once the major presidential candidates are nominated, they now receive more than $40 million in public funds for the campaign. In 1984, most of that money went to purchase television time, almost all of it to purchase commercials of thirty or sixty seconds. In the primaries, approximately $85 million was raised and spent by the candidates, mostly for commercials.

Presidents of the television age, starting with Presidents Eisenhower and Kennedy, saw the problem coming and urged reform. Now, more than twenty years later, the problem is more than twenty times worse. Why on earth should the American people spend millions out of the public treasury so that the Republican and Democratic candidates can flood the air with thirty-second television commercials contributing nothing to political enlightenment? If this money is to be spent, at least let us insist that the candidates appear live to deal with issues. I ask you to search for ways, constitutional ways, to eliminate this pollution of democracy, and use this great medium to inform and enlighten us.

Third, to shorten campaigns. If you've ever been in Great Britain during a political campaign, you saw campaign periods strictly limited to a three-week period, during which no candidate can buy television time. Instead, the parties are allocated an amount of political time on the air to use as they wish, with the parties sharing the time and taking their own cases to the voters. No commercials. No payments for time. And Western civilization was not impaired, and has survived.

Fourth, to assure basic access to television for all significant candidates for president and vice-president. As you know, our Federal Communications Act requires that all candidates for the same office be treated equally by broadcasters. This means that if a broadcaster gives or sells time to one candidate, time must be made available on the same terms to his or her opponent. There are certain exceptions for news programs and interviews. The presidential debates, with which I was deeply involved in 1976 and 1980, were conducted under regulatory and judicial interpretations of these exceptions—an interesting legal story, but too long to go into here. I believe that not *all* candidates need to be treated equally; there were 229 candidates for president in 1984; not all of them were serious. How can we distinguish between serious, significant candidates and the others? How do we do this under the law, under the Constitution, under our sense of fundamental fairness?

Courts have dealt with some of these issues. The law remains murky. The law has changed a great deal since I was a law clerk at the Supreme Court, but there is one thing I don't think has changed. Justice Jackson wrote an opinion when I was there in which he said, "The Constitution of the United States is not a suicide pact."

I do not believe the Constitution of the United States will cause our political institutions or our electoral process to commit suicide. But I suggest to you that's what is about to happen, unless we make some changes. Otherwise campaigns will continue to be contests between who can hire the best political consultant and ad agency. We will not see the candidates live, or hear what they have to say, and instead of having rational political discussion, our electoral politics will go steadily, steadily downhill.

Specific Proposals:
Text and Analysis

A. BICAMERAL NOMINATING CONVENTION (PARTY RULES)

Section 101

(A) The national convention to nominate candidates for president and vice-president shall consist of a popular chamber and a congressional chamber, composed of delegates as provided in paragraphs (B) and (C) of this section.

(B) The popular chamber shall be composed of delegates selected pursuant to sections _____ of these rules, provided that no person entitled to a seat in the congressional chamber shall be a delegate in the popular chamber.

(C) The congressional chamber shall be composed of:

    (1) candidates of the party for election to the House of Representatives and the Senate selected in state primaries and caucuses before the date of the national convention; and

    (2) members of the party holding the office of United States Senator whose terms do not expire within one year.

Section 102

(A) Delegates in the popular chamber and the congressional chamber shall be entitled to one vote each for the selection of the candidates of the party and for the approval of the party platform.

(B) Delegates in the congressional chamber shall not be bound to vote for any particular candidate.

(C) Delegates in the popular chamber shall be bound to vote for any particular candidate only to the extent provided in section _____ of these rules, provided, however, that delegates in the popular chamber shall not be bound to vote for any particular candidates in any runoff election pursuant to section 103 (C) of these rules.

Section 103

(A) Deliberations and balloting of delegates in the popular chamber and congressional chamber shall be conducted separately and simultaneously, and shall continue in each chamber until a majority of delegates cast ballots for one candidate.

(B) If a majority of the delegates in each chamber cast ballots for the same candidate, that candidate shall receive the nomination of the party for president or vice-president, as the case may be.

(C) If a majority of the delegates in one chamber cast ballots for one candidate and a majority of the delegates in the other chamber cast ballots for a different candidate, then each chamber shall conduct a runoff election between the two candidates. If, in such runoff election, a majority of the delegates of each chamber cast ballots for one of the candidates, that candidate shall receive the nomination of the party. If a majority of the delegates in each chamber cast ballots in such runoff election for different candidates, then the percentage of votes received by each candidate in each chamber shall be calculated, and the sum of such percentages of votes received by each candidate in each chamber shall also be calculated. The candidate receiving the higher sum of percentages shall receive the nomination of the party.

Section 104

The platform of the party shall require the approval of a majority of each chamber. If the popular and congressional chambers approve different platforms, then each chamber shall appoint _____ conferees, and the differences between the platforms shall be resolved in conference among such conferees. The platform agreed upon by such conferees shall require the approval of a majority of each chamber. If such approval is not obtained, the conference process shall commence again, and continue until such approval is obtained. The platform shall be adopted before the balloting for candidates begins.

Analysis

The proposed party rules would create a bicameral presidential nominating convention intended to enhance the role of a party's congressional wing in selecting the party's presidential and vice-presidential candidates. One chamber of the nominating convention would consist of delegates chosen, as presently is the case, by caucus and primary; the second chamber would consist of the party's candidates for the House and Senate, as well as all holdover Senators. If a candidate for the party's nomination for president received a majority of each chamber, that candidate would receive the party's nomination. If different candidates won in each chamber, a runoff ballot would be held between the two candidates. If one candidate won a majority in each chamber in the runoff election, he or she would receive the nomination. If the chambers were again split, then the proposed rules would require calculation of the percentage of the total votes received in each chamber by each candidate. The party's nomination would go to the candidate receiving the higher sum of such percentages.

The proposed party rules are designed to allow the selection of presidential candidates capable of forming a coherent national government and carrying out a coordinated legislative program. Under our present political party system, each party's congressional wing plays only a limited role in the process for nominating each party's presidential and vice-presidential candidates. Party experience and the view of party leaders play a much less important role in the presidential nomination process than do the financial resources, doggedness, political skill and TV techniques of the candidates in the primaries and caucuses that precede the convention. Deliberation within the convention itself is a memory of the past. Almost as often as not in recent times, the presidential nomination has gone to persons without prior connection to the congressional branch. (Since World War II, the major parties have had twenty chances to nominate a candidate for president; only three of those nominated—Kennedy, Goldwater and McGovern—were incumbent members of Congress when nominated. In only eleven cases did the nominee have prior congressional experience.) Moreover, even when the president and legislators are members of the same party, they have little incentive to agree on a comprehensive legislative program. The ultimate incentive for such cooperation—sharing the same political fate if the program succeeds or fails—is largely absent from our system, because legislators so often win reelection even though their party loses the presidential election. This disconnection between the presidential nomination process and the congressional wings of each party has resulted in the nomination for president of candidates whose ability to obtain the support of their party's congressional wing is far from assured.

The proposed party rules are intended to enhance cooperation between the White House and Capitol Hill, by giving the congressional wing of each party a major role in nominating the party's candidate for president. Under the rules presidential nominees would be likely to enjoy broad support among their parties' congressional candidates. A presidential nominee who prevailed in the general election would probably be responsive to the party's successful congressional candidates and holdover senators, owing to their role in his nomination. Likewise, the party's congressional wing would be likely to feel more accountable to the voting public for what the administration does. By thus linking the political fortunes of the president and the congressional wing of his party, the rules could result in greater cooperation between the two.

The proposed party rules also could produce genuinely deliberative conventions, rather than the current pattern of a winner emerging before the convention is even held. The delegates in the congressional chamber would not be bound by either caucus or primary to any candidate; delegates in the popular chamber could be bound by state law or party rule, but not if a runoff election became necessary. In both circumstances, delegates would be required to use their own best judgment in the selection of a nominee.

Many possible objections may be raised to the proposed rule. Some critics may argue that the voice of the voters, as expressed in state primaries and caucuses, should be controlling. Similarly, a congressional chamber consisting of all of a party's nominees for Congress might arguably give undue influence to hopeless candidates for the hundred or so seats that are usually safe for the other party. The chamber might therefore not be truly representative of the party's congressional wing. Critics may also argue that the bicameral convention would be procedurally cumbersome and that it might last too long. Proponents reply that our present conventions tend to be undeliberative and uninteresting; indeed, because it would be necessary to replace roll-call votes with electronic voting or written ballots in order to prevent inflation of the winner's percentage margin in runoffs, the bicameral convention could be shorter than current conventions. Finally, the proposed rules might still fail to produce the desired party cohesion because of the built-in institutional rivalry between Congress and the White House.

B. TWO-PHASE FEDERAL ELECTIONS
(FEDERAL STATUTE)

Section 101

(A) The electors for president and vice-president shall be chosen, in each state, on the third Tuesday in October, in every fourth year succeeding every election of a president and vice-president.

(B) Elections of members of the House of Representatives shall be held, in each of the states and territories of the United States, on the third Tuesday in November in those years in which elections of the presidents are held.

(C) In those years in which elections of the president are held, elections for the office of United States senator, the term of which commences on the third day of January next thereafter, shall be held, in each of the states holding such elections, on the third Tuesday in November.

(D) In those years in which elections of the president are not held, elections for the office of United States senator shall be held, in each state holding such election, on the date of the regular election in such state next preceding the expiration of the term for which any senator was elected to represent such state in the Senate.

Analysis

This proposed federal statute might accompany the proposed constitutional amendment fixing four-year terms for members of the House of Representatives, to run concurrently with the presidential term (see pages 175–177). The statute sets dates for presidential elections and requires that congressional elections be held four weeks after presidential elections. This change would permit voters to cast their ballots in congressional elections after learning the identity and party affiliation of the incoming president. The statute's purpose is to allow voters who wish to avert governmental deadlock to support congressional candidates belonging to the incoming president's party. Voters will remain free to vote for a House candidate of the party opposing the newly elected president, but they will possess the essential information necessary to avoid this result (the identity of the new president) if they wish to do so.

The proposed statute could increase the likelihood that the party winning the presidency would also win a majority of the House of Representatives. The statute might also strengthen party bonds between candidates for president and for the House, by linking the electoral fate of the latter more closely to the electoral fate of the president. For both these reasons, the statute would make it more feasible for the successful party to legislate and execute its program for governing.

Two principal objections have been raised to the proposed statute. First, voters might still choose not to support congressional candidates belonging to the incoming president's party. Rather, the electorate may be swayed by its appraisal of the contesting candidates and their positions on local as well as national issues or even by a desire to check one party's control of the presidency by granting control of Congress to the other party. This is of course true, but it is not a valid argument against the statute. By allowing a voter in congressional elections to vote with knowledge of the incoming president's identity, the statute permits the voter to make an [informed] choice, without requiring him to guess the effect of his congressional vote on the likelihood of creating executive-legislative deadlocks.

Second, opponents of the proposed statute contend that there might be a falloff in voter turnout in congressional elections held after presidential elections, just as there is generally a 20–30 percent falloff in voter turnout in off-year congressional elections held at the middle of the presidential term. However, this seems unlikely since House elections would be held only at four-year instead of the present two-year intervals, and since there is no comparable decline in the French run-off system of the "deuxieme tour."

C. AN OPTION TO VOTE FOR PARTY SLATES
(FEDERAL STATUTE)

Section 101

(A) In any election in which electors of the president and vice-president are appointed, candidates for the offices of president, vice-president, senator and representative may seek election on a political party slate.

(B) A political party slate in any election specified in paragraph (A) [may] [shall] consist in any state of (1) one candidate for the offices of president and vice-president; (2) one candidate for each of the offices of United States senator to be filled in that state in such election; and (3) one candidate for each of the offices of representative to the Congress to be filled in that state in such election.

(C) Each of the candidates comprising a political party slate shall satisfy all requirements for individual inclusion on the ballot on which the political party slate is placed.

Section 102

(A) Each state shall provide by law for the inclusion of any political party slate formed pursuant to Section 101 on all ballots, lists of candidates displayed in any voting booth or machine, and other voting tabulation mechanisms employed in any election specified in Section 101 (A). Each state shall provide by law that a vote for a political party slate formed pursuant to Section 101 shall be deemed a vote for each of the individual candidates for whom the person casting the ballot was eligible to vote.

(B) In any state in which ballots, lists of candidates displayed in voting booths or machines, or other voting tabulation mechanisms are prepared separately for each congressional district, a political party slate included on such ballots, lists or mechanisms in any congressional district need include, in addition to candidates for the offices of president, vice-president and senator, only that candidate for the office of representative to the Congress seeking election in such district.

Analysis

[Note: Beginning on page 177, there is a mandatory version of this suggestion, which would require a Constitutional amendment.]

The proposed statute is intended to reduce deadlocks between the executive and legislative branches by fostering party cohesion and increasing the likelihood that both branches of government will be controlled by the same party. If candidates choose to form a team ticket, they may be more likely, because of their linked electoral fortunes, to campaign on a single plan of government and, if elected, to pursue that plan. If team tickets were required to include a candidate for all contested House and Senate seats, party leadership might assert greater control over the identities and policies of individual candidates. The presence of team tickets on the ballot might also increase the voting public's consciousness of party differences and of the significance of forming a government capable of implementing its programs. If voters made use of their option to vote for team tickets, rather than individual candidates, the likelihood of the same party controlling both the presidency and Congress would be increased.

The proposed statute might be criticized on a number of grounds. First, there is a significant chance that locally popular candidates for the House and Senate would not join team tickets consisting of somewhat less popular presidential or congressional candidates. Moreover, because candidates would have the freedom to run independently, the availability of team tickets might do little to increase party control. Finally, there is some question whether voters will forego the opportunity to vote for locally popular candidates by voting for a team ticket, even if candidates choose to form such tickets.

D. PUBLIC FINANCING OF CAMPAIGN BROADCASTS
(FEDERAL STATUTE)

It is not practical to print here a draft of the statute, which would necessarily contain much technical language. In principle, it would amend the campaign financing laws to create a Congressional Campaign Broadcast Fund, similar to the existing Presidential Campaign Fund. This fund would be available to each party and its congressional candidates in the general election for broadcast expenses, on condition that they not expend any other funds on campaign broadcasts. Half or more of each party's share would go to the party itself, which could allocate its funds among its candidates so as to maximize its chances to win a majority.

Analysis

The proposed federal statute would establish a "political party broadcast fund" made up of amounts designated by taxpayers on their income tax returns and supplemented by federal matching funds. The statute would entitle each major political party to receive payments from the broadcast fund for use in federal election campaigns. (Major political parties are defined as parties that received 25 percent of the national popular votes cast in the preceding elections for senators and representatives.) Minor and new political parties would be entitled to lesser payments from the fund, calculated on the basis of the proportion of votes received by their candidates to votes received by major party candidates.

A political party that accepts payments under the statute would be obligated to distribute money received from the fund to the party's candidates for office in the House or Senate. The party's candidates might use money received from the fund only to defray "qualified broadcast expenses" incurred in general elections. "Qualified broadcast expenses" are defined as expenses "for purchasing radio or television broadcast time for a live appearance, to further such candidate's election." Money from the fund would not be available to presidential or vice-presidential candidates nor for use in primary campaigns for any office. Political parties would be given full discretion in deciding which of their House and Senate candidates would receive payments from the fund.

Candidates of major parties who accepted money from the broadcast fund would not be permitted to make any additional campaign expenditures relating to the purchase of radio or television time. Candidates of minor and new political parties who received payments from the broadcast fund would not be permitted to make expenditures relating to the purchase of radio or television broadcast time in excess of the payments received by the major party candidate receiving the largest amount of payments in a particular election.

The broadcast fund statute has several important objectives. Expenditures for radio and television broadcasts constitute a major portion of total expenditures by candidates in federal election campaigns. By providing public financing for radio and television broadcasts, the proposed statute would reduce the effect of private financial resources on the federal electoral process. The statute might thereby fulfill, at least in part, the objectives of the Federal Election Campaign Act, which were largely frustrated by the Supreme Court's 1976 decision in *Buckley v. Valeo*, 424 U.S. 1 (1976), holding important parts of the act unconstitutional.

The proposed broadcast fund statute could also enhance the ability of party leadership to maintain party cohesion. Under the bill, half of the funds available would be distributed directly to party nominees on a population formula basis. The remainder would be paid directly to the party's national committee (or its congressional campaign committee) to be allocated among the party nominees in the committee's discretion. This would enable the committee to concentrate its portion of the fund on close races in order to maximize the party's chances of winning a majority. Party control over half of the broadcast fund would increase the incentives for party nominees, if elected, to cooperate with the party legislative leadership in enacting the party's program for governing.

The proposed statute is also intended to improve the quality of the information received by the electorate in campaign broadcasts by political candidates. The statute might limit the use of money received from the fund to radio and television broadcasts of live appearances by candidates. This limitation would be intended to ensure that public funds are used for those types of political broadcasts that are most likely to provide valuable information about a candidate's view and capabilities.

Critics raise a number of objections to the proposed statute. They argue that too much money is already spent on political campaigning and that the statute would only increase such expenditures. Parties would direct money from the fund to candidates who could not independently raise the sums required by their campaigns, while candidates with adequate sources of funds independently raised would refuse payments and avoid the statute's expenditure limitations.

Opponents of the proposed statute also argue that the law would do little to achieve its objective of encouraging party cohesion. Party leadership would ultimately support even party mavericks, rather than allow the opposition party to win a particular seat. Some opponents of the statute also question whether live appearances by candidates are any more informative than other types of broadcasts. Finally, critics argue that the proposed statute would perpetuate the dominance of the major parties, by providing them with greater funding than new and minor political parties.

E. CAMPAIGN FINANCING LIMITS
(PARTY RULES)

Again, a draft-text would contain much technical language, so we confine ourselves to a summary of the leading principles.

The campaign financing system might be reformed by the adoption of party rules, modelled on the Federal Campaign Act, by the major political parties. These rules would impose restrictions on the size of the campaign contributions that party members could accept and the amount of total campaign expenditures they could make. The rules would establish a committee within the party charged with administering these restrictions. The committee would adopt procedures for investigating complaints regarding violations of the party's campaign financing rules and would be authorized to issue decisions and impose sanctions for violations of the rules.

The restrictions contained in the proposed party campaign financing rules would apply both to persons seeking party nomination and to candidates running on the party's ticket in general elections. The restrictions would be applicable in primaries and general elections for the offices of the president, vice-president, senator and representative. The rules would contain three principal restrictions:

1. *Expenditure Limitations.* The rules would limit the total campaign expenditures that could be made by candidates seeking the party's nomination for federal office and by candidates for election to federal office on the party's ticket. Following the model of the Federal Election Campaign Act, the limitations of campaign expenditure would vary depending on the federal office involved. Expenditure limitations would be lowest for campaigns for election to the House of Representatives, and would be progressively higher for senators, the vice-president and president. The limitations on expenditures in primaries would be lower than those for general elections.

2. *Limitations on Expenditures from Personal Funds.* The rules would place limitations on the amounts that candidates for party nomination and party nominees for federal office could spend from personal or family funds. The expenditure limitations would vary depending on the office involved.

3. *Contribution Limitations.* The rules would place limitations on the total campaign contributions that candidates for party nomination and party nominees could receive from any single person.

The party campaign financing rules would require that any contributions to candidates for party nomination or party nominees be directed to the treasurer of the party. Candidates receiving direct contributions would be required to forward the contributions to the treasurer. All contributions received by the treasurer would be held for the account of the nominee or candidate, and would be disbursed, in accordance with the expenditure limitations of the rules, as directed by the candidates or nominees.

Analysis

These proposed party rules regulate campaign financing by candidates for party nomination and by nominees running on the party ticket. The rules limit the size of contributions received by candidates for nomination and nominees, and require that all contributions be channeled through the party treasurer. The rules also place a ceiling on expenditures a candidate may make, either from personal funds or contributions.

The proposed rules are modelled on the Federal Election Campaign Act. That act was intended to combat both actual and apparent corruption of elected federal officials and to reduce the role that financial resources play in federal elections. Both these purposes have been largely frustrated. The Supreme Court's decision in *Buckley v. Valeo* striking down limitations on campaign expenditures by candidates and independent committees, seriously impaired the intended operation of the act. In addition, the Federal Election Commission has fulfilled its regulatory responsibilities less successfully than hoped. Consequently, there is now general agreement that the existing campaign financing system and regulatory structure are seriously flawed.

Although regulatory reforms by means of federal statute may well be foreclosed by the Supreme Court's decision in *Buckley v. Valeo*, there is no substantial constitutional obstacle to the regulation of campaign financing by political parties. Such regulation would serve a number of important ends. By limiting expenditures from personal and contributed funds, such rules would fill, at least in part, the gap left in the federal regulation of elections by *Buckley*. In so doing, the party campaign financing rules would serve the purposes of the original Federal Election Campaign Act, namely the reduction of the importance of financial resources in the American electoral process and the combatting of actual and apparent corruption. Moreover, in addition to correcting existing campaign financing abuses, the proposed rules would enhance party unity. Both the requirement that contributions to party candidates flow through the party treasurer, and the reduction in the importance of individual wealth and fund-raising efforts, would link party candidates more closely to the party structure than currently is the case.

Objections to adoption, by a party, of the proposed campaign financing rules will likely focus on the disadvantage that would result for candidates of a party adopting the rules. Although they have some merit, effective responses may be made to those concerns. Application of the proposed rules in campaigns for party *nomination* poses no danger of one party disadvantaging itself relative to another, since only party members are involved in the race. In general elections the major parties might agree to abide by the limits set forth in the rules, thus eliminating any relative disadvantage. Alternatively, one party might announce its intention to abide by the rules, provided the other party followed suit. In neither case would questions of relative disadvantage emerge.

Part 3

Reducing the Risk of Divided Government

In Part 1, we identified several areas of policy in which serious problems had mounted, but the government seemed unable to respond adequately. The deficit spirals upward. Everyone agrees that it should come down. Many politicians have ideas for reducing it. Yet the government cannot hammer out a policy for doing so. It is the same with urban policy, farm policy, immigration, tax reform, regulation, the nuclear industry, the cost of medical care, and a host of other unresolved issues. A broad consensus agrees that there are serious problems confronting the nation, and agrees, too, that enlightened, coherent public policy could help to alleviate them, but on the way to adopting these programs, the system falls into deadlock. (In some cases, enlightened policy might seek to reduce or eliminate the government's role in a particular area— but we cannot enact and implement policies to accomplish that goal, either.)

One of the obstacles to coherent policy-making is a spirit of suspicion, which stems in part from our individualism and our love of competition. In other words, it is partly our culture that makes our politics contentious and fractious, and no constitution could, or should try to, override the values that are part of that culture. But neither should a frame of government exacerbate these tensions. To the extent that our difficulties are attributable to the structure of our government, it constitutes an unnecessary and unproductive hindrance.

We have, as Richard Neustadt has written, a system of "separated institutions, sharing power." The separation of powers invites confrontation between the president and Congress, and between the House and Senate. Politicians in the government, seeking to enact and implement policies, may search for ways to cooperate with their peers in other branches, but, in doing so, they find themselves fighting against the dynamics of the constitutional system.

Why did the framers set the branches against one another? Why did they establish a system of "checks and balances"?

To understand their reasons, we must recall the circumstances in which they met. They met to reform a national government that had no executive branch. Its administration was carried out by small groups of men who worked directly for congressional committees. That produced a government that was weak, vacillating, and contemptible. Experience taught the framers that "energy in the executive is a leading character in the definition of good government," and that "a government ill executed, whatever it may be in theory, must be, in practice, a bad government." The framers were determined to create a strong, *independent* executive, to insure the energetic administration of policies enacted by Congress.

There was another major reason behind the separation of powers: a concern that the dominant faction in the legislature might use patronage for tyrannical and corrupt purposes. Again, note the circumstances in which the framers met. They had recently won a war for independence against Great Britain. Given the struggles of the previous half-century, it is not surprising that most of the framers learned what they knew about British government and politics from leaders of the British opposition and journalists critical of the ruling factions. (The major exception was William Blackstone, whose royalist *Commentaries* had a wide American readership, especially among those training for legal careers. But even Blackstone admitted that corruption was rife in eighteenth-century British politics.) According to these dissidents in England, leaders in Parliament were using the crown's powers of appointment to build powerful electoral machines by placing their cronies in lucrative government jobs. The result was tyranny, in the sense that politicians who were not part of this inner circle were excluded from any influence. Another effect was that Parliament often enacted programs whose primary purpose was to make "places" for agents of the dominant political faction.

The framers of the American Constitution were determined to prevent these abuses from developing here. The separation of powers was their main strategy. The idea was to keep law-making separate from administration. So long as the executive was independent from Congress, legislators would not be able to dictate who would occupy government jobs, and there would be no incentive to expand the size of the government just to make "places" for faithful political agents.

For many decades after the founding, the system worked essentially as the framers expected. In staffing the government, most presidents were able to retain considerable independence from Congress. But as the size of the government grew, particularly in the years after the Civil War, an opposition danger grew: that of presidential dominance. This led to the development of a civil service system, where appointments to most public positions was based on merit, rather than political considerations.

As the system moved into the twentieth century, the scope of government increased even further. This led to a demand for centralized planning and management. Significantly, it was during the administration of President Warren G. Harding, the Republican prophet of "normalcy," and at the insistence of a Republican Congress, that the federal government began to develop a capacity for centralized budgeting in the executive branch.

By the 1950s, in the wake of Franklin Roosevelt's New Deal and World War II, it was clear that the presidency had assumed a role of political leadership that was quite different from what the framers had intended. No longer was it the primary function of the presidency simply to see to the energetic implementation of policies designed by Congress. Political leaders of both major parties had come to expect presidents to assume leadership in defining public problems and in fashioning policies to meet them.

Despite these changes in public expectation and demand, however, the system still stubbornly kept the branches separated. It still operated to thwart the efforts of party leaders to frame coherent programs and gain popular mandates to implement them. It did not matter that national political parties were broad coalitions, rather than "factions" in the framers' sense of that term. The system still operated to fragment them, to pit congressional leaders of a given party against presidents of the same party affiliation. It still operated to encourage candidates to approach the electorate as individual political entrepreneurs, representing a district, rather than as members of a team with a coherent program for which they stood collectively accountable.

Americans still share the founders' commitment to checks on political power, but modern conditions have led to a search for ways to encourage cooperation, or at least to lessen the incentives for antagonism for its own sake. The selections in this Part reflect this search.

We begin with an essay by Woodrow Wilson, who at an early stage of his academic career was intrigued by the British system of "government by discussion" in parliament. Next comes a selection from Harold Laski, a British academic and politician who, on the eve of World War II, found merit in the American provision for presidential leadership. We round out these comments with a passage from a book by Thomas Finletter, serving then in the State Department, who urged Americans at the end of World War II to adopt aspects of the parliamentary system.

Next are three selections by members of CCS: a comprehensive plan of reform set forth by Charles Hardin; a suggestion by former Congressman Henry Reuss for including members of Congress in the president's cabinet; and an analysis by James M. Burns of the argument for party government. Finally, there are discussions of two current ideas for dealing with the problem of divided government: Governor Thornburgh's call for an amendment to require a balanced budget; and an analysis of the proposal for a single, six-year term for presidents.

Part 3 concludes with draft language and analysis of several specific proposals.

Woodrow Wilson

17. Cabinet Government in the United States (1879)

Woodrow Wilson was the twenty-eighth president of the United States, serving from 1913–1921. Prior to entering politics, he wrote several books about the American political system, taught at Bryn Mawr, Wesleyan, and Princeton, and was president of Princeton from 1902 until 1910, the year he was elected governor of New Jersey. The following excerpts are from an article first published in The International Review.

What then is cabinet government? What is the change proposed? Simply to give to the heads of the executive departments—the members of the cabinet—seats in Congress, with the privilege of the initiative in legislation and some part of the unbounded privileges now commanded by the standing committees. But the advocates of such a change—and they are now not a few—deceive themselves when they maintain that it would not necessarily involve the principle of ministerial responsibility—that is, the resignation of the cabinet upon the defeat of any important part of their plans. For, if cabinet officers sit in Congress as official representatives of the executive, this principle of responsibility must of necessity come sooner or later to be recognized. Experience would soon demonstrate the practical impossibility of their holding their seats, and continuing to represent the administration, after they had found themselves unable to gain the consent of a majority to their policy. . . .

[The president] would naturally resign; and not many years would pass before resignation upon defeat would have become an established precedent—and resignation upon defeat is the essence of responsible government. In arguing, therefore, for the admission of cabinet officers

---

Reprinted from *The International Review*, August, 1879.

into the legislature, we are logically brought to favor *responsible cabinet government* in the United States.

But to give to the president the right to choose whomsoever he pleases as his constitutional advisers, after having constituted cabinet officers *ex officio* members of Congress, would be to empower him to appoint a limited number of representatives, and would thus be plainly at variance with republican principles. The highest order of responsible government could, then, be established in the United States only by laying upon the president the necessity of selecting his cabinet from among the number of representatives already chosen by the people, or by the legislatures of the states.

Such a change in our legislative system would not be so radical as it might at first appear: it would certainly be very far from revolutionary. Under our present system we suffer all the inconveniences, are hampered by all that is defective in the machinery, of responsible government, without securing any of the many benefits which would follow upon its complete establishment. Cabinet officers are now appointed only with the consent of the Senate. Such powers as a cabinet with responsible leadership must possess are now divided among the forty-seven standing committees, whose prerogatives of irresponsible leadership savor of despotism, because exercised for the most part within the secret precincts of a committee room, and not under the eyes of the whole House, and thus of the whole country. . . . Under the conditions of cabinet government, however, full and free debates are sure to take place. For what are these conditions? According as their policy stands or falls, the ministers themselves stand or fall; to the party which supports them each discussion involves a trial of strength with their opponents; upon it depends the amount of their success as a party: while to the opposition the triumph of ministerial plans means still further exclusion from office; their overthrow, accession to power. To each member of the assembly every debate offers an opportunity for placing himself, by able argument, in a position to command a place in any future cabinet that may be formed from the ranks of his own party; each speech goes to the building up (or the tearing down) of his political fortunes. There is, therefore, an absolute certainty that every phase of every subject will be drawn carefully and vigorously, will be dwelt upon with minuteness, will be viewed from every possible standpoint. The legislative, holding full power of final decision, would find itself in immediate contact with the executive and its policy. . . .

We are thus again brought into the presence of the cardinal fact of this discussion—that *debate* is the essential function of a popular representative body. In the severe, distinct, and sharp enunciation of underlying principles, the unsparing examination and telling criticism of opposite positions, the careful, painstaking unravelling of all the issues involved, which are incident to the free discussion of questions of public policy, we see the best, the only effective, means of educating public opinion. . . .

The educational influence of such discussions is two-fold, and operates in two directions—upon the members of the legislature themselves, and upon the people whom they represent. Thus do the merits of the two systems—committee government and government by a responsible cabinet—hinge upon this matter of a full and free discussion of all subjects of legislation; upon the principle stated by Mr. Bagehot, that "free government is self-government—a government of the people by the people." It is perhaps safe to say, that the government which secures the most thorough discussions of public interests—whose administration most nearly conforms to the opinions of the governed—is the freest and the best. . . .

The apparently necessary existence of a partisan executive presents itself to many as a fatal objection to the establishment of the forms of responsible cabinet government in this country. The president must continue to represent a political party, and must continue to be anxious to surround himself with cabinet officers who shall always substantially agree with him on all political questions. It must be admitted that the introduction of the principle of ministerial responsibility might, on this account, become at times productive of mischief, unless the tenure of the presidential office were made more permanent that it now is. Whether or not the presidential term should, under such a change of conditions, be lengthened would be one of several practical questions which would attend the adoption of a system of this sort. . . . It is not hard to believe that most presidents would find no greater inconvenience, experience no greater unpleasantness, in being at the head of a cabinet composed of political opponents than in presiding, as they must now occasionally do, over a cabinet of political friends who are compelled to act in all matters of importance according to the dictation of standing committees which are ruled by the opposite party. . . . With a responsible cabinet—even though that cabinet were of the opposite party—he might, if a man of ability, exercise great power over the conduct of public affairs; if not a man of ability, but a *mere* partisan, he would in any case be impotent. From these considerations it would appear that government by cabinet ministers who represent the majority in Congress is no more incompatible with a partisan executive than is government by committees representing such a majority. . . .

A complete separation of the executive and legislative is not in accord with the true spirit of those essentially English institutions of which our government is a characteristic offshoot. The executive is in constant need of legislative co-operation; the legislative must be aided by an executive who is in a position intelligently and vigorously to execute its acts. There must needs be, therefore, as a binding link between them, some body which has no power to coerce the one and is interested in maintaining the independent effectiveness of the other. Such a link is the responsible cabinet. . . .

We should be less exposed to such fluctuations of power than is the English government. The elective system which regulates the choice of United States senators prevents more than one third of the seats becoming vacant at once, and this third only once every two years. The political complexion of the Senate can be changed only by a succession of elections.

But against such a responsible system the alarm-bell of *centralization* is again sounded, and all those who dread seeing too much authority, too complete control, placed within the reach of the central government sternly set their faces against any such change. They deceive themselves. There could be no more despotic authority wielded under the forms of free government than our national Congress now exercises. It is a despotism which uses its power with all the caprice, all the scorn for settled policy, all the wild unrestraint which mark the methods of other tyrants as hateful to freedom.

Few of us are ready to suggest a remedy for the evils all deplore. We hope that our system is self-adjusting, and will not need our corrective interference. This is a vain hope! It is no small part of wisdom to know how long an evil ought to be tolerated, to see when the time has come for the people, from whom springs all authority, to speak its doom or prescribe its remedy. If that time be allowed to slip unrecognized, our dangers may overwhelm us, our political maladies may prove incurable.

Harold Laski

18. In Defense of the Presidential System (1940)

Harold Laski was a British political scientist and politician. Educated at Oxford, he taught at McGill and Harvard, before returning to the London School of Economics in 1920. A member of the Labour Party Executive Committee from 1936 until 1949, he was its chair when Labour came to power following World War II. The material presented here is from The American Presidency, *a book which celebrated the virtues of the American system as the Atlantic alliance prepared for war.*

As long ago as February, 1864, Mr. Pendleton, a congressman from Ohio, sought to secure that "heads of executive departments may occupy seats on the floor of the House of Representatives"; and his proposal was strongly supported by James A. Garfield, then also a congressman from Ohio, in a remarkable speech. The committee to which the resolution was referred then introduced a bill containing two proposals: (1) cabinet officers were to have the right, in their own discretion, to attend debates when matters concerning their departments were under discussion; and (2) their attendance was to be made compulsory on certain days for the purpose of answering questions. An ardent discussion took place upon the bill, but it was not voted on. Fifteen years later, Pendleton, then a member of the Senate, raised the question a second time. The committee to which his resolution was referred produced a long and valuable report; but, as in 1864, no vote was taken upon the proposed measure. In 1886, Mr. J. D. Long, later a secretary of the navy, introduced a measure which permitted members of the cabinet to attend and speak, at their own pleasure, in the House of Representatives; but, on this occasion, the bill was not reported out of committee. The proposal then

Excerpted from *The American Presidency: An Interpretation*, by Harold J. Laski. Copyright 1940 by Harper & Row, Inc.; reprinted by permission of Harper & Row, Inc.

slumbered for twenty-five years. It was revived by President Taft who supported the idea of cabinet representation in Congress with considerable vigor; but his proposal came to nothing. It was renewed in 1921 and 1924; in neither case did it arouse any serious public interest or discussion.

The case for the Pendleton proposal has been well stated by President Taft. "Without any change in the Constitution," he wrote, "Congress might well provide that heads of departments, members of the president's cabinet, should be given access to the floor of each house to introduce measures, to advocate their passage, to answer questions, and to enter into the debate as if they were members, without, of course, the right to vote. . . . This would impose on the president greater difficulty in selecting his cabinet, and would lead him to prefer men of legislative experience who have shown their power to take care of themselves in legislative debate. It would stimulate the head of each department by the fear of public and direct inquiry into a more thorough familiarity with the actual operations of his department and into a closer supervision of its business. On the other hand, it would give the president what he ought to have, some direct initiative in legislation, and an opportunity, through the presence of his competent representatives in Congress, to keep each house advised of the facts in the actual operation of the government. The time lost in Congress over useless discussion of issues that might be disposed of by a single statement from the head of a department, no one can appreciate unless he has filled such a place."

The case is obviously a powerful one; and it has had the support of men so experienced as Mr. Justice Story, Senator Ingalls, and James G. Blaine. The case is the stronger with the immense growth, in recent years, of the congressional appetite for information from and investigation of the departments, much of which, if it is to be really effective, demands their friendly collaboration. There can be little doubt that it would greatly enhance the significance of congressional debate; and, thereby, it would give to it a character of responsibility and a popular significance which, compared to those of the House of Commons, are in considerable degree lacking. There is, too, much to be said for breaking down the antagonism between Congress and the departments; at present it is not untrue to say that many of the amendments each house makes to bills derive less from a knowledge of their value than from a desire to emphasize its power. I have myself heard Mr. Theodore Roosevelt insist that this method was not only likely to produce a wiser selection of cabinet officers; it was also, in his judgment, the best way to deal with the inherent difficulties of tariff legislation and of the "pork-barrel" bills which still remain a blot of no mean dimensions on the record of the legislature.

The argument, however, has not yet penetrated deeply into the popular consciousness. It is notable that in neither of his remarkable books on the American system did Woodrow Wilson think it worth while discussing, though he paid great attention to the relation between the executive and the legislature; while Lord Bryce, who knew Senator Pendleton personally, relegates it to a footnote in his *American Commonwealth*. The reason, I think, is clear. The change is not a superficial one. Its ramifications are, in fact, so wide that they might easily change the whole balance of power in the American system. They might change it, not merely as between the executive and the legislature, but within the elements of the executive itself. The failure to give the plan the consideration it deserves is not, I think, due to inertia, but rather, as Professor Cushman rightly suggests, to "the vaguely uneasy feeling that the plan would unwisely upset the traditional and established relationship between the executive and legislative departments with consequences that cannot be accurately foreseen and appraised."

Close analysis makes this at once apparent. If the cabinet is to sit in Congress, the president must choose its members from those who are likely to be influential with it. This at once narrows his choice. It makes him think of the men who already have some standing in its eyes, and some direct knowledge of its complicated procedure. But this means putting a premium on the experienced members of either house as cabinet material. It means, further, that the more successful they are upon the floor of Congress, the more independent they are likely to be vis-à-vis the president. They will develop a status of their own as they become known as the men who are able to make Congress take their views about the bills they promote. They are likely, in fact, to become rivals of the president himself for influence with Congress. The problem, in this situation, of maintaining cabinet unity would necessarily become a difficult matter. Congress might easily tend to weaken the administration by playing off the cabinet, or some part of it, against the president and some other part. The loyalty of the cabinet officer would be divided. Is he, for example, to support the president on a scheme like the Court plan, and thereby to weaken his standing with Congress; or is he discreetly to make known his dislike for the plan in the hope that he may thereby win approval for some bill in which he is interested?

The president's problem of changing his cabinet would, moreover, be immensely intensified. Is he to keep an officer about whose full loyalty he is dubious, but whose influence on Congress is clearly great? Can he prevent such an officer's so nearly rivaling his own authority as to make his own position exceptionally difficult? Would not the position of a president like Lincoln, whose hold on his own colleagues was small when he assumed power, become virtually untenable if

Congress were in a position to play them off against him? Is there not, indeed, the danger of a powerful cabal of cabinet officers' becoming the effective mediator between the president and Congress with a vital shift, as a consequence, in the present delicate balance of power? Would it not, further, be likely that a tendency would rapidly develop for any cabinet officer who became outstandingly influential with Congress to become the rival of the president himself, and, where the latter was weak, in actual fact his master?

More than even this is, I think, involved. There would develop the tendency for the president to choose his cabinet from Congress in order to maximize his influence with it, and thus to transfer the leadership of his party there to a room, so to say, of which he only had the key. There would be a tendency for cabinet officers to use their relation with Congress as a platform from which to reach the presidency, with all the difficulties of colleagueship of this position, and more, that Polk emphasized. It is difficult, moreover, not to feel that, in these circumstances, the advice of the cabinet member upon questions of patronage would be given under conditions altogether different from and inferior to those upon which they now depend. The danger of trading posts for measures is already profound enough in the American system; it is difficult not to feel that it would be greatly intensified if a cabinet officer were independent of the president in his power to influence Congress. The coherence that is now given to administrative action by the supremacy of the president might easily be jeopardized by this aspect alone.

The Pendleton scheme suggested that cabinet members should have access to debates upon the floor of the House. But in fact, the main business of Congress is performed in secret committees to which the public has no access. No cabinet officer could adequately look after his measures unless he penetrated the committee rooms also. But were he to do so, the control over him of the president would be still further diminished; and the relation between him and Congress would rival in closeness that with the executive of which the president is the head. This seems scarcely desirable in a system where there is no collective cabinet responsibility, and where the unity of the executive structure is supplied by presidential control. In these circumstances, no cabinet member can be transformed into an automaton who merely reflects the presidential will. For first, in such a transformation as this innovation portends, he would have been chosen just precisely because he is not an automaton; and second, to the degree that he seeks to act like one, he defeats the whole object of the innovation.

There are two further difficulties in the scheme, moreover, to which adequate attention has hardly been given in discussion of it. It raises most delicate and complicated questions of the relation between the cabinet officer, as a quasi-member of Congress, and the senator or congressman who is in charge of the bill in which he is interested. By whom is the concession to be made to a proposed amendment? How will chairmanships be arranged so as to secure a proper harmony in congressional proceedings between the cabinet officer and the chairman of his committee. On a bill, for example, like that of President Roosevelt's Court plan, the position of the attorney-general would be well-nigh intolerable unless he were at one with the chairman of the judiciary committee. The fact is that, on the present system, where the chairmen of the important committees of both houses form a kind of quasi-executive within the two branches of the legislature, the position of cabinet officers would be impossible at every point where they disagreed with that quasi-executive. Either they would be tempted into a position of continuous inferiority for the sake of agreement, in which difficult questions of loyalty to the president would be involved; or they would differ openly with the official chairmen of the legislative committees, in which case, they would greatly add, by that difference, to the burden the president had to carry.

Nor is this all. The Pendleton scheme seems to assume that each cabinet officer is to sit in Congress merely in relation to his own department. But the categories of government are far from being as simple as this view would make them appear. The range of modern legislation makes the secretary of the treasury as ubiquitously relevant as the chancellor of the exchequer in relation to most government proposals. The interrelations of modern problems of defense make half the issues which arise matters of co-ordination to which the secretary of the treasury, the secretary of war, and the secretary of the navy are all relevant. On foreign affairs, every vital matter is at least a joint operation between the president and the secretary of state; the latter could hardly offer an opinion in Congress save as he affirmed that outlook for which he had prior approval from the president; and in matters of supreme importance it is the president only whose attitude it is vital for Congress to know. There, as the Wilson administration makes clear, he supersedes the secretary of state far more emphatically than, in an analogous situation, the prime minister of England supersedes (he rather supplements) the foreign secretary. Similar difficulties arise as between the Departments of Commerce and Labor; and the Department of Justice, especially in the context of prosecutions such as those under the Sherman Act, has a vital relation to many other departments. It is, in fact, difficult to see how any cabinet officer except the postmaster-general could be confined within any rigidly defined domain. In the result, most cabinet officers would—whatever the system started as—be bound to develop roving commissions of general relevance not very different from the part that a cabinet minister plays in the British House of Commons.

It must, moreover, be remembered that in the American system the initiative in legislation does not lie, as with Great Britain, for effective purposes in the government only. No doubt a special preeminence attaches to bills which have, so to say, the imprimatur of the president. But the source of a good deal of important legislative action lies in the hands of individual senators and congressmen; in this respect it is only necessary to remember how much has been done, often despite the administration, by men like the late Senator La Follette and by Senator Norris. It would be far from easy to adjust the delicate relations which would arise from this dual relationship, not least if the president were in the minority in Congress. And if members of the cabinet were admitted only to the floor of both houses, they would, for the most part, miss the chance of participation in the pivotal consideration of bills; while, if they were permitted their full share in the committee processes, the duality of leadership would create almost insoluble problems.

The Pendleton scheme, in short, does not meet the real problems created by the presidential system. The facts of American life have concentrated literally enormous power in the hands of the president; and it is no doubt true that the exercise of this power produces, above all in a second term, grave congressional doubts of the wisdom of its extent. At some time in the tenure of a president with a majority, the accusation of autocracy is almost bound to arise. But the real outcome of the Pendleton scheme, or any variant upon it, would be, I think, to transfer the essential features of presidential leadership to the cabinet. Its operations in Congress would be bound, sooner or later, to become the axis upon which the authority of the administration turned. I believe, indeed, that properly to perform its function in Congress the cabinet would be bound to try and discover the terms upon which it could become a unity; a unity, be it noted, not only against the Congress, but against the president also. The latter would be compelled to spend a good deal of his energy in maintaining his authority against colleagues who would have developed an interest and prestige at least parallel to his own, and, conceivably, different from it. None of them could fail to be aware that outstanding success in the handling of Congress was the highroad to the kind of reputation out of which a presidential nomination could be secured. Some of them, at least, would be bound to play for that nomination; and the problem, in those circumstances, of maintaining presidential supremacy would be at every point delicate and complicated.

The real result, in a word, of the adoption of such a scheme as Senator Pendleton proposed would be very rapidly to transform the president into a person more akin to the president of the French Republic than to that of the United States. He could not avoid the certainty that his colleagues who became pivotal in Congress would soon become indispensable to him. He could hardly avoid the concentration of public attention upon their activites in Congress rather than upon his relations with it. He would have to watch those activities with a jealous eye lest they impinge upon the sphere of influence that is at present his own. The man among them who became the congressional leader of the cabinet would soon become a figure akin in character and influence to the prime minister; the president would be dependent upon him for every legislative move in the fulfillment of his program. Indeed, I think it not unlikely that the president would become rather the adviser than the master of the man to whom Congress looked for the formulation and defense of the presidential program; he would be moved to second place. He would find it difficult to resist the pressure of a cabinet officer who was influential with Congress; he might well jeopardize his own position if he asked for his resignation. A hostile Congress might even play off the cabinet, or some section of it, against him.

On any showing, this is to say, the Pendleton scheme would wholly alter the balance of forces history has evolved in the American system of government. I do not say that it would necessarily alter them for the worse; any such estimate depends upon a comparison between the presidential and parliamentary systems that is here out of place. All I am concerned to argue is that latent in the scheme is a revolution in the historical conception of the presidency. As it now operates, the nation looks to the president for executive leadership, and, in the long run, circumstances make it difficult for that leadership to be found elsewhere. Such a scheme as Pendleton's inherently threatens that authority. While it separates him from his cabinet, on the one hand, it builds a bridge between the cabinet and Congress, on the other; and the president cannot walk across that bridge. It gives the cabinet an interest against him, not only with the legislature, but also with the party. A generation which has seen the vice-president of the United States use his influence in Congress to intrigue against the president should have no difficulty in seeing what his position might become if to his influence were joined that of any considerable part of the cabinet. At present, at any rate, when the president and Congress are at odds, the former's power of direct appeal to the nation makes the issue between them a clear one upon which public opinion can make up its mind. A cabinet that moved toward independence of him would make such a clarity of choice a difficult matter. It would, almost necessarily, divert a good deal of attention away from the case the president has to make. It would offer the possibility of great rewards to those about him who were prepared to risk the penalties of disloyalty to him. Anyone who reflects upon the position that might have arisen if Stanton had been able to utilize Congress as a platform against Andrew Jackson can see the potentialities that are latent in this change.

It may be, as I have said, that it should be attempted; for it may well be that the burden which the present situation imposes upon the president is greater than any statesman, above all in a democratic community, should be asked to bear. But the change should not be attempted without a full knowledge that it will profoundly alter the historic contours of the presidential system. It may not, in the first instance, transform it on the lines of the parliamentary system; it is bound, I have argued, in the long run to move it toward those lines. It cannot do so, on all experience, without two results. It must first depreciate the position of the man who cannot directly influence the congressional process; those, to use my earlier metaphor, are bound to be nearer to it who cross the bridge than those who stay on the other side. And if men are sought who can influence Congress, men are bound to be sought by whom Congress is prepared to be influenced. That does not only mean the device of a different kind of cabinet officer from those of the past. It means also, in the long run, men who realize that the way to influence a legislative assembly is to be responsive to its will; and that is the first step toward responsibility to its wishes. Fundamentally, this is to alter the whole balance of the American Constitution. It is to make it desirable to build a cabinet which can sway Congress. That makes the main lever of executive authority resident in the cabinet rather than in the president. While this may be a better scheme than the present one, its possible merits cannot conceal the fact that it is a constitutional revolution of the first magnitude. It is to dig into the foundations of the state; and that, as Edmund Burke insisted, is always a dangerous adventure.

Thomas K. Finletter

19. Cabinet Members on the Floor of Congress (1945)

Interest in having cabinet members and agency heads appear in Congress to answer questions was revived during World War II, when Representative Estes Kefauver offered a resolution that would have amended the House rules to this effect. Thomas K. Finletter, serving at the time as special assistant to the secretary of state, made the following comment on Kefauver's proposal in an appendix to his book, Can Representative Government Do the Job?

Justice Story thought the appearance of cabinet members on the floor of Congress desirable for several reasons. First, unless the heads of departments have the right to speak in person before Congress they have no way of proposing or vindicating their own measures in the course of debate. The greatest security and strength of republican government, open and public responsibility for measures, is thus lacking. "If corruption ever eats its way silently into the vitals of this republic, it will be because the people are unable to bring responsibility home to the executive through his chosen ministers." Moreover, without this right to debate its proposals before Congress, "the executive is compelled to resort to secret and unseen influences, to private interviews, and private arrangements . . . instead of proposing and sustaining its own duties and measures by a bold and manly appeal to the nation in the face of its representatives." Also, unless members of the executive are allowed to debate on the floor, "measures will be adopted or defeated by private intrigues, political combinations, irresponsible recommendations, and all the blandishments of office, and all the deadening weight of silent patronage." Finally, if the cabinet members were obliged to appear on the floor of Congress, "it would compel the executive to make appointments for the high departments of government, not from personal or party favorites, but from statesmen of high public character, talent, experience, and elevated services; from statesmen who had earned public favor and could command public confidence. At present gross incapacity may be concealed under official forms, and ignorance silently escape."

The proposal was reviewed in 1881. In that year the Senate (Pendleton) Report supported a bill to admit cabinet members to the floor for debate. The arguments of Justice Story were used. The report met squarely the objection that the powers of government must be kept separate and that the appearance of members of the executive on the floor of the legislature might be said to violate this principle.

> Your committee is not unmindful of the maxim that in a constitutional government the great powers are divided into legislative, executive, and judicial, and that they should be conferred upon distinct departments. These departments should be defined and maintained, and it is a sufficiently accurate expression to say that they should be independent of each other. But this independence in no just or practical sense means an entire separation, either in their organization or their function—isolation, either in the scope or the exercise of their powers. Such independence or isolation would produce either conflict or paralysis, either inevitable collision or inaction, and either the one or the other would be in derogation of the efficiency of the government. Such independence of co-equal and coordinate departments has never existed in any civilized government, and never can exist. . . . If there is anything perfectly plain in the Constitution and organization of the government of the United States, it is that the great departments were not intended to be independent and isolated in the strict meaning of these terms; but that, although having a separate existence, they were to cooperate each with the other, as the different members of the human body must cooperate with each other in order to form the figure and perform the duties of a perfect man.

. . . Any proposal to create an orderly procedure for giving Congress full information of executive operations will meet a deep resistance from both branches of the government. Tradition will form a large part of this resistance. And the opposition will be the stronger for the fact that it is not entirely unreasonable. It is not self-evident that a full interchange of information between the two branches will necessarily make for better government.

Looking at the question jurisdictionally—that is, from the limited point of view of its effect on the authority of the two branches in relation to each other—the improvement of the channels of information would strengthen Congress. The Kefauver plan should receive a favorable reception there. Isolation from what the executive is doing does not make for greater power in Congress. On the contrary it is because of this isolation that Congress has little part in the creation and indeed is inadequately informed of the great policies which are made under the executive policy-making power.

The argument that the members of the executive would be able to bring overriding pressure to bear on Congress by the force of their speeches delivered in person on the floor of the houses is not convincing. This objection was successful in one precedent-making case when Alexander Hamilton was denied the right to present his views on the floor of the House; but the fears of the First Congress do not commend themselves today. The modern president already has and uses many ways of appealing directly to the people over the head of Congress when the two branches are deadlocked on policy. The arguments of cabinet members and agency heads at the question hour would add little to the power of the president to bring contested points before the people.

On the contrary, the question hour would have the merit from the point of view of Congress that the opinions of the congressmen and senators would be published along with those of the executive, thus presenting both sides of any contested point. And, since one effect of the question hour would be to provide a central point for airing differences of opinion between the executive and legislative branches, it would be expected that the number of unilateral appeals by the executive to the people over the heads of Congress would be lessened.

From the point of view of the executive, the case for the question hour is less clear. The standard argument against the proposal from the executive side is that it would weaken the position of the president by building up the stature of the members of the cabinet; but it is difficult to give much weight to this argument. The president has the power to dismiss any member of the cabinet at his discretion. No cabinet member, an appointed official, could stand up against a strong president chosen by the vote of the people.

There is however an important consideration which weighs heavily against the question hour from the point of view of the executive branch. Any procedure for keeping Congress currently informed of executive plans and operations might well interfere with the already difficult task of the executive in the creation of positive policy. The executive branch is the body which has to get things done. When legislation is needed to implement a policy, Congress of course has to be consulted. But there is the large field of pure executive action where policy can be made without the legislature. And the doctrine of the separation of powers justifies the executive in making policy by executive act without consulting Congress in advance. The classic fallacy that the executive merely administers the laws in a mechanical way and that major policies are made only by legislative action conveniently supports this important power of the executive.

If however we put classic dogma aside and face the fact that executive acts often create policies at least as important as those embodied in congressional legislation, especially in foreign affairs, we necessarily reach the conclusion that the deliberative power of Congress should extend to these executive policies as well as to policies created by legislation or treaty.

There is, though, an objection of great weight to such a course. Under our form of government Congress is not responsible in the exercise of the deliberative function since it cannot be held immediately accountable for its actions. With the fixed terms of office of the House and Senate, if Congress rejects a proposal of the executive there is no way in which the executive can challenge the decision before the judgment of public opinion. The result is freedom on the part of Congress to be irresponsible, that is to yield to pressures or parochial considerations which might not control it if its members had to stand for an immediate election on the issue in question. And if the Kefauver plan were adopted, every important policy of the executive branch would be known to Congress as it developed. Differences of opinion, or even obstructive tactics if the majority in a house were hostile to the president, would thus be injected into the one area of action where now the executive has a relatively free hand. It is understandable that opposition to the Kefauver resolution is found most strong in those members of the executive branch who have had experience as members of Congress.

But if we look at the Kefauver proposal not from the limited point of view of its effect on Congress or the executive but rather as to its possible influence for good on the government as a whole, the proposal has great merit. It would democratize executive policy-making by subjecting it to the jurisdiction of Congress' deliberative function. It would give the public greater knowledge of what its government is doing. It would make for more co-operation between Congress and the executive on legislation and treaties. For it may be assumed that if Congress were no longer excluded from information about executive policy-making it would be more co-operative on those matters which do require the approval of the legislature. The only troublesome point is that the Kefauver plan might subject executive policy-making to the same uncertainty and cyclic disturbances which now prevail in the case of bills and treaties.

This latter objection should not prevail. For if we examine it, it is an argument that our system of government will not work if Congress has the power which any legislation must have in a regime of self-rule. The argument for keeping things as they are rests on the proposition that positive government cannot exist if Congress is to be consulted about policy. It asks us in effect to carve out the great field of executive policy-making and to exempt it from the processes of representative government. For by so doing we would have one area at least in which positive and consistent policies could be had.

The need for a free hand is especially strong in those matters which are the subject of executive policy-making. It may therefore be argued that foreign negotiations, which are the subject of a large part of this kind of executive action, cannot be carried on within the limitations of full debate in Congress and with the delays and obstructions that inevitably will come if the legislature is consulted on foreign policy during its formative stage.

There is great doubt whether in fact our foreign policy would be hampered if Congress were brought into it in this way. But even if it would be, there is little to be said for keeping Congress out of it. The price for the additional effectiveness is too high. The royal prerogative whereby the king had the sole right of making war and peace has never been accepted in this country. It is expressly denied by the Constitution through the grant to Congress of the war-declaring power and the right to deliberate on treaties. All that remains of the royal prerogative is the practical consideration that in foreign relations the right of initiation and of negotiation must of necessity lie in the executive. The power of final decision on the great policies of foreign affairs should be in the legislature. . . .

I have emphasized executive policy-making in foreign relations because the most important policies which are made by the executive without consultation with Congress are those which have to do with foreign matters. There is of course much policy-making by purely executive act in domestic matters as well, and there is the same need for orderly deliberation on these issues as in the case of foreign policy. Executive action in foreign affairs is however the more important, for it carries with it the great issue of the national security.

It may be that the fears of those who oppose the question hour are well founded and that the result of keeping Congress fully informed of executive acts would be to weaken our foreign policy by injecting the conflict between the two branches of government into it. The lack of any method of making Congress immediately responsible to the judgment of public opinion might create that result. But the remedy would seem to be to face that problem if it arises and to change our procedures to correct it, by constitutional amendment if necessary. The alternative of avoiding the issue by excluding Congress from one of the most important areas of policy-making is to revert to the ways of the past and to follow the methods of the peoples who have been unable to maintain a regime of self-rule.

The solution which must be reached is to subject the whole field of executive action to the deliberative power of Congress and at the same time prevent that power from being used in an irresponsible manner.

Charles Hardin

20. Toward a New Constitution (1974)

Charles Hardin (see page 3), having traced the problem of divided government to its roots in the structure of the Constitution, offers the following re-design of the system as his remedy.

Proposals for Reform

I am less sure of the proposals for reform than I am of the previous analysis. To make basic criticisms of present institutions implies a conception of a better alternative, one that I have called presidential leadership and party government. The change will require major surgery. One cannot stop short of bold and decisive departures. And yet a guiding principle should be to write the new Constitution in a way that permits considerable leeway. The ideal is to create conditions so that the conduct of government itself will be ruled largely by conventions rather than by fixed laws. . . .

1. Presidents, senators, and congressmen should all be elected on the same date for four-year terms. The date would be fixed at four years from the inauguration of the last government, but with the provision that the government, by law, could change the date and call an election.
2. The House of Representatives (hereafter, the House) should be elected from single-member districts as now, but should be supplemented by approximately 150 members elected at large. Each party should nominate 100 candidates. The party winning the presidency should elect the entire slate. The losing party should

Reprinted by permission of the University of Chicago Press, from *Presidential Power and Accountability*, by Charles Hardin. Copyright 1974.

elect a maximum of fifty at-large candidates, diminished by whatever number is required to give the winning party a majority of five in the House. At-large candidates would be nominated by committees of forty-one in each party, composed, for the incumbent president's party, of the president, the ten ranking members of his cabinet (rank being determined by the party), and thirty congressmen nominated by the House members of the president's party who are not in the cabinet and who are elected from single-member districts. The opposition party's nominating committee for at-large House members should be composed in the same way, substituting the leader of the opposition for the president and the ten ranking members of the shadow cabinet for the cabinet members. Methods of nominating single-district House candidates should not be stipulated except for the proviso that the same committee that nominates at-large candidates should have the right to reject local nominees on the ground that they have refused to accept party discipline.

3. Presidential candidates should be nominated by committees of the parties composed of all House members from single-member districts as well as all candidates for election in such districts. In the event of presidential disability, either physical or political, the nominating committee of his party should be empowered to suspend him temporarily or to discharge him, but in either event it should be required to replace him. The office of vice-president should be abolished.

4. The Senate should be deprived of its power to approve treaties and presidential nominations. Bills would continue to be examined in the Senate, but if the Senate rejects a bill that has passed the House twice in the same form, sixty days having elapsed between the first and second passage, the bill would go to the president.

5. The president's veto would be retained, but could be overridden by an adverse majority vote in the House; the Senate could force the House to reconsider but could be overridden by the House after sixty days.

6. That part of Article I, section 6, clause 2 of the Constitution that prevents members of Congress from serving in other offices of the United States should be repealed, but the proscription should be retained on the federal judiciary.

7. The runner-up in the election of the president should be designated leader of the opposition and provided a seat in the House with privileged membership on all committees and privileged access to the floor. The opposition leader should have an official residence, adequate offices, and funds for staff, for travel and transportation,

and for other expenses essential to the vigorous operation of his office. Like the president, the leader of the opposition would be removable by the presidential nominating committee of his party, with the power of removal matched by the obligation to replace.

8. Presidential elections should be by national ticket, with the winning party identified by securing a national plurality of voters.

9. All parts of the present Constitution in conflict with the foregoing proposals should be repealed or modified to conform to them. The twenty-second amendment should also be repealed.

Discussion of Proposals

Coterminous elections of president and Congress would go far to strengthen the voters' feelings, now systematically diminished by the separation of power and the methods of nominating and electing federal officials, that they are sharing in the creation of the government and the opposition. The voters should thereby have a sense of participation in the awesome and necessary task of governing the nation. Voters would be linked to the government or to the opposition by bonds of partisan feeling. Enabling the national parties to veto the nominations of persistent mavericks in Congress would both strengthen parties and also educate the voters to the governing function of parties—that the winning party is elected to govern and the individual congressman is supposed to share in concerting policies necessary to govern rather than to make a career of independence.

The electoral system should both empower the president and subject him to new controls. He would be empowered by winning a national election with an assured congressional majority whose members would have strong incentives to support the administration's position. At one stroke, this move would revolutionize the organization of Congress. Seniority and senatorial courtesy would disappear. The "whirlpools" in which bureaucrats and strategically located congressmen develop virtual autonomy in various agencies would be overridden by the steady flow of political power within the governing party. But if all these developments increased presidential influence, there would also be new controls. Control of the president should derive from the fact that he would now be the choice of a majority rather than of "the people"; he and the country would be continually reminded of that fact by the presence of an opposition headed by a leader who commands resources second only to the president's to publicize his party's position and to dramatize his leadership. Moreover, while the president would continue to enjoy preeminence, he should now be viewed as the leader of a team in which the necessarily collegial approach demanded of governments by modern conditions is orchestrated. The team would be largely composed of politicians like himself, who retain their congressional offices but are no longer prevented from sharing in the government; many of them would exhibit their ambition to succeed the president someday, and this should also teach the public that the president is the first person in a government, rather than a lone leader of nearly imperial dimensions.

In addition to strengthening the government against the bureaucracy, the changes would increase its ability to resist private pressures for the following reasons. First, House members would know that they were elected for four-year terms coterminous with the president, that their own electoral fate and that of their presidential candidate (who must win if their party is to control the government) will commonly be closely tied to the electorate's appraisal of the performance of the parties as wholes. Second, the electoral turnout will be uniformly high—the mid-term drop of 20 to 30 percent in the total vote for congressmen would disappear—and this fact will decrease the leverage organized interests have on candidates by threatening to punish them at the polls when the vote is light; such interests would be submerged in the tide of voters who, less specifically informed about candidates, are more inclined to vote their approval or disapproval of the government. Third, knowing that their use of the party label will be denied if they persistently oppose the party's legislative policies, House candidates will perceive their political survival and political future to be bound up much more with the success of the national party than (as now) with their own ability to build a local political organization and to nurse local interests. Fourth, the new rules should diminish the expenditures in campaigns by cancelling off-year elections and later on, it is hoped, by leading to a substitution of elections following dissolutions for fixed calendar elections. In addition to strengthening the national orientation of voters and putting more muscle in the national parties, this last step would greatly shorten campaigns and thereby slash campaign expenditures.

Party government and short electoral campaigns will enable us to smother the viper of corruption that threatens to poison this country. In the United States it has well been said "elective offices can be purchased; . . . votes of federal, state and local officials are bought and sold every day; . . . access of the people to their government is blocked by a Chinese wall of money." There was a time when similar corruption flourished in Britain. But it came to an end. "Thus, old corruption was cleaned up by a combination of methods. . . . Above all, a highly organized party which claims for its leading members the responsibility of government has to proclaim all the political virtues and dare not practice secret vices."

The addition of at-large House members has been suggested by others in order to increase the national point of view of Congress. I propose to manipulate the device to ensure that we will have party government. In this way the party capturing the presidency will also control Congress. Under the suggested formula, the Republicans would have been allotted 100 congressmen-at-large in 1968 and the Democrats forty-three; the Republicans would then have had 290 congressmen and the Democrats 285. In 1972, the Republicans would have been allotted 100 congressmen-at-large and the Democrats forty-five; the Republicans would then have had 292 congressmen and the Democrats 287.

Under this proposal, voters would know that they are electing a government and an opposition. Let me admit at once that the election would be rigged to produce a majority government even though some voters seem to prefer, or at least to be indifferent to, divided government. But let me also insist that elections are now rigged to produce divided governments. It is true that ticket-splitting voters, measured by the number of congressional seats with split electoral results, has doubled since the 1930s. But it is also true that the overwhelming majority of the electorate still vote for candidates for the presidency and for Congress who bear the same party label. In 1956, an exceptionally high year for ticket splitting, 79 percent of the voters preferred presidential and congressional candidates of the same party. The facts are that divided governments are foisted on the public by a minority of not more than 20 to 25 percent of the voters.

More controversial will be the proposal to reduce the power of the Senate that has many admirers among scholars and perhaps has increased its public support by the Watergate investigation of 1973. The chief reason for the change is, once more, to create conditions favorable to party government. In this way there will be one prime forum for debating public policy, for seating the opposition, and for registering the confidence reposed in government by the national legislature (and, through the legislature, by the public). It is extremely difficult to have two theaters for testing the viability of government as the moves of both Britain and France to reduce the power of their second chambers show. It compounds confusion if the government has to fight for its program in two chambers with entirely different power bases. More important, it disturbs and perhaps destroys that perception of government that the voter must have in order to develop a sense that he is sharing, through his party, in running the country. It might also be pointed out in an age that places great emphasis on the principle of one person, one vote, that the Senate becomes increasingly anomalous. In 1790 half the states with the smallest populations (dividing South Carolina, the middle state) had 22 percent of the total population of the United States; in 1970, the smallest half of the states had only 15 percent of the total.

What would happen to the many able senators? They would move into the reconstituted House. Political talent gravitates toward power. In the House, under the new rules, they could aspire to be members of the cabinet or of the shadow cabinet; their honorable ambitions to be president would find a natural outlet in the House. There, too, they would gain not only the legislative experience but also the administrative experience demanded by modern government.

Election of the president—and of congressmen-at-large—in a national constituency would end the special leverage now enjoyed by more populous states by virtue of the unit rule that gives the entire electoral vote of each state to the party with a plurality of the presidential vote. The past justification of this leverage as needed to countervail the rural-small town advantage vested in Congress is losing credibility because of changes in the economy and would be demolished by the new government with its congressmen-at-large and its emphasis on disciplined parties. The extraordinary influence now vested in racial, ethnic, economic, or regional blocs by their strength in critical states would disappear or be transferred in a diminished form to the national arena. In view of the vast electoral turnout that the new scheme would ensure, such leverage would be much more difficult to organize into plausible threats. Moreover, efforts to identify a national voting bloc and to use its powers to pressure candidates or parties would have to be heavily advertised. Inevitably, this would court counterattacks. At the same time, the new scheme would give every voter everywhere a sense of equal significance in the vital act of creating a government.

21. To Encourage Cooperation (1979)

Henry Reuss, one of the founders of CCS, was a Democratic Congressman from Wisconsin for twenty-eight years and chair of the Banking and Joint Economic committees at the time of his retirement in 1983. During the 1970s, he proposed a number of constitutional amendments designed to bring about closer collaboration between the legislative and executive branches of government. The following discussion is taken from a memorandum to his constituents.

Proposed Constitutional Amendment
To Permit Members of Congress
To Serve in Key Executive Branch Offices

A possible constitutional amendment would permit senators and representatives to serve in the executive branch, and thus emphasize cooperation rather than stalemate in Washington and bring a "home town touch" to federal agencies now too often isolated in Washington.

Many Americans feel that their government—president and Congress—is failing them. Presidential appointees are often perceived as lacking skill in the art of government. Congress in turn is frustrated because of its inability under the Constitution to participate fully in decision-making on vital questions like inflation, energy and employment.

Article I, section 6 of the Constitution prohibits members of Congress from being "officers" of the United States—cabinet or sub-cabinet officials. All the other major democratic governmental systems—Germany, Japan, Canada, Great Britain, France, Italy, the low countries, the Scandinavian countries—have governments comprised of leading legislators.

The proposed amendment would allow Congress to legislate a list of up to fifty top administration jobs which *could* be filled by senators and representatives. The president, in consultation with Congress, would prepare a slate of such jobs at the start of the new Congress every two years, and the slate would have to be confirmed by a majority of both houses. The individual appointments, of course, would be subject to the usual Senate confirmation.

The amendment would make service in Congress more attractive, and put the emphasis on cooperation, by giving its members a chance at holding posts of executive responsibility without interrupting their congressional careers. It would also give the president a wider choice of executive leaders, now denied him. Executive-legislative stalemate is a luxury we can no longer afford.

Legislators named under the new arrangement to government posts would retain their congressional roles, particularly that of constituent service. To give them time for their executive branch duties, they would be excused from congressional committee work (while retaining committee seniority). In addition, the time consumed by voting on the floor would be compressed by clustering votes.

This proposal, while borrowing the joint legislative-executive feature of the parliamentary systems obtaining in all the other great democracies, would *not* incorporate two other features of so-called "parliamentary democracy"—the selection of the chief executive by the legislature rather than by the people, and the power of legislators to topple the government at any time by a vote of lack of confidence. The amendment would do what needs to be done, and no more.

The proposed amendment involves an important modification of the constitutional principles, often attributed to Montesquieu, of separation of powers and checks and balances. We will have to weigh carefully whether such a modification is justified. Many other questions are raised. Could members of congress, now subject to discipline and expulsion only by the house in which they sit, be impeached, a process from which they are now exempt? To whom would the federal officer/member of Congress owe his first loyalty—to the president who appointed him, or to his constituency and house of Congress? How would the proposed amendment work when the president and Congress were of different parties, or when the Senate and House were controlled by different parties? What effect would the assumption of executive branch duties by a number of legislators have on the conduct of legislative business, including quorums. Should there be a limit on the number of members of each House who can be given executive branch appointments? Would the proposal improve or worsen "party discipline"?

James M. Burns
_____

22. The Power to Lead (1984)

> James M. Burns (see page 59), in his 1984 book, The Power To Lead, stresses the inability of our weak parties to take control of the government and stand accountable for the results.

The oldest and toughest problem of our governmental system is the relationship of president and Congress. In no other area has there been greater intellectual confusion. The very term that schoolchildren learn for that relationship—the structure of powers—causes mental mischief, for nowhere else in the constitutional separation did the framers more artfully *intermix* power than in the legislative-executive connection. Congress could pass laws, president veto them, Congress pass them over his veto. The president could draw up treaties, one-third plus one of the Senate could veto them. The president could nominate executive heads, the Senate could veto them by majority vote. Legislative and executive power has become even more scrambled in the two centuries since the Philadelphia convention as Congress accumulated vast authority over foreign and military policy, and Congress in recent years seized much of the executive appointment power and retrieved some of its authority over war making, the budget, and administrative organization.

But if the framers required some kind of holy wedlock between the legislative and executive departments in the practical, mechanical, day-to-day handling of public affairs, at least for an activist government, they built powerful tendencies toward unholy deadlock in the very foundations of political system. Nowhere did they apply Madison's strictures more craftily than in the different modes of selecting and empowering president and legislators—Madison's strictures, we recall, that the "great security against a gradual concentration of the several powers in the same department consists in giving to those who administer

_____

each department the necessary constitutional means and personal motives to resist encroachments of the others," that "ambition must be made to counteract ambition," and that the "interest of the man must be connected with the constitutional rights of the place."

So, when we call for more teamwork between president and Congress, we cannot pretend that we are trying to bring together two disciplined armies and hence need only work out agreement on issues between the leaderships of each. Rather, we are seeking to unify a considerably decentralized executive army with a collection of guerrilla militias in the legislature. We might as well try to coordinate quicksilver. Greater unity between and within Senate and House, moreover, often produces greater disunity between legislature and executive. Thus presidents have often been able to marshal much more support in faction-ridden Congresses, where the "chief legislator" could exploit weak legislative leadership in House and Senate and play faction against faction, than in more centrally led chambers. On the other hand, on occasions when legislative leaders did have considerable power, and when that legislative leadership supported the president, as before 1910, he could maximize his influence in that kind of situation as well.

So the question of presidential-congressional teamwork is really a set of questions: Are we talking about an equal and creative partnership between the leaderships of the two branches—the kind of partnership ritualistically acclaimed at both ends of Pennsylvania Avenue but rarely put into practice? Or are we really talking about the kind of "teamwork" that results when one side dominates and directs the other—when the Congress exerts mastery over the presidency or vice versa?

Each side can marshal a formidable battery of powers against the other, when so minded. Congress not only possesses the basic legislative and fiscal authority; it has developed, as part of the intermix of powers, a number of extraconstitutional or de facto powers. One of these is influence over the administration through legislative oversight. In passing laws or appropriations, Congress can narrow the discretion it grants administrators, consult with administrators as to future plans, and threaten legislative retaliation if certain policies or procedures are not followed. Congress may even prescribe systematic oversight in the authorizing law itself. After a law is passed and its administration established, Congress may review, probe, and assess, with an eye to interesting the media and arousing a critical public opinion. At any point Congress can expose, harass, praise, threaten, coax, browbeat in trying to influence administrative policy and action.

Overall the results are mixed at best. I refer to the oversight of "Congress," but in practice oversight breaks down into numberless committees, subcommittees, and individual senators and congressmen engaged in numberless small fishing expeditions, hearing-room tussles, publicity campaigns, and even genteel blackmail, as they seek to gain some influence over the vast federal bureaucracy. But, as Sundquist points out, the result is often frustration: legislators "cannot ordinarily anticipate, and so take measures to forestall, administrative actions of which they disapprove; they lack information and authority to intervene while the action is going on; and while they can punish administrators afterwards, and propose corrective legislation, by then the damage will have been done." The fundamental problem is the diffusion of power in Congress itself, with the result that would-be "overseers" intervene here and there, in a spasmodic, ad hoc, uncoordinated, and often undisciplined manner, with little of the steady, comprehensive, continuing, and balanced examining and assessing that true oversight demands.

On the most crucial matters of all—war making and peace making— the partnership between president and Congress is more rhetoric than fact. From the start Congress has conceded the primacy of the president in precipitating as well as conducting hostilities. As wars have dragged on, senators in particular have become clamorous in their demands for more consultation between executive and legislature during the "road to war," but earlier, amid the precipitating crisis, members of Congress have tumbled over themselves to rally around not only their flag but their president. After World War II a series of controversial presidential interventions—Cuba, Dominican Republic, and especially Vietnam— produced a hostile reaction in Congress, culminating in passage of the War Powers Resolution of 1973; under its terms the president, in committing armed forces in a national emergency resulting from an attack on the United States or its military, must report the facts at once to Congress and consult with it. Within sixty days the troop commitment must be ended unless Congress declares war, or otherwise indicates its concurrence in continuing hostilities. The president is allowed another thirty days to withdraw troops if they are in jeopardy. The resolution further provided that after ninety days Congress, by concurrent resolution not subject to presidential veto, may direct the chief executive to withdraw the troops, but the constitutionality of this provision is now in doubt.

President Nixon vetoed the resolution, labeling it an unconstitutional intrusion into presidential authority and an action that would seriously undermine the "nation's ability to act decisively and convincingly in times of international crisis." Congress passed the resolution over his veto. Other presidents besides Nixon have opposed congressional restraint on their war-making (and war-preventing) authority, and their reasons, like his, have been as much practical as constitutional. If the White House is to consult with Congress, with whom does it consult? All 535 members? The several score members of foreign and military policy committees? The chairpersons of the same? The elected leaders of House and Senate? And how much delay and loss of secrecy can be tolerated in such consultation?

Gerald Ford, just after leaving office, described the problem of simply *finding* congressional leaders to consult with during the Danang evacuation. "Without mentioning names," he said later in a public lecture, "here is where we found the leaders of Congress: two were in Mexico, three in Greece, one was in the Middle East, one was in Europe, and two were in the People's Republic of China. The rest we found in twelve widely scattered states of the union." Congress happened to be in recess, he granted, but added caustically, "events, especially military operations, seldom wait for the Congress to meet."

To organize consultative machinery for crisis situations, it has been proposed that each chamber select a key person to serve as contact with the White House, or that an ongoing committee, on the alert to meet at short notice and capable of keeping military secrets, be authorized to represent the whole Congress in crisis consultations with the president. But Congress, always fearful of "centralization," and even more respectful of established leadership, has failed to organize, or even reorganize, consultative machinery. In a situation where the president is left with— from the standpoint of Congress—a still one-sided War Powers Resolution, and Congress with its usual diffusion of power, teamwork lags. . . .

The conclusion is inescapable: it is difficult to reorganize machinery to create more partnership between the executive and legislative branches because of the diffusion of power in both branches, especially the legislative. It is almost impossible to centralize authority, and hence make it more accountable and responsible, in House and Senate. And even if machinery were changed, the pattern of political motivations, perceptions, ambitions, rewards, deprivations, and other behaviors surrounding that machinery could not so easily be transformed.

Congress, in short, can tinker with machinery, but it cannot fundamentally reform or reorganize itself from within. This is also true of the executive branch, though to a lesser degree. Both are subject to the power forces, the political pressures, operating on them and through them and within them.

Let us face reality. The framers have simply been too shrewd for us. They have outwitted us. They designed separated institutions that cannot be unified by mechanical linkages, frail bridges, tinkering. If we are to "turn the founders upside down"—to put together what they put asunder—we must directly confront the constitutional structure they erected. . . .

What is the prospect, then, of achieving a constitutional system that fosters majority rule, firm governmental authority, consistent policy, collective leadership, vigorous and principled opposition, open and responsible government? Our only chance, I believe, lies in beginning with modest efforts to strengthen both the constitutional and party structures in the hope that gradual renewals and reforms simultaneously in both the party and constitutional spheres would set up a symbiotic relationship out of which might come major changes. This is a strategy for gradual structuralists.

I would start with the force that serves as the indispensable cutting edge in social or structural change—ideas. In this case the ideas would be policy proposals embodied in party platforms, candidates' promises, and official utterances by leaders in office and in opposition. No basic change is possible, and no change if adopted would work, unless each set of party leaders stands united behind a coherent and balanced set of foreign and domestic policies. A few years ago even this small idea would have seemed quixotic. But now the Republicans have provided a case study in the capacity of the Grand Old Party to find itself ideologically, to renew itself organizationally, to win office on the basis of a relatively clear program, to support its leadership, and, to a considerable extent, to enact its program.

Now the shoe is on the Democratic foot. No real structural change is possible in the long run unless the Democratic Party, in the short run, carries through the current process of party realignment and formulates and fights for a clear, comprehensive, and radical alternative to Reagan rule.

Once both parties have made up their mind, efforts to strengthen the linkage between grass-roots cadres and national leadership could be stepped up. Increasingly, party nominating caucuses could be substituted for "party" primaries; local recruitment, organization, and leadership could be strengthened; county, state, and national conventions could gain stronger financing and organization as well as powers; the politics of House and Senate could be grounded more firmly in national party politics; campaign funding could increasingly be channeled to candidates through responsible party organizations; and the national party committees and leadership could be immensely improved. Here again the Republicans have led the way and the Democrats, if only for competitive reasons, must follow suit.

Once renewal was well on its way in both parties, modest efforts to amend the Constitution could be initiated. If the parties had managed sharply to reduce the number of state presidential primaries in which delegates were chosen, it would be safe to amend the electoral college to make it more equitable, dependable, and more clearly representative of popular majorities. The presidential impeachment process might be strengthened to allow Congress to encourage or effect a resignation or removal of a president who had as clearly lost the confidence of the country for personal or political reasons as Richard Nixon had for moral dereliction. We might adopt the Reuss plan allowing the president to choose for high executive posts members of Congress who would retain their seats, from which they could seek to unify the executive and legislative efforts at collective governing. The "team ticket" might be established, at least covering presidential and House candidates.

Effective party renewal combined with a set of moderate constitutional "process" changes would bring about some modest improvement, at least, in our governance; and each would fortify the other. The question is whether it would be necessary, or even possible, to proceed to *structural* change. This is hard to predict. If the initial moves toward party renewal and moderate constitutional change worked well, the pressure for major constitutional restructuring, such as adoption of a parliamentary system, might be lessened. Indeed, these party and constitutional changes might be enough to make the system work tolerably well. If they did not, some leaders would want to return to the old system of divided powers and individualistic leadership.

Others might press for major constitutional restructuring. I doubt that Americans under normal conditions could agree on the package of radical and "alien" constitutional changes that would be required. They would do so, I think, only during and following a stupendous national crisis and political failure. By then any reform might be too late, but if not, at least we should have done our homework. And we can watch the unfolding constitutional experiments abroad. If we should ever make fundamental changes, the remarkable French combination of presidential and parliamentary government may be especially relevant to the American situation. I doubt that we would ever import the pure, classic form of parliamentarianism, as in Britain.

One thing is clear in all this murk. Major changes in process and structure will not be brought about by spontaneous action on the part of the mass public. People as a whole are not interested in the complexities of party organization and constitutional structure; they are interested in practical results. Changes will be brought about by leadership, as in the drafting and adoption of the Constitution of 1787. But today such changes will not be allowed to remain in the hands of a small set of elites, like the fifty-five men who drew up the Constitution. The second and third cadres of American leadership must be fully involved. The most heartening precedent for constitutional change today goes back to the thousands of grass-roots activists who took part in the state constitutional ratifying conventions of 1787–1788.

Do we have a third-cadre leadership of similar intellectual power and creativity today? The answer can be found in the civic and religious groups, in the local Leagues of Women Voters and local bar associations, in the unions and Chambers of Commerce, in the professional organizations, in the schools and colleges and universities of America.

23. Balance the Budget (1985)

Dick Thornburgh, a Republican, has been governor of Pennsylvania since 1979. The following piece was originally published in the Los Angeles Times.

Washington's continuing inability to deal with federal deficits of about $200 billion a year (and rising) renews the determination of those of us who support a constitutional amendment requiring a balanced federal budget to press our case even more vigorously during the current congressional session. Such a proposal is increasingly viewed as necessary to impose long-overdue fiscal discipline on the executive and legislative branches of the federal government, which have become addicted to easy credit-card spending with no eye toward the day when the bills must be paid.

Thirty-two state legislatures have called for a constitutional convention to adopt a balanced-budget amendment. In 1982 Congress came close to approving the amendment, when more than two-thirds of the members of the Senate and more than a majority (but less than the necessary two-thirds) in the House voted for inserting a balanced-budget requirement into the Constitution.

Doubters remain, however, despite this strong show of support. I have heard certain objections more often than others, and these are my responses:

"The amendment would 'clutter up' our basic document in a way contrary to the intentions of the founding fathers." Wrong. The founding fathers clearly contemplated that amendments would be necessary to keep the Constitution abreast of the times, and that process has already been used 26 times. Moreover, one can certainly speculate that the notion of a federal government consistently spending more than it took in was so alien to the thought of 1787 that a balanced-budget provision might well have been deemed to be superfluous in the original document. Indeed, one of the major preoccupations of the constitutional convention was to liquidate the post-revolutionary war debts of the states in an expeditious manner. It is worth noting that the Treasury did not begin systematically to incur annual deficits until the mid-1930s, nearly a century and a half after the adoption of the Constitution.

"The adoption of the amendment would not solve the deficit overnight." Right, but no such claim has ever been made by serious proponents of the amendment. Obviously a period, perhaps five or even ten years, would be required for the full phase-in of a reduction to a zero deficit. But, during this interim period, budget-makers would be disciplined to meet declining deficit "targets" in order to reach a final balanced budget by the established date.

"Such an amendment would necessitate vast cuts in social services or (if you will) military or other categories of expenditure." Not necessarily. It would be required that these programs be paid for on a current basis. Certainly difficult choices would have to be made about priorities and levels of program funding in all areas, but the amendment's purpose is to discipline the executive and legislative branches actually to make these choices and not propose or perpetuate vast spending programs without providing revenues to fund them.

"A balanced budget requirement would prevent or hinder our capacity to respond to national defense or economic emergencies." This is an easy one. Of course any sensible requirement would feature a "safety valve" to exempt the incurring of deficits to respond to national defense and economic emergencies—perhaps one requiring a two-thirds or three-fifths vote of the members of both houses of Congress. There would also be nothing to prevent Congress from instituting "rainy-day" funds that would set aside current revenues during good times to be used for countercyclical purposes during economic downturns. This is currently done in twenty-three states.

"A balanced budget amendment would be 'more loophole than law' and could be easily circumvented." Probably wrong, if the experience of the nation's governors is any guide. Such requirements are now in effect in all but one of the fifty states and have served them well. The inclusion of a presidential line-item veto, which is available to most governors, would ensure that any congressional overruns could by dealt with by the president. And public clamor, the elective process and the courts would provide backup restraint on any tendency to ignore a constitutional directive.

In the final analysis, most of the excuses raised for not enacting a constitutional mandate to balance the budget seem to rest on a stated or implied preference for solving our deficit dilemma through the "political process"—that is, responsible action by the president and Congress.

This has been tried and found wanting, again and again. The last attempt to establish guidelines for such a "political process," the 1974

Budget Reform Act, has given us nothing but mounting deficits, higher interest rates, a huge negative trade balance and further discredit to the governmental process.

Isn't it time to adopt the simple directive of a constitutional amendment to force elected officals to honor their fiscal responsibilities? Thus far, no good reason has been suggested for not doing so, and years of experience at the state level argue persuasively in favor of such a step.

24. The Single, Six-Year Term for Presidents (1984)

The Jefferson Foundation was organized to promote discussion and debate about constitutional issues during the bicentennial period. The following excerpts are from a pamphlet, one of a series which set forth the pros and cons of leading proposals for constitutional amendment, intended for use by meetings of citizens around the country.

The term of office of the president and vice-president of the United States shall be six years. No person shall be eligible for more than one term as president or vice-president.

The founders created the president as the representative of the entire people, the one who would lead, protect, and uphold the American vision of its nationhood. The office changed with the nation. In the last fifty years the executive branch has increased in size and stature beyond all initial expectation.

Modern attempts to reform the presidency are responses to recent developments, but they are not a new phenomenon. Hundreds of constitutional amendments affecting the executive branch have been proposed since 1787. Of the few that have passed, the 22nd, limiting the president to two terms in office, has had the greatest impact and sparked the greatest controversy. The proposal to create a single term of six years is a closely related reform which has had supporters in every political generation since the one that produced the Constitution. With each renewal of interest in the single six-year term, the debate over principles formulated in the eighteenth century is revived in an evolving political environment.

Reprinted from "So Great a Power to Any Single Person" by permission of The Jefferson Foundation, Washington, D.C.

The Formative Debate: Framing the Executive Branch

The framers of the Constitution looked to history for guidance as they confronted the task of creating an executive body. The ancient republics and the recent colonial experience supplied more negative examples than positive. The British monarch and the very idea of unappointed hereditary power were completely contrary to the right of self-government symbolized in the revolutionary success. It was clear that extreme caution had to be exercised when investing any individual or body with executive powers, especially the power of the sword, control over foreign affairs, and the ability to pardon and appoint officers of the government.

On the eve of the Philadelphia convention, the agitators for a change in the Articles of Confederation felt they were in danger of heading right for the "dictatorship" they had just escaped. The existing federal government was strapped by its lack of power and vulnerable to corruption, insolvency, and foreign attack. The situation demanded the attention of the framers and attracted the attention of the whole world. In their minds, the failure of the American experiment would signal the failure of self-government itself.

> It has been frequently remarked that it seems to have been reserved to the people of this country, by their conduct and example, to decide the important question, whether societies of men are really capable or not of establishing good government from reflection and choice, or whether they are forever destined to depend, for their political constitutions, on accident and force. If there be any truth in the remark, the crisis at which we are arrived may with propriety be regarded as the era in which the decision is to be made; and a wrong election of the part we shall act may, in this view, deserve to be considered as the general misfortune of mankind. (*The Federalist*, #1).

With the eyes of the world upon them and the fate of self-government in their hands, the founders were determined to avoid the mistakes of the past, to leave no room for the rise of an arbitrary despot.

The founders knew clearly what they did not want in an executive: neither a despot nor a figurehead, a puppet of foreign governments and an officer too weak to protect them from bad laws and schemes of the legislature. They faced a paradoxical problem: stability required a strong leader yet liberty could not be sacrificed. Few agreed on how both these demands should be met. "Publius," however, argued that strength did not have to threaten liberty; on the contrary, it was a necessary ingredient of sound republican government.

There is an idea, which is not without its advocates, that a vigorous executive is inconsistent with the genius of republican government. The enlightened well-wishers to this species of government must at least hope that the supposition is destitute of foundation; since they can never admit its truth, without at the same time admitting the condemnation of their own principles. Energy in the executive is a leading character in the definition of good government. It is essential to the protection of the community against foreign attacks. It is not less essential to the steady administration of the laws, to the protection of property against those irregular and high-handed combinations, which sometimes interrupt the ordinary course of justice, to the security of liberty against the enterprises and assaults of ambition, of faction, and of anarchy. (*The Federalist*, #70)

Could "good government" really be "free government" as well? "The true test of a good government is its aptitude and tendency to produce good administration," Publius said, and a good administration required an executive with the power to lead, the tools to manage, and sufficient time in office to become established.

Benjamin Franklin emphasized a very different set of criteria for the executive of his "free government."

In free governments the rulers are the servants and the people their superiors and sovereigns. For the former therefore to return among the latter is not to degrade but promote them.

The American executive, to satisfy the demands of stability and those of liberty, would have to be both energetic enough to lead and humble enough to follow. The founders had set themselves quite a task. . . .

The Debate Continues

It was with a decisive air that Publius pronounced in *The Federalist*, #72, that

There is an excess of refinement in the idea of disabling the people to continue in office men who had entitled themselves, in their opinion, to approbation and confidence, the advantages of which are at best speculative and equivocal, and are overbalanced by disadvantages far more certain and decisive.

And yet his was far from the final word on the subject of presidential terms. Ratifying conventions in New York, where *The Federalist* first appeared, and in North Carolina called for an amendment to limit the president to one term even as they gave their approval to the Constitution. These were the first in a steady stream of proposals to change presidential tenure. By far the most popular and frequently proposed has been the single six-year term, which continues to have its proponents today.

As the American style of popular politics began to take shape in the nineteenth century, a new specter appeared in the comments of observers such as Alexis de Tocqueville: the specter of the demagogue, who intrigued for power not by scheming with Congress, as the founders suspected, but by courting popular favor. To this French visitor, writing in the 1840s,

> . . . it is impossible to consider any course of affairs in the United States without perceiving that the desire to be reelected dominates the thought of the president; that all the policies of his administration tend to this point; and that his least movements are subordinated to this object. . . .

The danger of ineligibility was nothing compared to the danger reelection posed.

> If reeligible (and this is especially true at the present day, when political morality is relaxed and when great men are rare), the president of the United States becomes an easy tool in the hands of the majority. He adopts its likings and its animosities, he anticipates its wishes, he forestalls its complaints, he yields to its idlest cravings, and instead of guiding it, as the legislature intended that he should do, he merely follows its bidding. Thus, in order not to deprive the state of the talents of an individual, those talents have been rendered almost useless; and to retain an expedient for extraordinary perils, the country has been exposed to continued dangers.

A similar awareness of this desire for reelection led President Andrew Jackson to "earnestly invite" consideration of a single term limitation in every one of his eight annual addresses. Removal of the temptation to be reelected would save the country from the whims of mere popular favor and, Jackson seemed to be saying, save presidents from their own ambitions.

The proposal of a single six-year term continued to be part of nineteenth-century attempts to promote "good government" by preserving the presidency from the schemes of politicians courting popular favor. There was a notable shift in the support for the reform during the late nineteenth and early twentieth centuries, when it became a Progressive cause and gained a decidedly more populist ring. The schemers against the national interest were not the popular politicians but the monied interests and big corporations. The presidency was going to the highest bidder, and the highest bidder was inevitably the incumbent, as Senator Works of California said when he introduced a single six-year term bill in 1912.

> . . . under the present provisions of the Constitution, the people do not freely choose their presidents, but are prevented from doing so in great part by the conditions that enable a candidate for a second term to manipulate caucuses and conventions to subvert the will of the people and elect a candidate that the people do not want inspite of them. . . .

Senator Work's bill gained considerable public attention and, after a year-long debate, passed the Senate in 1913. Prospects for passage in the House looked good until President Woodrow Wilson, who had won on the 1912 Democratic platform that called for the single six-year term, threw his weight against it to preserve his reelection options in 1916. While he cited numerous reasons for opposing the reform, one point in particular turned the "protection of the people" argument on its head. First, he argued, the president was the one who needed protection, and second, it would be anti-democratic to take away the people's right to vote for the person of their choice.

> If you wish to learn the result of constitutional ineligibility to reelection, ask any former governor of New Jersey, for example, what the effect is in actual experience. He will tell you how cynically and with what complacence the politicians banded against him waited for the inevitable end of his term to take their chances with his successor. . . . We singularly belie our own principles by seeking to determine by fixed constitutional provision what the people shall determine for themselves. We cast a doubt upon the whole theory of popular government.

Whether swayed by Wilson's argument or not, Progressive interest in the six-year term diminished after Work's bill and similar attempts failed.

While a considerable part of the support for a six-year term is inspired by the desire to protect the presidency from too much politics, the proposal is also a part of attempts to control the presidency, one of which succeeded with the passage of the two-term limitation in the twenty-second amendment. During the 1947 hearings in Congress on the proposed twenty-second amendment, six-year term supporters argued that it would only be carrying the principles of limitation to its logical conclusion by removing the reelection option altogether. Their arguments, prompted largely by Franklin Delano Roosevelt's unprecedented election to four terms, focused on power and the need to control it.

President Harry Truman later deemed limitation an outright effort to disable the president.

> You do not have to be very smart to know that an officeholder who is not eligible for reelection loses a lot of influence. So, what have you done? You have taken a man and put him in the hardest job in the world, and sent him out to fight with one hand tied behind his back, because everyone knows he cannot run for reelection. (Testimony, Judiciary Committee, May 4, 1959)

The fear of a "lame duck" presidency echoes the founders' concern for the independence of the president from the legislature. But in limiting the president's term, it was Congress that was gaining protection from the accumulated powers of the executive, rather than the other way around. Protection, perhaps, but not absolute control, as Senator Mike Mansfield said in rejecting the idea that a single term could debilitate a president.

> Lameness is by no means inherent in a single term. It relates to the strength and quality of the man holding the office. If a president becomes a lame duck, it is not because of any inhibition imposed by a single term. An unlimited number of terms would not sustain such a man. (Testimony on single six-year term, August 26, 1973)

The Reform Today—Freeing the President

As its long history shows, the six-year term has become one of the "perennials" of the legislative process and is to this day discussed frequently in Congress, state legislatures, and other public forums. Support today is based on a combination of concerns of the past: the need to have a more efficient, less corruptible administration, to protect the people from the ambitions of a powerful incumbent, and to keep the office from being subordinated to the politics of reelection. But the overriding concern of current-day proponents is to free the president and his policies from what they see as a distraction from the real business of governing. The reelection campaign has grown to such length, cost and proportions that the president starts running again as soon as he takes office, they argue. The new cadre of election "experts" insulates the president and has entirely too much say in determining policy. What's good for the country and what's good for reelection are growing farther and farther apart, and while public expectations of the president increase, the president's ability to be a good leader declines. What six-year terms supporters are saying, then, is that reelection no longer serves the function it was intended to serve: rather than making the president independent of the legislature and accountable to his constituents, it threatens to turn the executive branch into a permanent campaign headquarters. . . .

In response, opponents of the reform charge that "taking the president out of politics" may lead to unintended consequences.

It is, of course, true that we would not have had the Watergate reelection scandal if we did not have reelections. Similarly, we would not have election scandals if we did not have elections. And that extreme solution flows from the anti-democratic logic of the argument for a single six-year term. (George Will, *The Washington Post*)

Arguments for the Single Six-Year Term

- First-term presidents are always looking to the next term and do not spend enough time truly leading the country. Six years could give the president enough time in office to carry out his policies in a single term and remove the diversion and disruption caused by the campaign for reelection.
- The president would pay more attention to the national interest and less attention to political popularity in making and instituting policies. A single term would free him to make courageous decisions.
- Without the prospect of an approaching reelection campaign, the president would feel less obliged to satisfy the demands of special interest groups.
- At the advice of their political advisors, presidents now tend to put off hard or controversial decisions until after their reelection campaign. This causes waste and inaction where we most need leadership.
- The campaign is financially and personally costly to a president and takes away from the dignity of the office. This is not in the best interest of the people.
- A six-year term would promote more consistency in foreign and economic policy because the administration would not fluctuate according to the barometer of public opinion.
- The presidency has grown tremendously since 1787, and especially so since the New Deal. Reforming the presidential term would recognize the increased demands on the office and produce more efficient administrative leadership.

Arguments Against The Single Six-Year Term

- The single six-year term would make the president an automatic lame duck.
- The need to be reelected keeps the president accountable to the people, an important check on an office that wields so much power.
- The whole idea of term limitation is anti-democratic because it restricts the right of the people to decide for themselves whether a president should be continued in office. Its supporters assume that paying attention to public opinion and what the people want is a distraction, when in fact it is what self-government is all about.
- Supporters of a six-year term are trying to take the president out of politics, when politics and reelection are integral parts of effective executive leadership. Giving up reelection for the sake of efficiency would further remove the president from his constituents.
- Six years is too long for a bad president to serve and too short for a good one. The single term limitation might arbitrarily remove a good leader from office in a time of crisis.
- Reelection is not the source of the troubled presidency, and the single six-year term is not the solution. We need better ways of attracting and nominating high-quality candidates for president.
- A single six-year term would be a step back in the direction of the "imperial presidency."

Specific Proposals:
Text and Analysis

A. COORDINATED TERMS OF OFFICE
(CONSTITUTIONAL AMENDMENT)

Article _____

Section 1. The House of Representatives shall be composed of members chosen every fourth year by the people of the several states.

Section 2. The terms of members of the House of Representatives shall end at noon on the third day of January in those years in which the term of the president ends; and the terms of their successors shall then begin.

Section 3. The Senate shall be composed of two senators from each state chosen every eighth year by the people of several states.

Section 4. In the year of the first election of a president and vice-president after this article takes effect, the Senate shall be divided as equally as may be into two classes. The first class shall consist of the senators whose terms expire in the following year, plus those senators of other states whose terms expire two years later. The second class shall consist of the remaining senators. The seats of the senators of the first class shall be vacated at noon on the third day of January of the year following such election of a president and vice-president. The seats of the senators of the second class shall be vacated four years later.

Section 5. This article shall take effect on the first day of January of the year of the first election of a president and vice-president occurring one year or more after the ratification of this article.

Analysis

The proposed amendment changes the length of terms of members of the House of Representatives from two years to four years, running concurrently with the term of the president. It also changes the length of terms of senators from six years to eight years and divides senators into two classes, with one class being elected every four years. Senate terms would begin and end in the same years as presidential terms (and, under the amendment, congressional terms). The amendment could be accompanied by a federal statute providing that elections of members of the House and of senators would be held two to six weeks after presidential elections [see page 117].

The proposed amendment is intended to serve several important interests. By establishing concurrent four-year terms for representatives and the president, the amendment would link the political fortunes of a party's presidential and congressional candidates more closely than currently is the case. Moreover, a four-year term running simultaneously with the presidential term would give House members the same electoral time horizon as the president, and permit members to support presidential initiatives requiring sacrifices for one or two years in order to achieve favorable results within four years. For both these reasons, presidents and legislators of the same party might be expected to achieve greater party cohesion and thereby enact the party's legislative program. The amendment could have similar effects in the Senate, since all senators would be chosen in elections held at the time of presidential elections and would not face new elections before the president. The enhanced party unity resulting from the amendment might lessen executive-legislative deadlock, at least in situations where the same party controlled both the White House and Capitol Hill.

The proposed amendment would also permit representatives to devote greater time and attention to legislative responsibilities and less to the currently unending task of campaigning for reelection. The increasing range and complexity of subjects dealt with by Congress add particular weight to this point. Moreover, the longer term could attract the most qualified persons to the House and might permit them greater freedom to support party positions opposed by a powerful single-issue interest group. In addition, a reduction by half in the number of elections faced by representatives would reduce expenditures on campaigns and would give persons of moderate means a better chance of winning election to the House.

Reelection pressures experienced by senators might also be marginally diminished by the lengthening of Senate terms, and, as with House seats, election costs might be reduced. By dividing the Senate into two, rather than three, classes the proposed amendment relieves senators from facing new elections before the president. By holding the presidential, House and Senate elections in the same year, the amendment increases the voting public's opportunity to elect a president and legislature responsive to its desires. The longer lifespan of each Congress resulting from the amendment (four years rather than two) would provide greater time for each Congress to complete its legislative tasks, and to do so without the distraction of upcoming biennial elections.

A number of objections can be raised to the proposed amendment. Since the House of Representatives is meant to be close to the people, the present system of biennial elections is the surest way to accomplish this goal. Biennial terms require a member to stay in touch with and be responsive to his or her constituency. Opponents also reject the notion that the president and the legislators of the same party should work more closely to carry out the party's legislative program, on the ground that party cohesion is less important than a legislator's independence and responsiveness to his or her constituents. Opponents also reject the argument that two-year terms deter qualified persons from running for the House and doubt that four-year elections will reduce election costs, reasoning that the higher stakes in each election will be reflected in increased campaign expenditures. In any event, they believe, the added cost of frequent elections is simply the price of a legislative body truly responsive to the popular will.

Critics of the proposed amendment also argue that, by reducing the staggered character of senatorial terms, the amendment dilutes an important constitutional safeguard. By providing for three staggered classes of senators with one class being elected every two years, the framers sought to minimize the dangers that a transitory electoral sweep could entirely dominate the government. Since the proposed amendment allows election of the Senate in only two stages, it increases the danger of pendulum-like swings in legislative programs.

B. THE TEAM TICKET (CONSTITUTIONAL AMENDMENT)

Article _____

Section 1. In any election for electors of president and vice-president and for senators and representatives, candidates for elector, senator and representative shall be required to run on a political party slate. The slate of a political party shall include, for each state in which a candidate of such party seeks election to the office of president, senator or representative, consenting candidates for all such offices to be filled in such state. No candidate for any such office may consent to run on more than one party slate. Each voter may cast a ballot for one such slate as an entirety, and votes cast separately for individual candidates shall not be counted.

Section 2. The Senate and the House of Representatives shall not adopt any law or rule or follow any practice which awards less than a proportional number, but in no event less than one-third, of the seats on any committee or subcommittee to members of the largest minority party, or which prevents the initiation and conduct of any investigation within the jurisdiction of such committee or subcommittee or the issuance of any subpoena supported by the vote of one-third of the members of such committee.

Section 3. The Congress shall have power to enforce this article by appropriate legislation.

Analysis

The amendment proposed here would require candidates for president, vice-president, senator and representative to run on political party slates. In each state in which a party's candidate sought election as president, vice-president, senator or representative, the party would be required to submit a slate including a candidate for each of such offices for which elections were to be held in such state. Voters could vote only for slates and not for individual candidates. Because the amendment would increase the likelihood that the same party would control both the White House and Capitol Hill, the draft contains a provision which safeguards the oversight functions of the Congress. The largest minority party is guaranteed the greater of one-third or a proportional number of seats on every committee and subcommittee. In addition, under the amendment one-third of the members of any committee or subcommittee could initiate and conduct investigations and issue subpoenas.

The proposed amendment is intended to reduce the risk of governmental deadlocks by strengthening party cohesion and by increasing the chances of a single party controlling both the White House and Capitol Hill. The amendment could also foster party cohesion by requiring candidates for executive and legislative offices to work together in formulating a common campaign strategy and platform. Once elected to office, the president and legislators belonging to the president's party would have an incentive to cooperate in framing legislative and executive programs, since their political fortunes would be linked to one another in the next elections. Because ballots would be cast for party slates, rather than for individuals, the amendment could also make party

---

Note: For a version of the "team ticket" which might be achieved by federal statute, see page 119.

platforms and programs more important to the voting public, thereby bolstering the influence of party leadership.

Finally, the amendment would virtually assure one-party control of the White House and the House of Representatives at least for the first two years of the president's term, thus reducing the chance of deadlock between the president and Congress and making the majority party clearly accountable to the voters for the success or failure of its policies.

Critics of the proposed amendment argue that it would substantially reduce voter choice by allowing voters to cast ballots only for political party slates. This could result in the election of less able persons, by preventing ballot splitting based on perceptions of competence. The amendment could also result in a less discriminating voting public, since the qualifications and positions of individual candidates would lose importance. The proposed amendment could also significantly handicap third-party presidential candidates, who would be required to assemble viable slates of candidates for Congress in order to compete against major party candidates. Third-party candidates for Congress would encounter similar difficulties.

C. BONUS SEATS FOR PARTY WINNING PRESIDENTIAL ELECTION (CONSTITUTIONAL AMENDMENT)

Article _____

Section 1. The political party whose candidate is elected president shall designate, as members of the House of Representatives, one person for every five congressional districts. The terms of such representatives shall commence on the third day of January in the years in which the term of the president commences and shall end four years later. Representatives designated under this amendment shall have all rights, privileges and duties of a member of the House of Representatives. No person shall be designated as a representative for any five congressional districts under this amendment unless such person is eligible to be elected as representative for one of such congressional districts.

Section 2. The political party whose candidate is elected president shall designate as senators of the United States one person for each state. The terms of such senators shall commence on the third day of January in the years in which the term of the president commences and shall end four years later. Senators designated under this amendment shall have all rights, privileges and duties of a member of the Senate. No person shall be designated as senator for a state under this amendment unless such person is eligible to be elected as a senator in that state.

Section 3. Not less than thirty days before election, each political party nominating electors for president and vice-president shall publish and file with the Clerk of the House of Representatives lists of persons whom, if its candidate is elected president, it will designate as senators and as representatives, together with the states and congressional districts, as geographically contiguous as may be, to be represented by each such person. Such lists may include persons standing for election as senator or representative, together with alternates for any such person who is elected to the office of senator or representative.

Section 4. The Senate and the House of Representatives shall not adopt any law or rule or follow any practice which awards less than a proportional number, but in no event less than one-third, of the seats on any committee or subcommittee to members of the largest minority party in such House, or which prevents the initiation and conduct of any investigation within the jurisdiction of such committee or subcommittee or the issuance of any subpoena supported by the vote of one-third of the members of such committee.

Section 5. The Congress shall have power to enact laws necessary to carry out this article.

Analysis

This draft constitutional amendment empowers the political party to which the president belongs to appoint fifty senators and eighty-seven representatives to the Senate and House respectively. Senators and representatives designated under this amendment would serve terms of four years, running concurrently with the term of the president, and would possess all the rights, privileges and duties of members of the house to which they were appointed. The amendment contains no express provision regarding removal of persons appointed to Congress, but the statements that the terms of senators and representatives "[shall] end four years later" carries the necessary implication that neither the political party appointing a legislator, nor the president, may remove such person.

Political parties are required to compile and publish lists of persons who will be designated senators and representatives if the party's presidential candidate is elected. Persons designated as senator for a particular state must be eligible to be elected as a senator in that state. Political parties are also required, to the extent possible, to divide the 435 congressional districts into groups of five geographically contiguous districts. Persons designated as senator of a state or representative of a particular group of districts are required to be eligible for election as senator of that state or a representative of one district within that group.

Since the amendment would virtually assure a majority of both houses to the party winning the presidency, the amendment also seeks to ensure that the majority could not control or suppress the oversight and investigatory functions of congressional committees and subcommittees. Section 5 guarantees that the largest minority party in each house shall receive the greater of one-third or a proportional number of the seats on every committee and subcommittee. Further, the section permits one-third of the members of a committee or subcommittee to initiate and conduct investigations and to issue subpoenas.

The proposed amendment is designed to prevent divided government and to enhance cooperation between the executive and legislative branches, and thereby to reduce the danger of governmental deadlocks. In half the time since World War II, one party has controlled the White House while the other party has held a majority in one or both houses of Congress. By awarding bonus seats to the party winning the presidency, the amendment would confer on the president's party the legislative majorities needed to win congressional approval of his programs. While fifty additional seats are more than the president's party would need to hold control over the Senate, this number has been chosen to meet the requirement that no amendment may reduce the "equal suffrage" of a state in the Senate without its consent.

The proposed amendment would also make it easier to fix responsibility for the success or failure of governmental programs. Armed with the bonus seats, which generally would enable the president to enact his party's programs, a president and his party would be unable to blame the shortcomings of their administration on the other party's opposition in Congress. The majority party's programs would be adopted and would be tested by their success or failure in actual operation. The proposed amendment could also strengthen party cohesion, by vesting the party winning the White House with the power to select the occupants of bonus seats. The loyalty of these additional members to the party's programs should be much stronger than that of constituency members less dependent on the party to retain their seats. The proposed amendment would also increase the information available to voters in presidential elections. Before voting, the public would know the identity of the persons who would receive bonus seats, and its vote for president would be informed by its knowledge of their positions, character and capacity. The parties would presumably compete for electoral favor by publishing the most appealing lists they could put together.

Finally, the proposed amendment could reduce the influence of single-issue interest groups over individual legislators. Persons chosen by the political parties would generally reflect the national concerns of a party and its presidential nominee, rather than the concerns of a single state or district. They would not be dependent on single-interest contributions or votes to win or retain office. Moreover, distinguished and experienced citizens, such as former legislators, cabinet members and governors, would probably accept party designations to serve as additional members even though they would not run for individual constituency seats. Their presence in Congress could contribute greatly to its deliberations and its emphasis on national over local and pressure group interests. Various combinations of constituency seats and additional seats filled from party lists are quite common in the democracies of Western Europe and have had these salutary effects.

Critics of the proposed amendment raise a number of objections to the bonus seat arrangement. The amendment rewards the party of a president elected by only a narrow national majority with almost certain control of the Congress. The additional members could be expected to be obedient party regulars whose votes would almost always adhere to the party line. Where the electorate has expressed its approval of a presidential candidate so narrowly, the bonus awarded by the amendment may be disproportionate. Critics also argue that the amendment vests far too much authority in political parties, whose decision-making may not be subject to an adequate degree of popular scrutiny and approval. Proponents of the amendment respond that publication of the list of potential designees to congressional office satisfies the demands for public scrutiny and control and would prevent the appointment of unreflective party members.

Critics of the amendment also argue that the bonus seat system could result in wide swings in legislative policy as first one party and then the other wins control of the presidency. The shift from nationalization to "privatization" of major industries in the United Kingdom is cited as an example. Opponents of the amendment also contend that the award of bonus seats will interfere with the legislature's responsiveness to local concerns, because of the substantial numbers of persons chosen on the basis of the national presidential vote.

Finally, opponents argue that both the House and the Senate are already large enough—if not too large—to fulfill their constitutional roles, and increases of 25 percent in the House and 50 percent in the Senate will make them even more cumbersome and less efficient.

D. LEGISLATORS IN THE EXECUTIVE BRANCH
(CONSTITUTIONAL AMENDMENT)
Proposal by Henry Reuss

Article _____

Section 1. Congress shall have the power by law to designate offices in the executive branch, not to exceed fifty in number, to which members of the Senate and the House of Representatives would be eligible for nomination and appointment, regardless of the time when the office was created or the emoluments whereof were increased, without being required to vacate their offices in the Senate or the House of Representatives.

Section 2. Immediately after the commencement of a Congress in a year during which the term of a president begins, and in the year commencing every two years thereafter, the president shall submit en bloc a list of the names of prospective nominees, whether members or not, to the offices designated pursuant to Section 1. hereof, to the Senate and the House of Representatives. If each house separately by a majority of its respective members present and voting, a quorum being present, concurs in such list en bloc, the president shall nominate and, by and with the advice and consent of the Senate, appoint those on such list to the designated offices. In the event of a failure of either house to give its concurrence, the president shall submit a revised list of names of prospective nominees until concurred in by the Senate and the House of Representatives.

Section 3. During the time that a member of the Senate or the House of Representatives serves in the designated office, his compensation shall be at the rate provided by law for the said office. In the event such senator or representative ceases for any reason in the designated office before the expiration of the term for which he was elected, his compensation shall be at the rate then provided by law for senators and representatives.

Section 4. The Congress shall have the power to enforce this article by appropriate legislation or rules of procedure, as relevant and proper.

ALTERNATIVE PROPOSAL

Article _____

Section 1. Any member of the Senate or the House of Representatives may be appointed to any civil office under the authority of the United States, regardless of the time the office was created or the emoluments whereof were increased, without being required to vacate his or her seat in the Senate or the House of Representatives; provided that nothing in this article shall permit the appointment of a member of the Senate or the House of Representatives as a judge of a court of the United States.

Section 2. Congress shall have power by law to designate not fewer than [twenty-five] and not more than [fifty] offices of the executive departments of the United States to which the president may appoint members of Congress; the president shall appoint no fewer than [four], and no more than [twenty-five], members of Congress to those offices designated by Congress.

Analysis

The proposed amendment removes the existing constitutional prohibition, contained in Article I, Section 6, on service by members of Congress in the executive branch. The United States is unique among the major democracies of the West in its prohibition of service by legislators in the administration.

Henry Reuss has written that the change would "emphasize cooperation rather than stalemate," and "bring a 'hometown touch' to federal agencies now too often isolated in Washington." The proposed amendment might also increase the attraction of a seat in the House of Representatives and thereby work to better the overall quality of the House. In addition, the amendment would somewhat expand the president's choice of executive officials.

The prohibition against service by legislators in the executive branch was termed "the cornerstone on which our liberties depend" in debates at the constitutional convention. Little explanation was offered for this judgment, which seems to rest on an exaggerated view of the separation of powers doctrine and the amount of money a legislator could make in 1789 if he won appointment as a postmaster or customs collector. From a practical perspective, the objection might be made that today both members of Congress and executive officials are fully occupied by their duties, and that requiring one person to fulfill both sets of responsibilities would be unwise. Such difficulties could be eased by appointing legislators to executive positions responsible for substantive areas where they hold committee or subcommittee assignments, but this might entail some loss of congressional oversight abilities and diminish the legislative "clout" of the executive appointees.

Two variations on the basic theme of permitting legislators to serve in the executive branch are presented. The amendment proposed by Mr. Reuss sets a specific, detailed procedure by which fifty executive offices, designated by law, would be filled by means of a single bloc appointment, requiring the approval of a majority of each house of Congress. The second proposal either permits the appointment of legislators to executive offices, with no requirement to do so [Section 1 standing alone], or permits such appointment and requires the president

---

France requires cabinet appointees to surrender their legislative seats to elected alternatives, but a legislator who leaves the cabinet is entitled to retake his seat.

to appoint a specified number of legislators to a list of offices designated by Congress [Sections 1 and 2 together].

E. CABINET SECRETARIES IN CONGRESS (CONSTITUTIONAL AMENDMENT)

Article _____

The president shall have power to appoint principal officers of the executive departments of the United States to the Senate and the House of Representatives, [provided that a majority of the house to which an officer is appointed concurs in such appointment]. No more than ____ principal officers of the executive departments of the United States shall serve at any time in the Congress, and, so far as possible, equal numbers of officers shall be appointed to each house. Any officer appointed to the Senate or the House of Representatives shall enjoy all the rights and privileges accorded members of that house, except the right to vote on bills. Nothing contained in this article shall restrict the power of the president to remove any person from executive office.

Analysis

The amendment is intended to reduce the likelihood of governmental deadlock by fostering a closer working relationship between the executive and the legislature. Cabinet officers participating in congressional debate would have the opportunity to explain presidential positions more quickly and directly than is currently the case. Proponents of the amendment cite Justice Story's arguments that the presence of cabinet officers on the floor would render the executive branch more accountable to legislative and popular concerns, would bring governmental decision-making more fully into public view, and would improve the quality of presidential appointments by requiring the president to appoint cabinet officers capable of withstanding attacks on the floor. The amendment's supporters note that President Taft saw similar advantages.

Several objections have been raised to the proposal reflected in the amendment. Both former legislators and cabinet officers have rejected suggestions permitting officers to take part in congressional debate. By a three-to-one margin, legislators interviewed in 1957 opposed such a measure on the grounds that it would enhance executive power and not benefit Congress, which was thought able to obtain information and advice from the president through committee hearings and other channels. A survey of seventeen former cabinet officers in 1957 revealed unanimous opposition to permitting or requiring executive officers to participate in congressional debate. The principal reason for opposition was the fear that Congress would gain power.

Among the opponents to the reforms proposed in the amendment, Harold Laski contended that even a statute permitting cabinet officers to participate in congressional debate, and requiring their attendance at specified question-and-answer sessions, "might easily change the whole balance of power in the American system." Under such a system, the president would be likely to select persons already influential with the Congress as cabinet officers; former members of one of the houses would be most likely candidates for appointment. Difficulties in maintaining cabinet unity could arise in such circumstances, particularly if Congress sought to play off the cabinet against the president. Laski also warned that cabinet officers, under this arrangement, would be more inclined to use their office as a platform to seek the presidency than currently is the case. All these considerations led Laski to the conclusion that the outcome of the proposal would be "to transfer the essential features of presidential leadership to the cabinet."

Some supporters of the proposed amendment agree that it would shift power from the president alone to the president plus the cabinet, but consider the change desirable. Woodrow Wilson believed such a change would foster accountability in the executive branch: if a cabinet were unable to implement its programs, it would be forced to resign in favor of a more promising coalition. Other supporters of the amendment's proposal dismiss the possibility that the president would lose significant power to his cabinet, citing the president's removal power and his popular mandate.

F. REPEAL OF TWO-TERM LIMIT ON THE PRESIDENCY (CONSTITUTIONAL AMENDMENT)

Article _____

The twenty-second amendment to the Constitution of the United States is hereby repealed.

Analysis

This amendment, abolishing the two-term restriction placed on persons holding the office of president by the twenty-second amendment, would serve several purposes, all aimed at avoiding governmental deadlock by strengthening the presidency. First, it would permit retention of capable leaders in the presidency. As Alexander Hamilton wrote, "How unwise must be every such self-denying ordinance as serves to prohibit a nation from making use of its own citizens, in the manner best suited to its exigencies and circumstances." Second, the proposed amendment eliminates the danger of "lame-duck" presidents. Under this view, the chief executive's effectiveness depends in large part on the support of his party. A president unable to seek reelection is arguably handicapped in maintaining party support, since his "coattails are permanently in mothballs." The twenty-second amendment imposes this handicap on any second-term president; by repealing that amendment, the proposed amendment is intended to increase the likelihood of effective second-term government. Finally, the amendment returns to the electorate the choice of chief executive.

Opponents of the amendment argue that "lame-duck" presidents are as effective as presidents able to seek reelection, citing Eisenhower's second term as historical evidence. Moreover, opponents argue that the amendment's supporters have advanced no positive evidence that "lame-duck" status handicaps a president, and that constitutional changes should not be undertaken without such evidence. Objections to the amendment also reflect concerns over vesting excessive power in the hands of a single individual. Under this view, the dangers of a single person slowly accumulating power in the course of several terms outweigh the benefits of an entirely free choice of presidents. Alternatively, lengthy service as president by one person is claimed to foster institutions and governmental processes tailored to a single individual, which will prove ineffective when new leadership inevitably emerges.

Part 4

Breaking Deadlocks

In the introduction to Part 3, we spoke of the tendency of the American political system to fall into deadlock when confronted by difficult and controversial issues. We traced this tendency to the structure of the Constitution, which was established by the framers to prevent "factions" from imposing "tyranny" on their fellow-citizens.

In that Part, we argued that political parties, as they have evolved in the American system, are not "factions" in the framers' sense of that term and that, far from posing the danger of "tyranny," they often seemed incapable of fashioning and implementing a coherent program of government. We noted that modern conditions often call for more positive government than the framers expected. To respond to this need without sacrificing popular accountability, we proposed various constitutional amendments which might reduce the tendency toward divided government and encourage the chance that a responsible team of public officials might take the reins of government and produce a program for which it could be held electorally accountable.

We turn now, here in Part 4, to a different set of concerns. The idea behind the writings and proposals in this Part is that the popular will is the ultimate arbiter in a constitutional democracy. In the course of government, disagreements among elected officials are bound to break out, no matter how they are chosen or how they divide their functions. Most of these disputes can and should be resolved by compromise.

Occasionally, however, differences occur which are so fundamental that they cannot be compromised. The president believes that it is time for a radically new set of budget priorities, but majorities in Congress block any coherent action on the budget. (That did not happen in 1981, but it very nearly did.) The country falls into severe economic depression, but the incumbent administration, with three years to go in its term, refuses to offer a remedial program, despite apparently growing popular demand. Or majorities in Congress become convinced that the president is incompetent or has grossly abused his powers, but no legally valid evidence can be produced to prove that he has committed "treason, bribery, or other high crimes or misdemeanors," the only grounds for impeachment.

In these circumstances—when the government is brought to a standstill by fundamental policy disagreements or by perceptions of gross malfeasance or incompetence—we have no mechanism for appealing to the nation for a decisive judgment.

This Part explores the need for such a mechanism and examines various proposals for supplying it. We begin with an analysis of the problem by Kevin Phillips, a conservative commentator who urges that we incorporate certain features of the parliamentary model into our system. We present next a brief excerpt from a recent book by Theodore C. Sorensen, a White House aide during the Kennedy administration, calling for coalition government. We conclude this introductory section with a suggestion offered by William Yandell Elliot, a Harvard professor during the New Deal period, that a president be empowered to take the dispute to the nation when Congress blocks his program.

President Nixon's resignation, following the Watergate scandal in 1974, gave rise to criticism of the impeachment process and stimulated the thought that we needed a mechanism for returning to the nation for a new mandate, to avoid an extended period of governmental paralysis. A symposium at the George Washington University Law School provided an occasion for analyzing the suggestion, made by Congressman Henry Reuss, among others, that we amend the Constitution by adopting a congressional vote of no confidence. We present several portions of that discussion here. We also include a brief excerpt from a conversation between a congressman and a law school professor on the problem of incorporating dissolution into the American system.

There have been other, less drastic attempts to accommodate our eighteenth-century Constitution to the demands of modernity. As Congress has felt compelled to delegate more and more discretion to the executive branch, it has sought means to retain a measure of control for the representative branch. One such mechanism was the legislative veto, which permitted administrators to take action, subject to reversal by congressional resolution, or (as it developed) by resolution of a single house, or even in some cases by a congressional committee. In 1983, the Supreme Court declared this device in its various forms unconstitutional and took the occasion, in the Court's opinion and in the dissent, to review the Constitution's provisions for interaction between the executive and legislative branches in the making of policy and to interpret the limits of accommodation to modern demands for efficiency. We here present portions of those Supreme Court opinions and a commentary by James Sundquist.

Part 4 concludes with draft language for several proposals for breaking deadlocks between the branches and a discussion of pros and cons.

Kevin Phillips

25. An American Parliament (1980)

Kevin Phillips is a lawyer, syndicated columnist, and radio commentator. He has served as a congressional aide and with the 1968 Nixon presidential campaign, and has written several books, including The Emerging Republican Majority *(1969) and* Post-Conservative America *(1982). The following is from an article published by* Harper's *magazine.*

The United States is in trouble that goes far beyond a single national election or its results. The dubious doctrine of "American exceptionalism"—based on the idea that this country is unique, or that God takes special care of babies, drunks, and the United States of America—is a misconception that may soon prove fatal. The notion springs from many sources, among them the belief that we are blessed with a peerless Constitution and brilliantly structured political system, designed for the ages in the candlelight of 1787. Yet the United States' success in coping with the 1980's may depend on the speed and intelligence with which we can transform a number of obsolescent, even crippling, political institutions, mechanisms, and relationships. Conservatives, by tradition partisans of the status quo, may find themselves charged with taking the reformist lead. . . .

Of all the malfunctions of the American political system, the most obvious is the entrenched counterproductivity of White House and congressional interaction. . . . In contrast to the parliamentary legislatures elected elsewhere in the west, the U.S. Congress not only operates on its own, but does so in a way to paralyze the executive branch. The White House has a national-security apparatus, a budget bureau, and a technology office, so Congress must have its own counterparts—and

Congress does, with some 19,000 employees to man its battlements and fortifications. The legislative branch has various quasi-executive functions, exercising control over major segments of the federal bureaucracy through auxiliaries of Senate committees, House committees, and allied lobby groups. Effective government is impossible.

Part of the predicament—the nominal separation of powers—is written into the Constitution. Much of the problem, though, is only a matter of paper, people, and procedures; it can be changed nonconstitutionally—not easily, but it can be done.

Senator Daniel Patrick Moynihan's suggestion of putting members of Congress in the cabinet is to the point:

> My thought is that the time is at hand to involve the legislative with the executive, and that this could be done by the practice of appointing members of the House and Senate to the cabinet. . . . The essence of the problem, clearly, was the constitutional decision to separate the executive from the legislative in a way not found in any other government, much less any other democracy. . . . The president (by appointing members of Congress to his cabinet) would have the advantage of devising legislative proposals that would be seen by Congress as partly legislative in origin, and the president's proposals would have advocates in the committees and on the floor.

Commentators generally inferred that the senator's suggestion would require a constitutional amendment. Not so. That *would* be necessary for any senator or congressman simultaneously to hold office as secretary of defense, secretary of labor, or whatever. Those are "offices under the United States," which members of Congress cannot occupy concurrently with their elected positions. But no prohibition exists against giving elected legislators cabinet status as, in effect, ministers without portfolio. The cabinet itself has no legal or constitutional status—anyone can be appointed. In such fashion, Capitol Hill leaders could join the president in devising legislative proposals, as Moynihan suggests, without assuming the administrative burdens of a departmental secretaryship. Several might also serve as administration floor spokesmen in their areas of competence. . . .

Lloyd Cutler, counsel to President Carter, sees progress along these lines as institutionally essential: "The separation of powers between the legislative and executive branches has become a structure that almost guarantees stalemate today." . . . Several prominent Republicans agree. Bryce Harlow, a respected senior GOP statesman who served both Dwight Eisenhower and Richard Nixon as chief of congressional relations, says, "It's not a people problem, it's a process problem. The executive and legislative branches are increasingly entrenched and unresponsive.

We have to shake up the bureaucracy, the parties, and Congress's self-perpetuation to make popular sentiment effective again." It is intriguing that both President Carter and Vice-President Mondale several years back also endorsed the notion of requiring the cabinet to appear before Congress to answer questions. In his 1975 book, *Why Not the Best?*, Mr. Carter urged that the president's cabinet "appear before the joint sessions of the Congress to answer written questions," and Mondale, as a senator, actually sponsored legislation to implement the idea.

Little current poll data is available, but an early-1980 national survey, conducted by the St. Louis-based Civic Service, asked: "Would you favor having major new legislation worked out in close consultation between the president and congressional leaders before it goes to Congress to help reduce confrontation and stalemate?" Of respondents, 60.7 percent said yes, while 20 percent said no. Clearly, separation of powers commands little fidelity at the grass roots.

At the risk of appearing unfairly pejorative, I point out that some of the greatest enthusiasm for a divided U.S. government is found in the Kremlin. A 1979 study by noted Soviet Americanologist Professor Yurdi I. Nyporko, entitled, "Constitutional Inter-relationships Between the President and Congress of the U.S.A.," announced appreciatively that "tensions now rise with greater frequency within the bourgeois governmental mechanisms." Nyporko noted that the "intensified struggle" between our legislative and executive branches had made checks and balances a reality. In his analysis, Soviet interests would be best served by a Republican president "balked" by a Democratic Congress, especially by the Senate. A Democratic president vying with a Republican Congress would rank second in favor, and least desirable would be an executive-legislative collaboration dominated by the same political coalition.

The presidential selection process itself contributes to the flawed structure of the executive branch. Lone wolves tend to emerge, ensuring the sort of White House that fortifies itself from hostilities with Capitol Hill. Quite apart from how presidents reach the Oval Office, the job they find there simply has gotten too big. It must be reduced, spread, or divided. If we can begin to move toward the quasi-parliamentary system advocated by Moynihan, Cutler and others, the role of the cabinet would necessarily increase in a way that would ease the burdens of the presidency. Cabinet government, pivoting on the department heads and on the major political legislative leaders of the presiding coalition, could redistribute presidential responsibilities. Such a government would be much more tenable than might be suggested by the results of the occasional, half-hearted cabinet upgradings of the "personal presidency" era. The upper echelons of the White House would become less the purview of home-state cliques and more the mobilization ground of national talent.

Redefinition of the vice-presidency is essential. When pursued recently by Gerald Ford and Ronald Reagan, such redefinition miscarried, but the basic idea of the vice-president assuming a role as chief operating officer of the government or being specifically responsible for certain areas of expertise is unlikely to be set aside. In the aftermath of the Detroit deliberations, Ford's former presidential press secretary, J.F. terHorst, suggested that "a truly worthwhile [constitutional] amendment might be an enlargement of the role of the vice-president so that he could take up some of the duties of the executive branch. . . . The aborted Reagan-Ford plan ought to spur some scholarly research into the feasibility of such an amendment."

Effective reform of the federal government would be best served by a quasi-parliamentary transition. A limited shift of the sort heretofore sketched, in considerable measure achievable without amending the Constitution, could set the scene for a stronger cabinet and reforms above and beyond better executive-legislative collaboration. It also would offer a possible vehicle for regrouping legislators and politicians in an era when the increasingly obsolescent Republican and Democratic parties may no longer be able to revitalize themselves.

In this respect, we are beginning to hear more and more about another device most familiar but not limited to parliamentary systems: the coalition. Arguably, the two party system can no longer produce ideological turning points because individual legislators have shaped themselves into communications age ombudsmen—constituency servants who rise and fall too little on party tides to make party tides effective or meaningful. If so, then progress must seek an institutional bypass. Four or five years ago, a number of conservatives seriously contemplated a new party on the right, and Gallup found 25–30 percent of Americans in favor of that option. More recently, spurred by John Anderson's independent presidential candidacy, Gallup polled the public on support for a new center party, and found 30–40 percent backing. Likewise, an early-1980 Opinion Research Corporation survey found 47 percent of those queried in agreement that a strong third party would revitalize our political system. But the question is probably moot. For all that the public seems to be searching for some new alternative, current federal election law is so stacked against the emergence of successful new parties that some strategists prefer a new avenue—such as the coalition.

The coalition can be approached on many levels. Foremost is the concept contemplated briefly in June by the Ronald Reagan forces—the idea of choosing Georgia's Democratic senator, Sam Nunn (or some other southern Democrat) as Reagan's running mate, with the goal being the first national-level coalition since Abraham Lincoln picked Tennessee Democrat Andrew Johnson in 1864. But the *Atlanta Constitution,* reporting the plan, quoted one Reagan aide as saying the Nunn approach was abandoned because GOP convention delegates had not yet perceived the institutional or national crisis: "We may indeed be reaching such a point, but the perception of the crisis has yet to take hold."

In times of turmoil and uncertainty, both parties have sometimes sought a degree of bipartisanship in cabinet appointments. Prior to World War II, Franklin D. Roosevelt added Republicans Henry Stimson and Frank Knox as secretary of war and secretary of the navy; in 1961, Democrat John Kennedy, after winning the election by the narrowest of majorities, appointed Republicans Robert McNamara and C. Douglas Dillon as secretary of defense and secretary of the treasury. Early-1980 polls turned up 54 percent in favor of a similar move by Jimmy Carter, with 26 percent opposed; and mid-1980 saw several senior Reagan aides float trial balloons on the possibility of naming some cabinet members a few weeks before the election so that voters might consider them in casting their November ballots and including several well-known Democrats in order to give the ticket a coalition coloration.

My own feeling is that much of the impetus toward coalitionism in Congress must come—if it is to come at all—from the quasi-parliamentary thrust and the perception of the inadequacy of separation of powers described earlier in this essay. To overcome the current extreme separation of powers, congressmen and senators will have to be brought into the cabinet; should that happen, the critical question becomes: in whose cabinet, with what kind of president, would conservative Democrats serve? The election of 1976 (probably an aberration) aside, many white southern Democrats locally vote Republican on the presidential level. Implement Lloyd Cutler's idea of having national and congressional candidates run together on a quasi-parliamentary ticket, and metropolitan Houston, Dallas, Tulsa, Shreveport, Jacksonville, Palm Beach, Charleston, Winston-Salem, and a dozen other cities would immediately shift to a conservative coalition representation.

Somewhat the same thing could result if conservative Republicans were to gain control of the White House, recognizing simultaneously that the name of the political game during the 1980s is institutional reform rather than traditional realignment. Suppose that a Republican president held out three cabinet posts to conservative Democrats, proposed that ten congressmen and senators (four or five of them sympathetic Democrats) sit without portfolio in an expanded cabinet, and expressed the simultaneous hope that Republicans and the sizable moderate-to-conservative minority of Democrats sort themselves into a majority coalition to take over the machinery of Congress and work in tandem with the new executive-level coalition. It just might work, and if it did, the result would have the political effect of a realignment combined with the structural benefit of institutional reform.

Accept the importance of quasi-parliamentary reform and a lot of other conditions become clear. Preeminent among them is the counter-productivity of current efforts to reinforce—or even freeze—the existing party structures. One can argue that once the potential realignment of 1972 was aborted by Watergate, the Republican and Democratic parties have become obsolescent groupings. Their ineffectiveness has been a factor in the poor performance of U.S. government in general and the hostility of the executive and legislative branches in particular.

Ironically, the more that Americans have cried out for institutional reforms catalogued again and again in Gallup polls, the more that the Republican and Democratic parties have tried to entrench themselves against displacement or competition. Since Watergate, that entrenchment has been intensified in an attempt to assure the permanence of a choice that only 56 percent of the 1976 voting-age population thought worth making. . . .

So long as politicians insist on trying to prop up the two major parties, they are almost certain to shrink from more serious institutional and constitutional reforms premised on the failure of the party system. From this perspective, reinforcement of the existing parties seems counterproductive.

Some of us have changed our perspective. Before Watergate and its dissipation of the GOP's possible 1972–76 opportunity of forming a new coalition, I thought that the existing party frameworks would suffice for realignment. Since then, changed circumstances have suggested otherwise. The public has lost too much faith in governmental and political institutions.

At any rate this writer, at least, has believed since Watergate that some new vehicle or arrangement would be necessary to harness the conservative trend that, albeit suspended for a few years, is reemerging to dominate the foreseeable political future. Exactly what that vehicle could or would be is, admittedly, still something of a question.

The best current options, preferable to reinforcing the existing party system, may be either to do nothing pending larger institutional reeval-uations, or to erase some of the recent major-party protections included in the federal election code (notably campaign subsidies and preferences). As for the cumbersome thirty-five-primary process by which we now nominate our chief executives, an initial element of reform seems obvious: let the states shift to a series of four regional primaries to be held in June or July, followed by conventions (of some sort) in August, then by the election in November. . . .

The sad truth is that most of our institutions and processes—not just two or three—need reform. With the federal judiciary having overstepped so many bounds, perhaps Congress, as authorized by the Constitution, should cut back on the jurisdiction allowed to the federal courts. This summer, the National Governors Conference passed a resolution deploring the substantial inroads Washington has made on federalism and the perversion of the system when Congress dictates minutiae. Surely a correction is in order here, too? And perhaps we would even do well to consider some form of national initiative and referendum, in the beginning no more than advisory in nature, to give the public a larger role in policy making.

Chief Justice Warren Burger, speaking at a 1978 seminar on legal history, summed up what should be the scope of our inquiry and concern.

It may seem premature to be thinking about the next significant bicentennial celebration in our national life, but our experience with the bicentennial of 1976 demonstrates the desirability of long advance planning. It is not too soon to turn our minds to the two-hundredth anniversary of the document [the Constitution] signed in Philadelphia almost exactly 191 years ago. I submit that an appropriate way to do this will be to reexamine each of the three major articles of our organic law and compare the functions as they have been performed in recent times with the functions contemplated in 1787 by the men at Philadelphia.

Others have suggested a more formal reexamination: Delaware Senator William V. Roth and some of his colleagues would like to see a second constitutional convention meet in this decade. Missouri congressman Richard Bolling, chairman of the House Rules Committee, has introduced legislation to set up a grand "Commission on More Effective Government" to "study the organization, operation and functioning of all aspects of the federal government."

The crisis is genuine. Futurist Alvin Toffler goes so far as to urge "a widespread, public, political debate about future forms of democracy" to head off possible bloodshed and totalitarianism. . . . Analysts are beginning to discuss parallels—malaise, military defeat, frustrated nationalism, loss of faith in institutions—between the United States and the Weimar Germany of the 1920s.

Be that as it may, the system is *not* healthy; pretensions that it is are nonsense. And the political irony—which may be simultaneously one of the decade's most decisive political vulnerabilities and opportunities— is that aging liberals are no longer the innovators, but the Bourbons and Hapsburgs of contemporary institutional failure. Theirs are the palaces under attack, and the restless crowds beginning to throw rocks into the Tuileries are populist conservatives of a sort. The challenge of the 1980s is that conservatives may find themselves obliged to preside, not over a traditional electoral realignment, but over a critical restructuring of U.S. political institutions.

Theodore C. Sorensen

26. A Coalition Government (1984)

Theodore C. Sorensen, who was special counsel to President Kennedy, practices law in New York City. He has written several books, including Kennedy, Watchmen in the Night: Presidential Accountability after Watergate, *and* A Different Kind of Presidency: A Proposal for Breaking the Political Deadlock, *from which the following is excerpted.*

Ineffectiveness in Washington is not new. Our recent presidents are not the first to find their authority diminished and their proposals impeded. The country has survived this kind of Washington power outage in previous eras. But this time the national problems not being adequately addressed are so deep-seated and far-reaching that the irreversible consequences of continuing drift could drastically alter our national future.

Specifically:

- If we do not in the next five years reach an agreement with the Soviet Union halting the nuclear arms race, both superpowers will undertake strategic weapon developments and deployments that will make meaningful limitation impossible and future confrontations unavoidable.
- If we do not in the next five years drastically reduce our federal deficits, this country's national debt and annual borrowing will grow to levels so disproportionate to the size of our economy and budget as to be insupportable.
- If we do not in the next five years begin to restore the ability of American industry to compete internationally, our prospects for

Reprinted by permission of Theodore C. Sorensen.

regaining world economic leadership, steady growth and high employment will be indefinitely lost.
- If we do not in the next five years develop with our allies and the
  international finance institutions a long-term restructuring of third
  world debt, a wave of government bankruptcies or debt repudiations
  will undermine the U.S. banking system and with it much of our
  economy and that of the Western world.
- If we do not in the next five years establish with our industrial
  allies fair and enforceable rules on trade barriers, subsidies, credits
  and exchange rates, a rising tide of protectionism and commercial
  warfare will wash away the institutional channels for trade expansion,
  painstakingly built over three decades, on which world prosperity
  is dependent.
- If we do not in the next five years develop with the government
  of Mexico a series of agreements on trade, immigration, credit,
  energy, population and economic stability for that nation, we will
  for the first time in this century face a serious security problem in
  our own border.

No doubt this list is incomplete. No doubt other national and international problems will reach such perilous proportions in the next five
years that failure to act will risk unacceptable consequences for our
country. But this list is long enough—long enough to make us realize
that we cannot go on as we are. . . .

Our immediate need is not to make any permanent or fundamental
alteration in the plan of those who framed our remarkable Constitution,
but to save that plan through *voluntary* and *temporary* adjustments
within that constitutional framework. . . .

To paraphrase a David Lloyd George memorandum of 1910 urging
a coalition, the built-in clash between the parties, and between the
president and Congress, has served us well in the past and will again
in the future; but the time has arrived for a truce.

Specifically, I believe the time has arrived in this country for a
temporary bipartisan "grand coalition" of national unity. . . . It would
go beyond anything previously attempted or seriously considered in the
United States. It would include, if adopted by the winner of the 1984
predidential election, regardless of party:

- a president and vice-president of opposite parties, each agreeing in
  advance to serve one term only and to decline all partisan activities;
- a cabinet and sub-cabinet equally divided between the two parties;
- a small but experienced bipartisan White House staff acting as a
  unifying force in government;

- a presidential advisory council of elder statesmen;
- a national council of economic cooperation and coordination, harmonizing the practices of private interests;
- a joint executive-congressional delegation to the U.S.-U.S.S.R. arms reduction talks; and
- a return to politics as usual at the end of four years.

William Yandell Elliott

27. Presidential Dissolution (1935)

William Yandell Elliott taught government at Harvard from 1925 until his retirement in 1962. As the New Deal took shape, he was among those who believed that the move toward positive government required fundamental changes in the American "political machinery." The following material is from his book, The Need for Constitutional Reform.

In order to keep his hold upon Congress throughout his administration or to learn whether the country has definitely turned away from his policies, the president should have the power to force the House of Representatives to stand one general election during his term of office. To make this power effective without making it too coercive on Congress, two changes would have to be made in the present organization of that body: first, the Senate should be given the power to delay the passage of money bills for only a month, but in no case beyond the end of the session. It should have taken away from it the power over bills appropriating money or raising revenue—a power which was given it at the dictation of the small states in 1787 by one of the bitterest and most unwise compromises of our famous constitutional convention. Normally the Senate has almost no party discipline whatever. It can and does upset the fiscal apple cart at the behest of small local interests or powerful sectional minorities. It is the entrenched stronghold of lobbying pressure groups, the most unrepresentative body, from the point of view of population, in the world today. To gain its support every president must play the patronage game, "gold-plate" the "silver senators"—that is to say, let them "gold brick" the rest of the country—and perform similar unedifying services for other interests. That the Senate contains outstanding political figures is true. But in shaping policy these men too often count for little more than the Senate's clowns and its nonentities.

If the House of Representatives is to become the controller of the national purse strings, and at the same time is to be made subject to an election if it blocks the executive's policies, its term should be lengthened to four years. The president's right to dissolve it at his discretion *once* within that period would help party discipline, but it would not render Congress slavish. If a president were genuinely out of touch with the country, he could be successfully challenged by Congress. After that he would have to accept their legislative will. In instances of overwhelming defeat, he might even feel forced to resign. This is not so hair-trigger a system as the parliamentary system. It leaves room for adjustment between the executive and the legislature along the lines of presidential leadership and compromise. But it does give our president, as a national leader, a power that would make our party system far more responsible, for with it he could resist pressure-group legislation successfully. A Congress that overrode him would have to face what amounted to a national referendum on his policy. Under those conditions successful resistance to the veteran's bonus, for instance, might be expected.

At present the president has the whip of patronage to crack—but in normal times not for more than one session of Congress. Then he loses his hold. But even were patronage an effective weapon of continuous party discipline, the price to pay would be a very heavy one. The temptation to buy support through a program of free spending and governmental expansion is very great. Until, however, we give our executive some effective substitute for the spoils system and the pork barrel as a means of party control, we shall continue to pay the price of an inefficient and partisan bureaucracy, subject by its very nature to every type of unwholesome pressure. The right of the president to force an election upon a recalcitrant Congress is the key to any effective effort to create an adequate civil service. It is certain that no deal, new or old, is going to be more than a reshuffling of the deck, unless this fundamental need is met.

These reforms could probably be forced only by a constitutional convention. It is too much to expect Congress to alter its present powers and to make itself more responsible to truly national opinion. . . .

In the United States we have had an executive who did not lose office when he lost control over Congress. In that way we have been spared the instability of European parliamentarism. But we have never had the advantages of the English system. A president who has lost his hold on Congress (as what president has not?) is an impotent and pathetic figure. He has to depend upon political patronage, appeals to the country, the usual logrolling, and the usual distributions from the pork barrel to get through the measures necessary barely to carry on the government. Can you think of a single president of the United States who has not come to that pass sooner or later? It was Will Rogers, I believe, who suggested that Coolidge alone had escaped—because since Coolidge did not know what his own policies were, it was difficult for Congress to defeat them! He may wrap himself in his dignity and sit back and sulk like a sick eagle annoyed by the crows. But once his hold over Congress is gone, his program is effectively "finished." A realization of this fact causes presidents to hold back patronage as long as possible in order to retain the bait.

Of course, loss of hold over Congress does not always mean that the president has actually lost his hold on the country. Presidents who have been completely stopped by Congress have been reelected by considerable majorities. The sectional nature of our federal system and the irrationality of the distribution of votes and power in our Senate help to account for that. It is really an impossible system that holds our chief executive responsible for failure while it does not equip him with the power necessary to carry out his own program. Mr. Hoover had a right to feel that most bitterly—though he seems to be too much a conservative ever to have got at the root of his own failure.

The result of this system—and a result fatally implicit in the system of separation of powers—is that each successful president must be primarily a politician. He must not merely keep his hold on the country at large. He must be able to hold "silver senators" in line, to keep his unstable party majorities in both Houses. If he is to have any foreign policy, he has to keep two-thirds of our irresponsible and recalcitrantly individualistic Senate behind him. Nothing is more extraordinary in human nature than the seriousness with which our elder statesmen of the Senate frequently take themselves. Yet it is, in a measure, both understandable and justifiable since the senator alone among our politicians is answerable only every six years, and then only to God, his conscience, and to a state machine which through his patronage he is in a very fair way to control.

If the president is to see the disappearance of the spoils system and the reform of the civil service, he must have some other control over the Senate to look to. Either he must be able to dissolve both houses of Congress and force their members to stand for reelection on their opposition to or their support of his policies; or power over money bills must be taken from the Senate, and its veto on treaties made dependent on ordinary majorities—not the present two-thirds. Then the president would be better able to deal with the House, which comes up for election every two years and usually reflects with reasonable adequacy the sentiment of the country. It would seem however to be preferable to give it a four-year term and allow the president to send it to the country only once—at his discretion—during their joint term of office.

With this power of dissolution as a whip to crack over Congress, the president would not need patronage. In fact patronage tends to be exhausted, under normal conditions, when he needs it most. Once he had the right to dissolve Congress, the retention of patronage—which in fact causes many of his enormous present difficulties—would become a liability. He could follow his natural desire as the chief executive to strengthen the administrative departments and turn their chief posts into permanent civil service positions open to career men. There should be a political secretary (cabinet member) and one or two political assistant secretaries in each department. But there should also be a permanent and complete staff, headed by an undersecretary and several assistant undersecretaries, as well as bureau and division chiefs—all within the permanent service. This will only be possible in any real sense when the president feels that he can forego patronage as a means of controlling Congress. Otherwise it will be difficult to build any real security of tenure, even though one succeeded during this administration in having a law passed creating these permanent positions. This is one of the most important points at which a change in our constitutional system seems necessary. We cannot reform the civil service without eliminating patronage. No president can surrender patronage unless he is given some other hold on Congress.

Henry Reuss

28. A Congressional Vote of No Confidence (1975)

In August, 1975, one week after the resignation of President Nixon, Congressman Henry Reuss (see page 155) introduced in Congress a proposed constitutional amendment which would have provided for a congressional vote of no confidence, followed by special elections for president, vice-president, senators and representatives. The January, 1975, issue of George Washington Law Review, *from which the next five selections (numbers 28 through 32) are excerpted, was devoted to a discussion of Reuss's proposal. We begin with Reuss's introduction of the discussion.*

For the next decade we will be spending much time analyzing and digesting the significance of Watergate. There are many lessons to be learned, affecting a broad range of public affairs.

One of the first questions that confronts us on the morning after is whether the impeachment process indeed "works." Presidential impeachment, used only once until 1974, was considered nearly a moribund constitutional process. A mountainous accumulation of evidence had been exposed to public view for many months; after much pain, public soul-searching, and deliberation, Congress finally initiated the impeachment process. Following the impeachment recommendation of the House Judiciary Committee, President Nixon resigned rather than face almost sure impeachment by the House, and probably conviction by the Senate.

Optimists conclude from this that presidential impeachment *does* work, that the constitutional method of removing a president *is* a viable one, and that the status quo should be retained.

I recall 1973 and 1974 somewhat differently. I recall that members of Congress found it very difficult to discuss publicly the possibility of impeachment, let alone propose such an action. I recall that the process was finally initiated only after the "Saturday Night Massacre" inflamed the public and produced a Monday morning deluge of telegrams on Capitol Hill. I recall the long and slow investigation, and the haggling over the definition of "impeachable offenses." But above all, I recall that readiness to impeach Richard Nixon would probably never have been reached—in spite of the circumstantial evidence—without the existence of the taped conversations, something I doubt will ever exist again.

In my view, President Nixon's resignation is not proof that impeachment "works," but rather a hint that the opposite may be true. . . .

An alternative to impeachment would have to include four characteristics.

First, it would have to be a relatively fast process. Given the realities of the modern world, the United States cannot flounder in long periods of zero leadership, uncertainty, and transition.

Second, the process must allow for a broader review of presidential conduct, broader than "high crimes and misdemeanors." A president should be subject to removal in cases of general incompetence, misfeasance, abuse of power and even mental or emotional breakdown.

Third, the process must be safeguarded against petty party politics and personal grudges.

Fourth, the alternative must not disrupt the present constitutional system, one based on checks and balances. It must not be a first step towards congressional supremacy.

Some have suggested that one way to avoid the continuation of the "imperial presidency" would be by adopting a parliamentary system of government. Without going this far, we might properly begin our search as the drafters of our Constitution did, with a review of the British (and more generally, the parliamentary) system of government.

Such a review has led me to consideration of the vote of no confidence. This is the process whereby a government is incapacitated through loss of the support of a majority of the parliament. A vote of no confidence is quickly followed by either a new government (with a parliamentary majority), or by a new election. In such an election, the parliament itself faces the electorate. The election is a referendum of the leader and the parliament.

The vote of no confidence, then, meets the previously stated requirements of speed, general review of the government's conduct, avoidance of petty partisanship, and avoidance of congressional supremacy.

The proposal, which I introduced in Congress on August 15, 1974, is to adopt a constitutional amendment which allows a vote of no confidence by Congress. To pass, the motion would require a 60 percent majority in both the House and the Senate. Upon passage, the president would continue in office, with a national election for president and vice-president, and for the entire Congress, held within 90 to 110 days.

Should the vote occur during the president's second term, he would be allowed to run for a third term, notwithstanding the twenty-second amendment; he thus could seek vindication by the public. A president elected following a vote of no confidence would serve out the remaining years of that previous administration. The terms of congressmen and senators would be similarly modified.

Such a plan meets all requirements outlined earlier.

First, the vote of no confidence is quickly followed by a national election which resolves the issue.

Second, a vote of no confidence allows consideration of issues broader than "high crimes and misdemeanors." It allows for a general review of the conduct of an administration. It allows for reasonable inferences concerning executive responsibility—inferences which many members of Congress refused to apply in the quasi-criminal atmosphere of impeachment.

Third, since the Congress and the president would have to face the electorate, the vote of no confidence would not be lightly invoked. Members of Congress, including senators with long terms ahead of them, would have to lay their offices on the line. It would hardly be a useful weapon for partisan politics or personal vindictiveness.

Fourth, the vote of no confidence should not lead to parliamentary tyranny, due to the requirement of a 60 percent majority in each house and because the Congress would have to face reelection along with the president.

The vote of no confidence allows the public to be the final arbiter of this political confrontation. Following a vote of no confidence, both the president and the Congress must face the electorate for a final and definitive accounting. Issues could be resolved, the political air could be cleared, and the business of the nation could resume.

Hans A. Linde

29. The Inadequacy of Impeachment (1975)

Hans Linde has been justice of the Supreme Court of Oregon since 1977. Earlier, he had been clerk to Supreme Court Justice William O. Douglas and an aide to Senator Richard L. Neuberger, and taught law at the University of Oregon.

The question is how much the present constitutional arrangements can be modernized without losing their central value: the stability of the president's independent four-year mandate of political and administrative leadership, secured for that term against merely partisan opposition or policy disagreements.

It should be . . . clear that the choice need not be between the present elective four-year monarchy, vulnerable only to personal mortality or the legal equivalent of regicide, and the free-swinging ouster of an entire administration on a legislative vote of no confidence that we associate with parliamentary government in its Anglo-Saxon form. Undoubtedly the journalistic and political urge to invoke already familiar images would equate even a mild easing of the ironclad presidential term with the revolving and impotent coalitions of Italy. Of the recent proposals, those introduced in the House by Representatives Reuss and Dingell in fact would employ the form of a resolution of no confidence. There are intermediate stages of executive independence and security in office even in parliamentary systems, however, and useful steps toward greater accountability of the American president could stop far short of approaching such a system.

The design of an alternative constitutional procedure for replacing a discredited president can vary in a number of important and interrelated ways. These include variations in defining the grounds for removal, in the initiation of proceedings, in prescribing their duration, in the participation of the president or his representative, in the votes needed for a decision, and in the consequences of a removal vote. The choice among them can fall at many different points on the spectrum between impeachment and replacement by a majority vote of no confidence. Reformers leery of destroying the strength of the presidency need not pursue uncritically every old or new idea for revising the basic structure of the American government; a reasonable point of departure is to seek a design of presidential accountability without the fatal weaknesses of the impeachment device.

The Grounds for Removal

To a realist, it will seem more important how many votes are needed to remove a president, after what procedures, and with what consequences for the succession, than in what words the issue of the president's removal is formulated. On closer examination, the choice of the initial premise carries with it implications for the logical choice among the procedural variations.

If our recent experience demonstrates anything, it is that grounds for replacing a president should not require proof of his personal culpability. Such a personal charge, when made, is bound to call forth an equally personal defense. It forces decision into the format of an adjudication, with all its consequences of excessive legalism, procedural anomalies, and delay. Reducing these barriers to accountability is the central object of reform.

In deciding whether to stand pat with the mechanism of impeachment or to provide an alternative, the key question is whether the president is to be responsible for serious misconduct at the highest levels of his administration as well as for his misconduct—responsible for encouraging abuses in the use of executive power, or for ignoring them, or for condoning them when brought to his attention. Since only replacement in office is at stake, the issue should be the president's conduct of his office. The facts of the alleged abuses will often be in dispute, as will their legality. The important thing, however, is that the facts be established by the procedure of committee investigation, not by a trial. The issue of abuse of office calls for floor debate, not legal pleadings, briefing, and adjudication.

If abuse of power is to be the issue in a new constitutional procedure for replacing a president, how should this issue be phrased? Proposals for a simple resolution to no confidence do not attempt to focus congressional debate by a new constitutional standard for measuring cause to remove a president; relying on the requirement of a three-fifths vote in both houses and the incumbent's opportunity to triumph in a new election, the proposals count on political practice to evolve the criteria for invoking this power.

A different approach is taken in a proposal introduced by Representative Edith Green that was endorsed by former Justice Abe Fortas and attracted a substantial number of co-sponsors. It would trigger a special election upon enactment, by two-thirds votes, of a joint resolution

> that the president has failed or refused faithfully to execute the laws enacted by Congress; or that he has willfully exceeded the powers vested in him by this Constitution and the laws of the United States; or that he has caused or willfully permitted the rights of citizens of the United States to be trespassed upon in violation of this Constitution, the laws of the United States, or treaties made, or which shall be made, under their authority. . . .

The flaws in this text are the opposite of a simple no confidence resolution; its verbosity invites more legal hairsplitting about probably unintended ambiguities than the ancient "high crimes and misdemeanors." . . .

Nevertheless, that proposal does move in the right direction by focusing on the president's constitutional duties rather than on his commission of unlawful acts. In principle it is this issue that can be investigated and debated rather than pleaded and tried. . . .

The Consequences of Removal

The occasion for contemporary discussion of alternatives to impeachment is the demonstrated need for a better way to remove a discredited president from office. The focus of the discussion is bound to be on the criteria and the procedures for removal. But constitutional reform, however necessary, might be shipwrecked in providing for the succession.

When a president can be removed only by impeachment and conviction, it is logical that the vice-president should take over the presidency. Since the premise of impeachment is the personal misconduct of the president, his downfall does not discredit the vice-president unless he is himself shown to have participated in the misconduct. . . .

The situation is different, however, after a successful no confidence vote. Such a vote would be a congressional repudiation, not specifically of the president's personal conduct, but of his leadership and that of the political party and the administration which he heads, and of which the vice-president is inescapably a part. Representative Reuss's resolution accordingly provides for a special election of both the president and vice-president, leaving the incumbent administration in office during the interim.

A special election is also the proper sequel to the removal of a president upon a congressional determination that he has defaulted in the exercise of his office. It alone can bridge what is otherwise a difficult ambiguity in the position of the vice-president during and after consideration of this issue in the Congress. . . .

Moreover, since such a congressional determination may rest on grounds less personal to the president and more susceptible to public debate and ultimate decision than are "high crimes and misdemeanors," a special election offers the displaced president an opportunity to debate the issues and to attempt to vindicate his record if the public approves of the conduct that has been condemned by the Congress. The version of a "presidential abuse" amendment introduced by Representative Green and her co-sponsors in fact provides for a special election. However, a congressional finding of presidential default of the seriousness contemplated in this approach would be so grave and extraordinary that the vice-president and not the president should be acting president pending the election.

The idea of a special election of the president and vice-president may at first meet with public surprise, yet it is a return to the oldest constitutional assumptions. Last year, three Harvard Law School scholars, Paul Freund, Abram Chayes, and Raoul Berger, drew attention to the fact that, in the constitutional convention, James Madison expressly secured congressional authority to provide for an election when both offices were vacant, and that the Second Congress in fact included such a special election in the Succession Act of 1792, which remained in force for almost a century. In 1945, President Truman recommended return to this system, and Senator Hathaway (D., Maine), relying on this history, introduced a bill to the same effect following the replacement of Vice-President Agnew by Gerald Ford in 1973. Indeed, Arthur Schlesinger, Jr., recently pointed out that the constitutional convention's original plan was to fill the unexpired term of a president by special election, the president of the Senate serving in the interim, and the office of vice-president being an afterthought. . . .

Provisions for a Special Election

The premises of the foregoing discussion have been that it should be possible under extraordinary circumstances to replace a president before the end of a four-year term by means other than impeachment, and that such an extraordinary removal should be followed by a timely election of a new president. These simple, although far-reaching, objectives may founder on secondary problems of conducting a special election. Thus, Representative Reuss's plan first included only a special election of the president and vice-president, but in its later version, truer to the parliamentary analogy, a resolution of no confidence would lay the jobs of representatives and senators on the line along with those of their prey. Representative Green's proposal, on the other hand, requires that the special election be by direct popular vote. . . .

The real problems are more political than legal. Candidates would have to be nominated rapidly and entirely outside the normal seasonal rhythm of presidential politics. Political candidacies would not await the outcome of congressional proceedings against an incumbent president; they would have to anticipate them. Indeed, public speculation with respect to possible candidates would rise with the first stirring of serious congressional protests against alleged presidential abuses. The natural leaders of the opposition party would find it embarrassing to take an active role in pursuing abuses that might lead to the downfall of the incumbent administration for the same reasons that kept past or potential Democratic presidential candidates off the Senate Watergate committee. I mentioned at the outset that our inexorable calendar of elections has vitiated both the need and the opportunities for personal leadership in the opposition party between leap years; the possibility of a presidential election in mid-term would likely remain too remote to change this.

The administration party, on the other hand, would have to begin considering alternative nominees, including the vice-president who is due to become acting president, without jettisoning its incumbent president, while waiting to see how bad the case against him ultimately proves to be. If a system of removal and special election had resulted in a congressional vote against President Nixon by the end of the Senate Watergate hearings—which is the reason for creating such a system— how would the Republican party then have decided whether to risk renominating him or splitting the party between his defenders and advocates of a new and untarnished leadership?

Finally, if the nomination of truly national candidates under these circumstances can be managed at all, the nominees would be obliged to finance and conduct campaigns in far less than the accustomed time, against the backdrop of the crisis of legitimacy that caused the extraordinary congressional vote to remove a president in mid-term and with the full exposure and legal pursuit of the alleged abuses still in process. It would be no ordinary election. Indeed, it might prove an extraordinary opportunity for a candidate outside the traditional two-party structure, if not outside politics altogether and far from Washington, D.C.—a candidate who could long since have begun his campaign against the

Capitol and all its works without being constrained by the conflicting obligations of those on the scene.

Troubling as these reverberations appear, they pose political, not constitutional problems, and they would find political solutions. Insofar as procedures for nominations and elections, even for financing, require legal solutions, these can and should be left for statutes.

Conclusion

The device of a simple no confidence resolution, whatever its merits, has no prospect of approval in the Congress, particularly when it requires a special congressional as well as presidential election, and no prospect of ratification in the states, all of whom are accustomed to governorships patterned on a presidency not defeasible by the legislature. Less politically hopeless is the case for a usable modern alternative to the anomalies of a quasi-criminal trial by legislature.

Such an alternative must offer the public two advantages over impeachment. It must promise a speedier resolution of serious charges against the president's conduct of his office, with adequate time for good faith inquiry, defense, and deliberation; and, consistent with extending the president's political accountability beyond personal guilt, it must provide an early opportunity for the public to render its judgment in a presidential election. . . .

Samuel Beer

30. The British Experience (1975)

Samuel Beer was professor of government at Harvard from 1938 until his recent retirement. He is an authority on British politics and has been active in the Democratic party in Massachusetts.

I have been asked to evaluate the Reuss amendment in the light of British experience. The revised Reuss proposal provides that if three-fifths of both houses of Congress vote no confidence in the president, a general election will be held in which not only a president and vice-president will be chosen, but also members for all seats in the Senate and House of Representatives. It makes sense to look at British experience, since the no confidence vote is borrowed from the parliamentary system and since it was Great Britain that provided the model for that system which has been imitated with variation by many other countries. The procedure that Representative Reuss envisages is modelled on the "appeal to the country" that has sometimes taken place in Great Britain when the executive has lost the support of the legislature.

In Great Britain a vote of confidence is a vote of the House of Commons which, if it involves defeat of the government, leads either to the resignation of the government or to a general election in which a new House of Commons is chosen. The procedure presupposes the existence of a government, that is, a body of ministers in charge of the executive branch of the state, and is a means by which collective ministerial responsibility to the legislature is enforced. The motion may have originated with the opposition or with the government itself.

Several principles of the British constitution are involved. One is the convention of the constitution that "ministers resign when they have ceased to command the confidence of the House of Commons." This convention manifests the connection between legislature and executive that makes the regime parliamentary, distinguishing it from a regime of separated powers, such as the American, where the chief executive achieves power by a separate election and holds it whether or not he has the confidence and support of the legislature. Supplementing the parliamentary with the democratic idea, a further convention gives a government defeated on a vote of confidence the option of appealing to the country instead of resigning. If the government fails in this appeal, it must resign, in contrast with the method of operation of the Reuss amendment which would leave a reelected president in power even though the new Congress remained hostile to him.

A third important characteristic of the British system, partly the result of convention and partly the result of law, is that most ministers, and certainly the prime minister, are members of the House of Commons, where they spend a great deal of time proposing laws, answering questions, defending government policy and generally providing political leadership. Their presence in the house is important, but one can imagine it being arranged without the necessity for membership in the house. The regime is parliamentary because of the first convention which requires confidence as a condition for acquiring and retaining executive power.

A crucial fourth convention subordinates this plural executive to a prime minister. Particularly important to the way the vote of confidence operates is the prime minister's power to decide whether and when the government will resign and whether and when it will appeal to the country.

To summarize: The Reuss amendment combines elements of the first two principles. It does not require that the executive have the confidence of the legislature to hold office, but it does give the legislature the power to force a dissolution. It does not provide for the appearance of the chief executive before the legislature, and it does not give him the power of deciding on a dissolution.

Since the Reuss amendment does not attempt to define the grounds on which votes of confidence may be moved, it is worth asking what the British do. Rather than talk in generalities I will give some examples; only in that way can we hope to get any instruction from their experience.

Given the seriousness of the consequences of defeat, one might expect that only the weightiest questions of public policy would be regarded as involving votes of confidence. Sometimes attempts to describe the British constitution are put in these terms and it is said that governments are obliged to resign or dissolve when defeated on important matters of policy. This does not state the matter quite correctly. One authority writes: " . . . most divisions are regarded as votes of confidence." *A fortiori*, they cannot be confined to weighty matters. Being frequent, almost daily, occurrences, motions involving confidence range from life-and-death questions of foreign and domestic policy to the trivia of parliamentary in-fighting.

A good example of the latter occurred in 1952 when the Conservatives, just returned to power after six years of Mr. Attlee's Labour government, were reversing Labour's nationalization of the iron and steel industry. During a debate on the bill, Labour MPs forced the adjournment of the House by refusing to answer a quorum call. When the government made up the time by lengthening a sitting of the House, Labour protested vociferously and Mr. Attlee exercised the undoubted right of the leader of the opposition to put down a "motion of censure" on the government and get parliamentary time to debate it. The motion's grounds were that the government had dealt with the business of the House "incompetently, unfairly and in defiance of the best principles of parliamentary democracy and the national interest" and lacked "adequate support in the Parliament and the country" for its measures. As everyone expected, the Tory majority showed up in force and won the division by a vote of 280 ayes to 304 noes.

At the opposite pole on the seriousness-levity axis was the vote terminating the grim debate of May 7 and 8, 1940, that took place after the disastrous failure of the British to stop the Nazi seizure of Norway. The motion being debated was nominally a motion to adjourn. It was turned into a vote of confidence only when on the second day a spokesman for the Labour party, then in opposition, declared that he was neither satisfied with Prime Minister Neville Chamberlain's explanation of the government's failures, nor confident that the government was aware of its shortcomings. The prime minister replied: "I accept the challenge . . . and call upon my friends to support us in the lobby tonight." In spite of its ghastly failures in the war and the violence of the attack upon it during the debate, the government won this vote of confidence by a majority of 81 and, strictly speaking, under the convention of parliamentary confidence, it was entitled to hold onto power. The temper of the debate, however, and the large defections from the normally huge majority of the government obliged Chamberlain to attempt to broaden his government. When Labour refused to join, he resigned, making way for Winston Churchill as head of a coalition government. The vote in the House was the crucial event in the change of governments.

As these examples show, the subject matter of votes of confidence is various. So also is the verbal form. From time to time, the question is posed in explicit and unmistakable terms. The term "confidence" in motions asserting the necessity that ministers have the confidence of the house has been used since the eighteenth century. An example from

1841 will illustrate the verbal form. A Whig government had been in office since 1834, during which time it had been defeated 59 times in the House of Commons, without feeling impelled to resign or dissolve. The leader of the opposition, Sir Robert Peel, then moved:

> That her Majesty's ministers do not sufficiently possess the confidence of the House of Commons to enable them to carry through that House measures which they deem of essential importance to the public welfare, and that their continuance in office, under such circumstances, is at variance with the spirit of the constitution.

Again defeated, although by only one vote, the government responded to these words by a dissolution. Variations on this language are still used in substantive motions of confidence. With motions of this sort anyone can tell what is at stake. Usually, however, the verbal form alone will not reveal whether a motion involves confidence. As in the Norway debate, the motion may be, in terms, merely a motion to adjourn; or it may be an amendment to a piece of government legislation, or a motion to reduce the appropriations for a department. Moreover, it may not be only the verbal form of the motion that is confusing. Examples can be found where participants in the debate did not and could not know, because the government did not decide whether confidence was involved until after the division. For instance, in 1895, while the House was debating appropriations, an amendment was voted to reduce the salary of the secretary of state for war by 100 pounds to draw attention to what critics thought was a shortage of small arms ammunition. The defeat was accomplished by a trick, additional members of the opposition being brought into the House surreptitiously, and under ordinary circumstances the government would have disregarded it. But his majority already being precarious, the Liberal prime minister chose to regard the vote as a vote of censure and resigned. The opposition formed a government, dissolved and won a substantial majority [in the ensuing general election].

Governments sometimes say in advance what they will regard as involving confidence. The simplest case is when the government provides ad hoc for a certain measure. For instance, it will say that since a question coming before the House is not a matter of government policy, the division will be treated as a "free vote" and the government will not put on its whips. This has frequently been done with regard to questions that have cut across party lines, such as divorce, capital punishment, and homosexuality.

A more general statement may be made by a minority government, as was done by Ramsay MacDonald when he formed the first Labour government in January, 1924. The Conservatives had the largest party in the House, but had resigned when defeated by the combined votes of Liberals and Labourites. Since Labour was the second largest party, the king called MacDonald, the new prime minister, who informed the House that he would treat as votes of confidence motions explicitly putting the question to a vote and other motions involving "substantial issues, issues of principle, issues which really matter." Between January and October the government was defeated ten times before its defeat on a motion on which it had explicitly staked its existence, causing it to go to the country. In light of the three-fifths requirement of the Reuss amendment, it is worth noting that in this vote the government was defeated by a majority of 64 percent.

In contrast with MacDonald's declaration is the position taken by Harold Wilson when he formed a minority government after the general election of February, 1974. In that curious election the Liberals and an assortment of smaller parties picked up support, while both Conservatives and Labourites lost seats, leaving the House without a majority party. As leader of the largest party, Wilson formed a government, informing the House that he would not necessarily regard as a matter of confidence a defeat on "a snap division or even, perhaps, in some cases, a more substantial one." If such a defeat did occur, he indicated that he would ask for another vote, posing the question of confidence explicitly. "In other words," he said, when pressed to clarify the rule, "we shall provide a recount. . . ." During the next six months, his government was defeated numerous times, a half a dozen occasions involving matters of importance. While he did not, as he had promised, then table votes of confidence to provide a "recount," the political weakness manifested in these votes was a major reason why he called the general election of October 10. In a quite real sense, defeats in the House led to that dissolution.

With regard to the balance of power between the legislature and the executive, the parliamentary system in Great Britain has had different consequences, depending upon other circumstances, especially the number of parties and the strength of party ties. In the years 1846 to 1860, parliamentary independence reached its peak, the House of Commons administering eight major defeats to successive governments. On six occasions, defeat led to resignation, and on the other two occasions to a solution. In these fourteen years there were five different governments with an average life of less than three years. In 1924 and again in 1929, the presence of three sizable parties in the House forced the formation of minority governments, as happened again in February, 1974. These episodes in British experience are reminiscent of the instability of cabinets in Weimar Germany and in France during the Third and Fourth Republics.

Representative Reuss intends that the vote of confidence be used only against presidents with grave deficiencies: "[I]nability to lead, loss of moral leadership, presiding over an administration in shambles, possessing an aptitude to choose the wrong aides and subordinates." As British experience suggests, political leaders continually find deficiencies of this magnitude in their opponents. This is the daily meat of partisan politics. But if partisanship were to control the vote, the three-fifths requirement would not be a sufficient guarantee against frequent dissolutions. With the recent great rise in ticket-splitting, divided government in Washington is increasingly likely. Yet the Democratic preponderance in the legislature continues. Both Eisenhower and Nixon occasionally had three-fifths majorities against them as does President Ford in the 94th Congress. One cannot rule out government instability as a probable consequence of the Reuss amendment.

British experience also suggests another and opposite possibility; namely, that the vote of confidence would be turned to the advantage of the executive. A dissolution of the legislature punishes not only the executive, but also the members who must risk their seats in a new campaign. In Great Britain, the prospect of a dissolution helps to keep rebellious backbenchers in line behind the government, and many observers think that the power to threaten dissolution has had a good deal to do with the extraordinary party discipline displayed by members of the House of Commons. Votes of confidence are continually being moved, but in the twentieth century they have almost never succeeded. In 1924, as noted previously, a government suffered a defeat that precipitated an election. The last time a government resigned because of a defeat in the House, however, was 1923, but that was because of the three-party situation. To find an instance when a government originally enjoying a partisan majority lost on a vote that caused it to resign, we must go back to 1885 when Gladstone's Liberals were defeated on the budget.

Ordinarily, under the British system the prime minister chooses when there is to be a general election, subject, of course, to the five-year limit on the life of a Parliament. Fortified by the knowledge of voters' attitudes provided by opinion surveys, an incumbent leader can and normally does adjust the timing of the dissolution to favorable swings of public opinion.

The Reuss amendment appears to exclude this aggrandizement of executive power because it provides that only a vote in Congress could bring about a general election. Yet the ways in which a popular president might so manipulate the Reuss provisions to force Congress to give him a dissolution are not hard to imagine. For instance, he could defy recalcitrant majorities to appeal to the country, holding back his own supporters, if necessary, in order to put it in the power of his opponents to pass the no confidence vote. It is relevant that, when in the past, reformers have proposed the importation of parliamentary features into the American system, they have usually aimed at strengthening the presidency.

The lesson of British experience, and indeed of comparative government generally, is that the vote of confidence device might unduly weaken the executive, or unduly strengthen the executive, or, possibly, bring about the nice adjustment that Representative Reuss desires. In short, the consequences of the proposed reform are incalculable. In view of the further fact that the impeachment process did work in the case of President Nixon, these prospects indicate to this author that Congress should leave things the way they are.

Allan Sindler

31. A Critique of the Reuss Proposal (1975)

Allan Sindler has been dean of the graduate school of public policy at the University of California, Berkeley, since 1977. He taught previously at Duke, Yale and Cornell universities, and is the author of a number of books and articles on political institutions and public policy.

It is no accident that the Reuss plan fails to provide any meat on the bare bones of its no confidence notion. Presidential impeachment deals with designated categories of serious wrongdoing; the twenty-fifth amendment deals with physical or other disabilities which make the president "unable to discharge the powers and duties of his office." What situations are supposed to raise considerations of no confidence? Surely not every instance of congressional rejection of presidential policy, in the manner of parliamentary regimes. And hopefully not because there has been a sharp or durable decline in the standing of the president in public opinion polls. Not only are such surveys an inexact and volatile barometer, but ours is not a plebescitary democracy. A fixed term of office provides the president with a degree of insulation allowing him to do other than popular things. Coercing the president to look over his shoulder at the opinion polls at every major decision point sets his incentives in ways that, contrary to the intent of the no confidence plan, may unduly expand the status and claims of the office.

Failure to delineate the characteristics of no confidence situations derives from no special weakness of the Reuss plan, but rather, from the deficiency of the concept itself. There are no effective measures to determine the degree of loss of public confidence in the president or whether his leadership position has become too eroded, and without possibility of renewal, to permit him to discharge his responsibilities adequately. The play of partisan and personal motives in determining so ambiguous a matter would necessarily be high, or thought by the public to be high, and the decision Congress rendered could not help but be suspect to many. Although quite neglected by Representative Reuss, this is no small concern. Public doubt about the legitimacy of congressional use of no confidence may easily provoke a crisis of system loyalty and maintenance focusing on political succession, one of the most critical and fragile components of any political system.

Most other nations have severe problems of political succession which in some cases persistently promote instability of the basic regime. America, by contrast, has been able to operate by rapid and legitimated succession, even under such trying circumstances as assassination or impeachment of the president. No small virtue of the present system, it should not be taken for granted as a practice either easily developed and maintained or assured to Americans no matter what. Quite the contrary is the case. Consider the following possibility: a president, deposed and/or forced to run in a special election because of a no confidence vote adopted largely by action of the opposition party, mounts a crusade/vendetta against his opponents in a highly emotional, bitter and divisive campaign for personal vindication in the special election. How many such occurrences would it take to unsettle what is commonly assumed to be our settled practices of political succession, to provoke deep societal cleavages on the legitimacy of our governmental institutions, to sour the trust of the people in the good faith of their public officials?

Political succession arrangements, in short, lie close to the heart of political systems. Hence, proposals to alter those arrangements must be assessed by a suitably broad and sensitive perspective and not by application of a tunnel view which isolates both the problem it identifies and the remedy it proposed from the larger context. Even if the supporters of Representative Reuss's plan could pinpoint the kinds of situations for which no confidence was designed, and even if they could confine its use entirely to such situations, the plan's high potential for destabilizing the political succession process still would have to be confronted rather than ignored. Since the Reuss proposal meets neither contingency condition, however, its danger in this regard merits rejection. . . .

The no confidence proposal is ostensibly a lesson drawn from the Watergate experience, but it can draw little sustenance from it. Perhaps in February 1974, when H. J. Res. 903 was introduced, an arguable case could be made for the need to supplement the impeachment process by a no confidence mechanism. But by mid-August 1974, when H. J. Res. 1111 was introduced, Nixon had resigned, Ford had succeeded to the presidency, and the impeachment process had proved itself to most everyone's satisfaction. Reviewing Watergate in retrospect, one of the invaluable contributions of the impeachment process to its acceptable resolution was the thoroughness, deliberateness, gravity and nonpartisanship of the impeachment inquiry. These characteristics, together of course with the hard evidence gathered, produced and interpreted through the inquiry, were indispensable to legitimate the findings, the articles of impeachment and the forced resignation of President Nixon. Had the impeachment process been displaced by a no confidence inquiry, debate and vote, a much faster decision would have been reached. But that decision, whether in favor or opposed to no confidence, would likely have fanned public discord rather than laying the controversy to rest. The premise quite appropriate for such a no confidence move—that Nixon, regardless of his innocence or guilt, had lost his capacity to govern adequately because of the spreading and unresolved Watergate scandals—was exactly opposite to what was required to bring the controversy to a publicly acceptable close. And had the no confidence inquiry taken on the task of investigating and producing evidence, there would be no reason to prefer that those functions be performed by other than the impeachment process. The Watergate situation, in sum, suggests that the American system ultimately profited from the unavailability of any suspect, shortcut moves, such as a no confidence arrangement, and from the necessity to go the slower, more tortuous, but more appropriate, route of impeachment.

If in the Watergate controversy a no confidence inquiry could not likely have done as full or effective a job as the impeachment inquiry in fact did, is there something the latter failed to do which the former could be expected to handle well? Other than the third article of impeachment, dealing with President Nixon's noncompliance with subpoenas issued by the House judiciary committee, the impeachment process sidestepped or explicitly rejected the bringing of charges relating to inflated presidential power or presidential invasion of congressional authority. The first two impeachment articles, alleging obstruction of justice and political misuse of several sensitive executive agencies, do not properly fall in either category. What might have been included were such disputed charges as claims of executive privilege excessive in scope and in coverage of executive personnel, persistent impoundment of appropriations authorized by Congress or the secret bombing of Cambodia, accompanied by denial or falsification of information to the Congress.

Would the supporters of the Reuss plan consider such disputes as apt occasions for no confidence moves by Congress? If so, it would be hard to maintain that a special election focusing on the controverted issue, such as would follow Congress's adoption of a no confidence resolution against the president, is a desirable or even a sensible way to settle the conflict. Interinstitutional quarrels over authority relations are invariably complicated and ambiguous. Their resolution is best accomplished not by imposing final boundary definitions from the outside, whether from voters in special elections or courts through litigation, but by an ongoing series of unstable compromises on particular disputes, grounded in the give-and-take of pragmatic politics. Even if voters were capable of intervening in such conflicts with the requisite sensitivity, the form of the election makes that virtually impossible. Not only are voters confined in effect to registering a simple "yes" or "no," but they must do so in a choice between candidates and not directly on the issue itself. Could the dispute over impoundment of appropriated funds be settled, or settled satisfactorily, by holding a special recall election on Nixon or a special contested election between Nixon and, for example, Edward Kennedy? . . .

Perhaps the most puzzling aspect of the rationale noted for the Reuss proposal is how its supporters can reconcile a desire to curb inflated presidential power with provision of a new mechanism that channels congressional and public attention even more fixedly on the president as the sun-center of the governmental universe. Have the supporters of the Reuss plan considered that in a no confidence showdown between Congress and the president on a controversial issue the latter might well win? What of the possibility that a highly popular and aggressive president, if opposed by Congress, might seek a special election to gain public re-endorsement by challenging the Congress to vote no confidence? And what of the provision in H. J. Res. 1111 which mandates a special election for representatives and senators as well as for the president and vice-president, thus tying the fate of congressional incumbents to the public's view of the president? The presidentialization (to coin a clumsy word) of congressional politics, in combination with the plebiscitary character of the special election called to judge an incumbent president, could go far to produce a horse for a "man or horseback." Here again, then, the Reuss proposal could promote the reverse of what it sought.

Rather than burden the Congress with a new authority it neither needs nor can use effectively, and which threatens to be counterproductive in its effects, Representative Reuss would serve his goal better by tackling more directly the problem of the relative weakness of Congress. The recent reform of Congress's handling of the federal budget is an apt, if limited, example of what might be explored and done. Increasing Congress's expert staff resources, providing for stronger collective leadership, promoting a less fragmented and parochial view among individual legislators, reducing its overwhelming dependence on the executive branch to set the policy agenda, improving the quality of its monitoring/

review/oversight of executive agency performance—all these problems and more merit the attention of those seriously concerned about correcting the imbalance in congressional-presidential relations. However well intentioned the no confidence proposal, and even if it were to operate solely as expected by its sponsors, it would be only marginally relevant to the goal of strengthening the Congress or of improving the vitality of the checks-and-balances system. When so modest a maximum benefit is set against the array of potential serious costs discussed in this article, the Reuss plan must be awarded a resounding vote of no confidence.

James L. Sundquist

32. The Case for an Easier Method to Remove Presidents (1975)

James Sundquist (see page 89) here presents the case for the Reuss amendment as a check on presidents made necessary by recent unavoidable increases in the power of the executive office.

The question Representative Reuss presents is whether the Constitution should be revised to broaden and simplify the present extremely limited procedures for removing presidents. His resolution rests upon the premise that the United States needs at all times an effective government, that it cannot afford to wait for as long as three or three and a half years if its president loses his ability to lead and govern for any reason. It does not take high crimes or misdemeanors to destroy the capacity of a president to lead, inspire and unify the country, as he must. Misfeasance that is not malfeasance in the impeachable sense can fatally impair the presidency. The people need to be safeguarded not just against the president who commits or tolerates crime but against the one who is incompetent, or negligent, or rash, and against the one who loses his stability, his capacity to make sound judgments. For all these kinds of circumstances, short of obvious incapacitation, the Constitution now provides no remedy. . . .

The Failure of Checks and Balances

The complacency of the American people over the years about the lack of a broad and general power of presidential removal is attributable

---

in part, I suspect, to a popular misunderstanding of the nature of governmental institutions growing out of an understanding of more familiar institutions. In other words, the people know that the Congress sits in Washington, watching and checking and balancing the president, and from that they draw the comfortable feeling that a president will be prevented from overreaching himself and will be brought to account quickly if he does—much as in their local school systems, chambers of commerce, and social agencies.

We all learned in elementary school that the unique American contribution to the art of government was "checks and balances." And when we became adults, we got the idea that the checks were really checking and the balances balancing because we were accustomed to reading in each day's newspaper about how the president and the Congress were at each other's throats, each blocking and stalemating the other.

The point we missed is that the effective stalemating is wholly in one field of governmental action—legislation. The legislative power is divided, with each branch given a veto over the other. But not so the executive power. The Constitution puts all the executive power in a single branch of government—the executive branch. It does not give Congress any right to participate at all in the exercise of that power, or even any right to be consulted.

That does not mean that the Congress does not find ways of "horning in," but it does so with very blunt and indirect instruments. Sometimes, if the Congress does not like the way the president is executing the laws, it can deal directly with the matter by passing new legislation to make its intent clear. The president, however, can veto the new legislation and, if upheld by one-third plus one of either house, he can continue doing as he pleases. Normally he can expect to have at least that much support; Nixon, with a hostile Congress, was overridden only once—on the War Powers Resolution. Moreover, this recourse is of no avail if the intent of the Congress was clear all along, which seems to be the case most of the time (in the case of the War Powers Resolution, it can be argued, even the Constitution was clear), and the president is just choosing to ignore it. Take, for instance, the president's attempt to liquidate the Office of Economic Opportunity in open defiance of the law and of clear congressional intent. There is not much point in the Congress passing still another law reiterating that intent. The limitations, indeed, the futility, of congressional oversight when a president is adamant is well illustrated by the fact that the members of Congress could stop the dismantlement of OEO only by bringing suits in the courts like any ordinary citizen.

The power of the purse is similarly limited. It can really be used only to curtail functions. It might have been used, for instance, to compel an end to the war in Vietnam; but if the problem is, say, the use of the FBI or the Internal Revenue Service by a president against his political enemies, the Congress cannot get at that matter by cutting the budgets for those agencies. That would only mean that more criminals would run loose and more tax evaders remain undiscovered.

There is another check, the power of the Senate to confirm presidential appointees, but this is even more ineffectual. At the time an appointee comes up for confirmation, the Senate rarely knows what kind of an administrator he is going to be and what commitment it needs to extract from him. One need only point to the number of Watergate figures who had been confirmed easily by the Senate, for the simple reason that no one could know how they were going to behave in circumstances that had not arisen and could not be foreseen.

Finally, there is the general right of the Congress to inquire and to expose—the congressional investigation. The Congress can be frustrated here, too, by the exercise of executive privilege to withhold information, which the Nixon administration claimed to be an unlimited right. Even when the Congress obtains the information it wants about what the executive is doing, however, it cannot order him to change his ways. It can heckle, it can entreat, it can bulldoze, it can threaten, but it cannot tell him what to do. A congressional investigation is essentially an appeal to public opinion, which a determined or obsessive president can ignore. In the end, the president has the sole responsibility under the Constitution for the execution of the laws.

Thus, what the Congress is compelled to do, most of the time, if it wants to restrain the president, is resort to a kind of blackmail: the members who are aggrieved threaten to use against the president the powers they do share with him, namely, the legislative powers, including the power of the purse. Sometimes this works, but more often it does not, because the president's position is infinitely stronger. In the first place, threats work both ways: the president can bring senators and congressmen into line by using his powers of granting or withholding all kinds of favors, in appointments, projects, legislative compromises and all the rest. In the second place, the Congress is not organized to bargain effectively with the president; the 535 members are divided into two houses, two parties, and a multiplicity of committees and subcommittees; they have no way of arriving at a common strategy to combat a monolithic executive branch, and they have not delegated to their leaders the responsibility to strike deals on their behalf.

That leaves the courts. Some people are contending that Watergate proves how well our checks and balances work, because the people responsible for Watergate have been indicted by grand juries, brought to trial and some, at least, are or soon will be in jail. True enough, judicial processes provide some check, if executive secrecy can be breached—which, as has been demonstrated, is not easy—and if retribution is all that is sought. If, however, the object is to prevent the damage from occurring in the first place, that is, to forestall the abuses of power that cause the loss of confidence of the people in their government, then putting people in jail long after the damage has been done is not quite good enough. Moreover, the legal processes only cover outright violations of the law. In the wide range of circumstances where presidential power is used legally but unwisely, the courts are useless. They have essentially the same limitations as has the impeachment process, which is the ultimate form of the judicial type of check.

So much for the restraints upon the executive power that reside in the other branches of the government. Characteristically, except for the confirmation power, which operates long before the fact, they operate after the fact, that is, after the damage has been done. They do not operate during the fact, while the executive power is being used, and abused, and that is the crucial time if the damage is to be prevented. They can be marginally improved within our present constitutional system, the War Powers Resolution and the anti-impoundment provisions of the new budget control act being two improvements, but basically they are barriers to presidential power made of very thin stuff.

The Presidency Cannot Be Dismantled

What of checks and balances provided internally within the executive branch? At one time, the cabinet meant something. During the first century of the republic, the United States had cabinets somewhat on the model of the British. Presidents chose as department heads men who represented a broad spectrum of the party's top leadership. Prominent members of the Senate were commonly appointed, along with political leaders from the major states. Often presidents named to their cabinets men who had been their principal rivals. So men of the stature of Hamilton and Webster, Clay and Calhoun, Seward and Sherman and Bryan—some of the greatest names in our history other than presidents— sat in presidential cabinets.

Cabinet members, in short, had independent power bases. Furthermore, they were used as a consultative body. Presidents made decisions after consulting the cabinet, rather like kings-in-council. They could still ignore or overrule their cabinets, of course. Lincoln could say, "Seven noes and one aye; the ayes have it." But at least he asked his cabinet's opinion and he took a vote.

Everyone knows what has happened to the cabinet. Presidents discovered, in these days of direct communication between presidents and the electorate, that their political strength is highly personal. It is not increased by the strength of other party leaders assembled in a cabinet. And they realized that, as a result, it was certainly much more comfortable not to have as department heads men or women who had independent sources of political strength. Such men or women can be defiant and cause trouble; they have to be conciliated, because if they resign they can do so with a splash. Far better, presidents learned, to appoint nameless and faceless men, men without their own power bases, who are wholly dependent upon the president who took them from obscurity and made public figures of them; men who consequently will not defy the president. Or, if by any chance they should and he is forced to fire them, their departure will not be noticed and they will not be missed. The ideal cabinet member in recent days seems to have been the one described by John Ehrlichman shortly after the Miami convention in 1972: "The cabinet officers must be tied closely to the chief executive, or to put it in extreme terms, when he says jump, they only ask how high." A president obviously does not see much purpose in using such a group of men as a collective consultative body to serve as a check upon his judgments, and the three presidents who followed Eisenhower did not even try.

Accordingly, there is now much talk about finding ways to dismantle the powerful presidency that has been built up during this century. Senator Hatfield, for example, has advanced a proposal that the principal members of the Cabinet be elected in order to make them independent of the president. Some have proposed that the department of justice be taken out of the executive branch. Some have suggested that the size of the president's White House staff be tightly limited by law. But these approaches seem to be looking for the answer in the wrong direction. The fact is that the country does need a powerful presidency. The aggrandizement of the office has not been without reason. Governmental functions do need to be directed and coordinated from a single point of leadership, so that within limits set by law there can be worked out a coordinated economic policy, a comprehensive energy policy, a coherent national growth policy, a military policy and a foreign policy and a food policy consistent with one another, a coordinated system of intergovernmental relations, and all the rest. If the functions of the executive branch were to be scattered among persons of independent authority, any chance of the government's making sense with what it tried to do would be abandoned, and the cry would immediately rise: give the president the authority to make order out of this shambles. A strong argument can be made for granting some additional powers to the president; for instance, giving him clear control over the personnel management, as distinct from the inspection and policing, functions of the Civil Service Commission; or control over the activities of the Federal Reserve Board, which now has the authority to pursue a monetary policy that can cancel the president's fiscal policy and thus prevent the government from having any effective economic policy at all; or the power to raise and lower tax rates, within limits, for fiscal policy purposes. In short, there is no substitute for the powerful presidency in the complex modern world.

That is what makes it so important to strengthen the removal power. A powerful presidency can exist with safety only under equally powerful control.

What Forms Should the New Proposal Take?

The problem is to strike exactly the right balance in making presidential removal easier. If the process is made too easy, it could destabilize the presidency too much. Nobody wants a system like the Third Republic of France, or even the Italian Republic today, where prime ministers are turned out of office every year or two, or even every few months. The British system comes closest to the model; there a prime minister normally serves his full five-year term, but when a prime minister botches his job and loses the confidence of the country, and hence of the House of Commons and its governing majority, the majority does have means to force him out and get the country off to a fresh start under a leader who can lead and a government that can govern. This happened after Narvik, when Neville Chamberlain was forced to give way to Winston Churchill, and again after Suez, when Anthony Eden was persuaded by his colleagues to step down. Under our system a Neville Chamberlain would stay in his office for his full term even if that meant losing a war and the very freedom of the nation.

The Reuss resolution, in its current form, may well strike the balance that is necessary. The key was the addition to his earlier version of the provision that, when the president is removed by a no confidence vote, all members of both houses of the Congress also stand for reelection. They would have to take their decision, in effect, to a referendum. That would surely be a very great restraint upon the exercise of the congressional prerogative. Perhaps it would be too great; some may contend that under no conceivable circumstance would the members of the Senate voluntarily subject themselves to an election unnecessarily. (House members could avoid the dilemma by simply scheduling the new election to coincide with the regular midterm election.) But if the public were aroused—and that is the only circumstance in which the procedure would even be considered, or should be—a senator would have to think twice about basing his vote simply upon personal convenience. In any event, the error should be on the side of making the procedure an unattractive one. The important thing is that the procedure be available to a national majority as expressed through the Congress—available as a last resort, to be sure, but nevertheless available to be used when it is absolutely, and incontrovertibly, necessary.

The remaining flaw in the Reuss resolution, I believe, is the provision that after the Congress has voted no confidence in the president he remains in office for a period of not fewer than ninety days and under some circumstances for more than seven months, from June 1 to the following January 20. In most instances where the leadership capacity of a president has deteriorated to the point where the Congress, unquestionably reflecting the public or it would not dare to act, has determined that the president is no longer fit to stay in office, that is far too long a period for temporizing. The resolution should be revised to deprive him of his power at once, so that he would be gone as quickly as Chamberlain after the Narvik campaign exposed his failures or as quickly as Nixon after his culpability was unmistakably revealed, and the country could be rallied behind new leadership the following day. Both those occasions showed how quickly a poisonous national atmosphere can be purified, and how salutary that it be done at once. During the period pending the election, whether five months or seven, it is better to have the vice-president assume power as an interim leader than to continue to rely on a discredited president, whose personal instability may constitute grave risk.

Opponents will argue, as has Arthur Schlesinger, Jr. recently, that if this provision had been in the Constitution since the beginning some presidents would have been deposed for taking stands that, in the eyes of history, proved to be right. Schlesinger refers to John Adams' resistance to a war with France, and Harry Truman's firing of General Douglas MacArthur. Perhaps so. A risk of democracy is that in a system where the popular will prevails, the popular decision may be either right or wrong. But democratic systems are predicated on the proposition that decisions made undemocratically are even more likely to be wrong, and so the gains of democracy outweigh the losses. If the Reuss amendment had been in the Constitution throughout the last half century, it would have permitted the removal not just of Harry Truman but of Herbert Hoover and Lyndon Johnson, both incapacitated as leaders well before their terms expired, and of Richard Nixon sooner and with far less of a national ordeal. If one has to choose between losing both Truman and Hoover, say, before their time, and losing neither one of them, I suggest the national interest would lie in losing both. For Truman, however right he was and however much later generations may admire him, did not possess much capacity to lead the nation in his last two years. Vice-president Alben Barkley, as a caretaker president for a few months pending an election, would have done as well. Also, if either Truman or Hoover had chosen to fight the congressional decision and seek vindication at the polls, under the Reuss proposal he could have done so. Hoover, in all probability, would have won the nomination and then gone on to sound defeat. The transition that took place in 1933 would have come two years or so earlier, and that could only have been advantageous to the country. In the case of Truman, who knows? He would have chosen to fight, presumably. One may speculate that the Congress, recalling vividly what had been accomplished by that same determined underdog in 1948, would itself have backed away from a showdown and let the president finish out his term.

The mere existence of a no-confidence procedure could not help but have a continuous restraining influence on presidents, and this too would have results that would be, on balance, desirable. The effect would be to bring the president into closer consultation with the Congress that held the ultimate power over him. He would have to keep the confidence of Congress, and to keep its confidence he would have to take its leaders into his. He could not hide essential information from them. He could not abuse his powers and then defy them to do anything about it. He would have to make sure, through consultation in advance, that major decisions met with their concurrence. This would restrain his individual power to do great deeds both good and ill, but those who reflect upon the headstrong acts of recent presidents taken without consultation outside their immediate, sycophantic circles may well conclude that more bad deeds than good ones would be forestalled by the kind of collective leadership that a degree of enforced collaboration would bring about.

The new responsibilities of the congressional leadership should result, in turn, in a higher degree of congressional discipline internally. The members would have to repose more power in their leaders whose job it would be to contain and restrain the president and then hold those leaders effectively accountable. All this, I admit, is conjectural, because one never knows how any reform will actually work out in practice, but its effect would surely be in these directions.

Perhaps better schemes than the Reuss resolution will be found as this whole problem is considered. The most important thing, I think, is that the country begin talking seriously about the question of what should be done about the presidency. The alternatives to the Reuss proposal seem to be two: to leave the presidency as it is—powerful but unrestrained—and trust to luck, or attempt to reduce its power. Both these alternatives involve risks that seem to me to be greater than the risk involved in leaving great power in the president but subjecting its exercise to the ultimate restraint of quick removal if, in the judgment of the people as expressed through their elected representatives, he defaults grievously in his responsibilities.

Bob Eckhardt and Charles L. Black, Jr.

33. No Confidence Will Not Work in America (1976)

Bob Eckhardt was Democratic Congressman from Houston, Texas, for sixteen years, until his defeat in 1982; Charles L. Black is Sterling professor of law at Yale. The following exchange is taken from their book, The Tides of Power, *which is presented in the form of an extended conversation between old friends about the practical workings of the American constitutional system.*

ECKHARDT: In the recent troubles [over Watergate], one of the things which we heard recurrently suggested, on which we have touched briefly, is some sort of borrowing or adaptation on our part of the British system. That suggestion centers around the fact that by vote of "no confidence" in the House of Commons, a prime minister, and indeed his entire governmental entourage, can be thrown out of office, and this required no judgment of anything resembling criminality; it totally skips the technicalities of our impeachment process. Within the past few years some people have tended to look on this system rather admiringly, and I think we ought to talk a bit about what it would entail to substitute this system for ours. . . .

BLACK: This certainly opens up the question of the difficulties of adapting a single feature of a foreign system to our own Constitution. What Congress would attain by a vote of the "no confidence," under our system, altered only by the transplantation of the "vote-of-confidence" feature of the British system, is the elimination of the president from office, but what happens then, unless we effect a further change in our system, is simply that the vice-president assumes the office. Now there are several problems about that. The first [is] because the enormous likelihood is (whether he be elected on the same ticket with the president or whether he be appointed, as in the case of Mr. Ford, and rather perfunctorily confirmed by the houses of Congress, on the ground that there was nothing deeply wrong with him) he's likely to be no more a sparkplug or a leader than the outgoing president was. This difficulty, therefore, without a further change in the system, would not be answered by the removal of the president. I think we face that even under the impeachment system as it stands. Insofar as the British system involves a possibility on the part of the House of Commons of insisting upon being presented at the time of removal with an alternative leader who is thought better of and who can remedy the defects, we can't do that without a still deeper cut into our constitutional system. The mere removal of the president doesn't really answer anything like the questions that would be answered in the British Parliament. . . .

The reason for the independence of members of Congress and senators is something that is absolutely basic within our Constitution, and something in which it disresembles the British constitution altogether—the firm territorial base which each congressman has. Now to go to the British model, as you know, there is a very considerable power, it's not true as to every constituency, every time, but there is a very considerable power in the party leadership heading up in the prime minister, when he's in office, to influence the choice of constituencies in which candidates may run, and often of somebody who is elected from a constituency which he visits from time to time simply as a matter of courtesy. This is what's called a "safe seat." A Conservative who is high in the party council would be likely to be assigned such a seat rather than to a swing constituency. That limited but important power of designating the candidacy of members is an important disciplinary weapon in the British system. It doesn't exist at all in the United States. It doesn't exist for multiple reasons. First as to the Senate, the state is the constitutionally designated unit, and while a senator may, of course, be interested in his institutional position in the Senate, he lives or dies on the basis of his ability to be elected in his state. If there's a conflict between the party leadership on the one hand, and the senator's estimate of what it takes to get reelected on the other, his constant interest has to be in his state. If it is not, and in some crucial cases maybe it hasn't been, then of course sooner or later that state is going to find a senator who matches up with it.

ECKHARDT: The same thing is true of membership in the House. The practice of districting for House elections is of course not of constitutional origin, but it is followed, and it is anticipatable that it will be followed for any measurable, foreseeable future. What this means is that the party leadership has only collateral and relatively unimportant things that it can do or not do with respect to a member, while the major political interest of that member has got to be, if he's going to stay in Congress, his own district at home.

I think a second reason is our *bicamerality*. If you could hold one of these wild horses straight, you sure can't hold two of them at the same time, going in the same direction. . . .

The accommodation that is now being sought in Congress is not a movement toward the British Parliament, but a movement toward the structure of the United States Congress prior to the advent of Sam Rayburn. And that is the revitalization of the majority party caucus. If we should strengthen the majority party caucus sufficiently in the House, it would move us *somewhat* closer to the British system, because the caucus, being related to the party's ideological position, and having certain authority over the committee's majority and their chairmen, could institute a certain degree of uniformity of direction and an organization of national effort that would approach the British system. Congress would never really come near to a parliamentary system—there would be no way for the caucus to actually impose its will on its members— but it would move toward a tighter organization to effectuate a majority party program.

BLACK: No, there's no way. Let's take the case in the Senate, or take several cases. Of course there have been many, but one conspicuous case was former Senator Frank Lausche of Ohio. He called himself a Democrat and voted with Democrats to organize the Senate, but at just about that point the connection stopped. He was a very conservative man, usually voting with the Republicans, and he found that this matched up with the people of Ohio. His whole style and set of views matched up with their wishes, and he was repeatedly reelected.

There wasn't anything wrong with this, there wasn't even any violation of conscience or any question of expediency involved. I think that's something many people don't understand about politics—constituencies and representatives tend to match up ideologically. It's not so much that a man like Lausche would go in and vote against his conscience in order to get reelected. There's no reason to think he ever did that. They had found a man, and he had found a constituency, which matched up and suited each other, ideologically and as a matter of conscience, but in any case there was no power whatever the Democratic leadership could exert over Frank Lausche with respect to voting on any issue. Now the Democratic caucus used to be powerful to be sure, and I think we need more power in the caucus, but it never was able to command the votes of any southern Congressman on any racial issue dear to the hearts of northern Democrats. It just wouldn't have made any difference to them which way the vote went in the caucus in those times, they would have marched on in and voted in obedience to their own ideas in the main and the wishes of their constituency against the fair employment practices bill or anything else, it wouldn't have mattered how many Democrats had voted for it in the caucus.

BLACK: On these leadership matters, we have come up with a different pattern with each president. What we have now is kind of a mix and maybe that mix could be changed somewhat by such devices as that of increasing the power of the caucus.

But leadership in our government is a scarce resource. It's not something we can afford to gamble with. Now I have been desperately afraid, in the recent crisis, that we were going to do the most foolish thing possible, and that is (to put it plainly) to remake the written law of the presidency and remake the unwritten law of the presidency, remake the practices that go with the presidency, remake these in such a way as to make the whole set of laws and practices suitable for a president such as Richard M. Nixon. Now that's a foolish thing to do. Because if we can't do any better than elect one president after another like Richard M. Nixon, then we should go out of business. We ought to look on his term in office as the rarest of the whole set of laws and practices regarding the presidency.

ECKHARDT: Let me go back a minute here to this question of the balance that exists because of the power of Congress constitutionally and the power of the president practically. I think in examining this we find that it really works well because of that balance when the presidency and the Congress are in the hands of the same party. But in order to maintain that real balance you must envisage the worst of all possible situations, when a government is virtually paralyzed; that is the situation when the president and Congress are in different parties. I don't take this as a fatal flaw, but it is a flaw which can cause a long period, or at least a substantial period, of near-stagnation in government. Sometimes, it doesn't do so. The situation existed in Taft's last term, and mild reforms were put into effect with the Democratic Congress and a Republican president. But then of course there was a great surge of sweeping innovative legislation when Wilson came in, beginning his term, very much like the New Deal era. It was the era of the Clayton Act and the institution of the Federal Trade Commission and many other things like that.

BLACK: One of the statesmenlike things about Lyndon Johnson was the way he operated as Senate majority leader under Eisenhower. What little was possible in that era, at least housekeeping and all that in this relatively calm era, was carried on to some extent with more neatness because Johnson didn't take the position of exploiting this party opposition.

ECKHARDT: Eisenhower deserved some credit for that too, not only as a man, but as a sort of an institution. He was a kind of nonpartisan president—the closest thing to a coalition government we've ever had.

BLACK: I think that the conclusion we come to is that our political problems have to be analyzed in this country in our own terms and on the basis of our own federal situation, on the basis of our traditional federal situation, on the basis of our traditional politics and political ideas, and that looking with longing on something across the ocean is not really going to get us anywhere. We're going to have to deal with this problem of the presidency and the Congress, and of leadership in counterpoint with constitutional power, in terms of our own Constitution. It's not going to do very much good, and may do very much harm, to subject the president to additional vulnerabilities superimposed on those which already exist. The president is vulnerable to all kinds of actions short of impeachment and removal. The Congress has innumerable powers over the executive branch which could be exercised in their full force if two-thirds majorities can be mustered, but which sometimes don't even need that because they're negative powers like the withholding of appropriations.

ECKHARDT: Well, suppose though we accept the proposition from the discussion we've had, that we should not attempt to devise a system moving toward a parliamentary structure merely because our situation at the present time, which is a rather unusual one, creates some very difficult problems of forward movement in the government.

34. *Immigration and Naturalization Service* vs. *Chadha* (1983)

In the case excerpted here, involving the deportation of an alien, the United States Supreme Court, by a majority vote, declared that it is unconstitutional for Congress to reserve the right to veto an administrative action. Chief Justice Warren Burger wrote for the majority; Associate Justice Lewis Powell, Jr., gave a brief concurring opinion; Associate Justice Byron White wrote the dissent.

The fact that a given law or procedure is efficient, convenient, and useful in facilitating functions of government, standing alone, will not save it if it is contrary to the Constitution. Convenience and efficiency are not the primary objectives—or the hallmarks—of democratic government, and our inquiry is sharpened rather than blunted by the fact that congressional veto provisions are appearing with increasing frequency in statutes which delegate authority to executive and independent agencies.

Since 1932, when the first veto provision was enacted into law, 295 congressional veto-type procedures have been inserted in 196 different statutes as follows: from 1932 to 1939, five statutes were affected; from 1940–49, nineteen statutes; between 1950–59, thirty-four statutes; and from 1960–69, forty-nine. From the year 1970 through 1975, at least one hundred sixty-three such provisions were included in eighty-nine laws.

Justice White undertakes to make a case for the proposition that the one-house veto is a useful "political invention," and we need not challenge that assertion. We can even concede this utilitarian argument,

77 L. Ed. 2d (1983), 317.

although the long range political wisdom of this "invention" is arguable.
. . . But policy arguments supporting even useful "political inventions"
are subject to the demands of the Constitution which defines powers
and, with respect to this subject, sets out just how those powers are
to be exercised. . . .

The Constitution sought to divide the delegated powers of the new
federal government into three defined categories, legislative, executive
and judicial, to assure, as nearly as possible, that each branch of
government would confine itself to its assigned responsibility. The
hydraulic pressure inherent within each of the separate branches to
exceed the outer limits of its power, even to accomplish desirable
objectives, must be resisted.

Although not "hermetically" sealed from one another, the powers
delegated to the three branches are functionally identifiable. When any
branch acts, it is presumptively exercising the power the Constitution
has delegated to it. When the executive acts, it presumptively acts in
an executive or administrative capacity as defined in Article II. And
when, as here, one house of Congress purports to act, it is presumptively
acting within its assigned sphere.

Beginning with this presumption, we must nevertheless establish that
the challenged action under Section 244(c)(2) is of the kind to which
the procedural requirements of Article I, section 7 apply. Not every
action taken by either house is subject to the bicameralism and presentment requirements of Article I. Whether actions taken by either
house are, in law and fact, an exercise of legislative power depends not
on their form but upon "whether they contain matter which is properly
to be regarded as legislative in its character and effect."

Examination of the action taken here by one house pursuant to Section
244(c)(2) reveals that it was essentially legislative in purpose and effect.
. . . Section 244(c)(2) purports to authorize one house of Congress to
require the attorney general to deport an individual alien whose deportation otherwise would be cancelled under Section 244. The one-
House veto operated in this case to overrule the attorney general and
mandate Chadha's deportation; absent the House action, Chadha would
remain in the United States. Congress has *acted*, and its action has
altered Chadha's status. . . .

The nature of the decision implemented by the one-house veto in this
case further manifests its legislative character. After long experience with
the clumsy, time consuming private bill procedure, Congress made a
deliberate choice to delegate to the executive branch, and specifically to
the attorney general, the authority to allow deportable aliens to remain in
this country in certain specified circumstances. It is not disputed that this
choice to delegate authority is precisely the kind of decision that can be

implemented only in accordance with the procedures set out in Article I. Disagreement with the attorney general's decision on Chadha's deportation—that is, Congress' decision to deport Chadha—no less than Congress' original choice to delegate to the attorney general the authority to make that decision, involves determinations of policy that Congress can implement in only one way; bicameral passage followed by presentment to the president. Congress must abide by its delegation of authority until that delegation is legislatively altered or revoked. . . .

Since it is clear that the action by the House under Section 244(c)(2) was not within any of the express constitutional exceptions authorizing one house to act alone, and equally clear that it was an exercise of legislative power, that action was subject to the standards prescribed in Article I. The bicameral requirement, the presentment clauses, the president's veto, and Congress' power to override a veto were intended to erect enduring checks on each branch and to protect the people from the improvident exercise of power by mandating certain prescribed steps. To preserve those checks and maintain the separation of powers, the carefully defined limits on the power of each branch must not be eroded. To accomplish what has been attempted by one house of Congress in this case requires action in conformity with the express procedures of the Constitution's prescription for legislative action: passage by a majority of both houses and presentment to the president.

The veto authorized by Section 244(c)(2) doubtless has been in many respects a convenient shortcut: the "sharing" with the executive by Congress of its authority over aliens in this manner is, on its face, an appealing compromise. In purely practical terms, it is obviously easier for action to be taken by one house without submission to the president; but it is crystal clear from the records of the convention, contemporaneous writings and debates, that the framers ranked other values higher than efficiency. . . .

The choices we discern as having been made in the constitutional convention impose burdens on governmental processes that often seem clumsy, inefficient, even unworkable, but those hard choices were consciously made by men who had lived under a form of government that permitted arbitrary governmental acts to go unchecked. There is no support in the Constitution or decisions of this Court for the proposition that the cumbersomeness and delays often encountered in complying with explicit constitutional standards may be avoided, either by the Congress or by the president. With all the obvious flaws of delay, untidiness, and potential for abuse, we have not yet found a better way to preserve freedom than by making the exercise of power subject to the carefully crafted restraints spelled out in the Constitution. . . .

Justice Powell, concurring in the judgment: The Court's decision
. . . apparently will invalidate every use of the legislative veto. The
breadth of this holding gives one pause. Congress has included the veto
in literally hundreds of statutes, dating back to the 1930s. Congress
clearly views this procedure as essential to controlling the delegation
of power to administrative agencies. One reasonably may disagree with
Congress' assessment of the veto's utility, but the respect due its judgment
as a coordinate branch of government cautions that our holding should
be no more extensive than necessary to decide this case. In my view,
the case may be decided on a narrower ground. When Congress finds
that a particular person does not satisfy the statutory criteria for
permanent residence in this country, it has assumed a judicial function
in violation of the principle of separation of powers. Accordingly, I
concur only in the judgment. . . .

Justice White, dissenting: Today the Court not only invalidates Section
244(c)(2) of the Immigration and Nationality Act, but also sounds the
death knell for nearly 200 other statutory provisions in which Congress
has reserved a "legislative veto." For this reason, the Court's decision
is of surpassing importance. And it is for this reason that the Court
would have been well-advised to decide the case, if possible, on the
narrower grounds of separation of powers, leaving for full consideration
the constitutionality of other congressional review statutes operating on
such varied matters as war powers and agency rulemaking, some of
which concern the independent regulatory agencies.

The prominence of the legislative veto mechanism in our contemporary
political system and its importance to Congress can hardly be overstated.
It has become a central means by which Congress secures the accountability of executive and independent agencies. Without the legislative
veto, Congress is faced with a Hobson's choice: either to refrain from
delegating the necessary authority, leaving itself with a hopeless task
of writing laws with the requisite specificity to cover endless special
circumstances across the entire policy landscape, or in the alternative,
to abdicate its lawmaking function to the executive branch and independent agencies. To choose the former leaves major national problems
unresolved; to opt for the latter risks unaccountable policymaking by
those not elected to fill that role. Accordingly, over the past five decades,
the legislative veto has been placed in nearly 200 statutes. The device
is known in every field of governmental concern: reorganization, budgets,
foreign affairs, war powers, and regulation of trade, safety, energy, the
environment and the economy. . . .

The history of the legislative veto also makes clear that it has not
been a sword with which Congress has struck out to aggrandize itself
at the expense of the other branches—the concerns of Madison and

Hamilton. Rather, the veto has been a means of defense, a reservation of ultimate authority necessary if Congress is to fulfill its designated role under Article I as the nation's lawmaker. While the president has often objected to particular legislative vetoes, generally those left in the hands of congressional committees, the executive has more often agreed to legislative review as the price for a broad delegation of authority. To be sure, the president may have preferred unrestricted power, but that could be precisely why Congress thought it essential to retain a check on the exercise of delegated authority.

The Court heeded this counsel in approving the modern administrative state. The Court's holding today that all legislative-type action must be enacted through the lawmaking process ignores that legislative authority is routinely delegated to the executive branch, to the independent regulatory agencies, and to private individuals and groups.

> The rise of administrative bodies probably has been the most significant legal trend of the last century. . . . They have become a veritable fourth branch of the government, which has deranged our three-branch legal theories. . . .

This Court's decisions sanctioning such delegations make clear that Article I does not require all action with the effect of legislation to be passed as a law.

Theoretically, agencies and officials were asked only to "fill up the details," and the rule was that "Congress cannot delegate any part of its legislative power except under a limitation of a prescribed standard." Chief Justice Taft elaborated the standard: "If Congress shall lay down by legislative act an intelligible principle to which the person or body authorized to fix such rates is directed to conform, such legislative action is not a forbidden delegation of legislative power." In practice, however, restrictions on the scope of the power that could be delegated diminished and all but disappeared. In only two instances did the Court find an unconstitutional delegation. In other cases, the "intelligible principle" through which agencies have attained enormous control over the economic affairs of the country was held to include such formulations as "just and reasonable," "public convenience, interest, or necessity," and "unfair methods of competition."

The wisdom and the constitutionality of these broad delegations are matters that still have not been put to rest. But for present purposes, these cases establish that by virtue of congressional delegation, legislative power can be exercised by independent agencies and executive departments without the passage of new legislation. For some time, the sheer amount of law—the substantive rules that regulate private conduct and direct the operation of government—made by the agencies has far outnumbered the lawmaking engaged in by Congress through the traditional process.

If Congress may delegate lawmaking power to independent and executive agencies, it is most difficult to understand Article I as forbidding Congress from also reserving a check on legislative power for itself. Absent the veto, the agencies receiving delegations of legislative or quasi-legislative power may issue regulations having the force of law without bicameral approval and without the president's signature. It is thus not apparent why the reservation of a veto over the exercise of that legislative power must be subject to a more exacting test.

If the effective functioning of a complex modern government requires the delegation of vast authority which, by virtue of its breadth, is legislative or "quasi-legislative" in character, I cannot accept that Article I—which is, after all, the source of the non-delegation doctrine—should forbid Congress from qualifying that grant with a legislative veto.

The Court of Appeals struck down Section 244(c)(2) as violative of the constitutional principle of separation of powers. It is true that the purpose of separating the authority of government is to prevent unnecessary and dangerous concentration of power in one branch. For that reason, the framers saw fit to divide and balance the powers of government so that each branch would be checked by the others. Virtually every part of our constitutional system bears the mark of this judgment.

But the history of the separation of powers doctrine is also a history of accommodation and practicality. Apprehensions of an overly powerful branch have not led to undue prophylactic measures that handicap the effective working of the national government as a whole. The Constitution does not contemplate total separation of the three branches of government. "[A] hermetic sealing off of the three branches of government from one another would preclude the establishment of a nation capable of governing itself effectively."

Our decisions reflect this judgment. As already noted, the Court, recognizing that modern government must address a formidable agenda of complex policy issues, countenanced the delegation of extensive legislative authority to executive and independent agencies. The separation of powers doctrine has heretofore led to the invalidation of government action only when the challenged action violated some express provision in the Constitution.

I do not suggest that all legislative vetoes are necessarily consistent with separation of powers principles. A legislative check on an inherently executive function, for example of initiating prosecutions, poses an entirely different question. But the legislative veto device here—and in many other settings—is far from an instance of legislative tyranny over the executive. It is a necessary check on the unavoidably expanding power of the agencies, both executive and independent, as they engage in exercising authority delegated by Congress.

I regret that I am in disagreement with my colleagues on the fundamental questions that this case presents. But even more I regret the destructive scope of the Court's holding. It reflects a profoundly different conception of the Constitution than that held by the Courts which sanctioned the modern administrative state. Today's decision strikes down in one fell swoop provisions in more laws enacted by Congress than the Court has cumulatively invalidated in its history. . . .

James L. Sundquist

35. The Implications of *Chadha* (1983)

James L. Sundquist (see page 89) offered the following interpretation of the Chadha *decision, which appeared in* The Brookings Review *for Fall, 1983.*

When the Supreme Court this past spring found itself forced to decide the long-simmering issue of the legislative veto, a majority of the justices took a "strict constructionist" approach. They asked themselves, "What did the founding fathers, when they met at Philadelphia nearly two hundred years ago, intend?"

After long and arduous deliberation—so arduous, indeed, that the question was carried over from one term to the next before the Court finally resolved it—a six-justice majority concluded that the founders did not intend to include the legislative veto in the constitutional design. If they had meant to permit it, Chief Justice Burger wrote for the majority, they would have said so. But they didn't.

Accordingly, the Court invalidated 207 legislative veto provisions in 126 laws. The decision, said Justice White in his dissent, "strikes down in one fell swoop provisions in more laws enacted by Congress that the Court has cumulatively invalidated in its history." Thus, said White, the decision was "of surpassing importance."

That may turn out, in the long run, to have been an exaggeration. The Congress is sure eventually to find other, valid ways of controlling the executive branch in as many of the 207 areas of governmental activity as it still wishes to control. Until the new and substitute laws are written, there will be much uncertainty, and in some areas a temporary increase in authority for presidents, administrative agencies, and independent regulatory commissions.

The substitute devices for congressional control will be, unfortunately, more cumbersome and awkward. As the Chief Justice conceded, the legislative veto has been "a convenient shortcut . . . an appealing compromise." Some of the certain results of the decision, then, will be a loss of governmental efficiency, a heightening of the level of conflict between the Congress and the executive, and exacerbation of the normal tendency toward stalemate and deadlock in the policy-making process. Less certain, but highly probable, is a net ultimate loss in the authority and discretion of the executive branch.

Why the Legislative Veto Grew

In the concept of the founding fathers—and of the Supreme Court strict constructionists—the Congress writes laws authorizing the executive branch to do things, and the executive branch then does them. The trouble is, the Congress does not always know precisely what it wants done—and usually for very good reasons. Sometimes, the means to an objective are simply too uncertain. Sometimes, the executive branch must be authorized in advance to cope with events that have not even happened. In such cases, where the activity to be authorized cannot be defined exactly, the Congress has two choices: either it can give the executive branch a broad delegation of power to do as it sees fit, or it can withhold the power until such time as it is prepared to be precise.

It is because the Congress has so often found this to be an unhappy pair of choices that the legislative veto was invented. The device has permitted the Congress to steer between the alternatives, delegating and withholding power at the same time. The legislators say to the executive, in effect, "Go ahead and act, but if we disagree with what you do, we reserve the right to disapprove."

Using this proviso, the Congress often found itself ready to delegate powers to the executive that it had never been willing to grant before. The case that came before the Court is a typical, although relatively minor, example of such a delegation. Until 1940, the Congress had always regulated immigration through precisely-written statutes that the Justice Department was directed to enforce to the letter—a relationship between the branches conforming exactly to what the founders had in mind. But letter-of-the-law enforcement affecting thousands of illegal aliens resulted in severe hardship in many individual cases, and administrators and legislators agreed that some deserving immigrants ought to be exempted from deportation orders. Whenever they identified a worthy case, the exemption was made through an act of Congress—termed a "private law"—that named the excepted individual.

The system worked, but it was cumbersome. The private bills had to be drafted, approved by committees in both houses, passed on the floor of each house, then signed by the president. On occasion, they could be controversial; one day the House spent five and a half hours debating four private bills. Eventually, someone said: let's simplify all this. Whenever the two branches agree, let the attorney general do on his own what has heretofore been done through private bills; when they disagree, reserve for the Congress the power that it has always had to say no. So a two-house legislative veto was written into law in 1940, and converted to a one-house veto in 1952. It was when the attorney general excepted one Jagdish Rai Chadha of Kenya from deportation in 1974 and the House of Representatives disapproved his action that the historic legislative veto case started its long journey to the Supreme Court.

Most of the legislative veto provisions, of course, involve far more significant delegations of power. The earliest, enacted in 1932 and renewed at intervals thereafter, permitted government departments and agencies to be reorganized by presidential actions subject to a congressional veto—instead of by statute, as had always been the case before. Few presidential plans have been rejected, and, consequently, much reorganization has been accomplished. Two veto provisions enacted during the Watergate era helped to resolve the central issues in the stormy confrontation between President Nixon and the Congress. One was contained in the Congressional Budget and Impoundment Control Act of 1974, welcomed by the president, which authorized him to defer, subject to disapproval by either house, expenditure of appropriated funds: Nixon had freely impounded billions of dollars in appropriations during the preceding two years, but the courts had found that he had seized the power unconstitutionally. The other was the heart of the War Powers Resolution of 1973, enacted over the president's veto; that act authorized him to involve U.S. forces in combat but required him to withdraw them if the Congress did not approve the action within sixty days.

After its clash with Nixon, the Congress began writing legislative veto provisions into new grants of administrative authority much more frequently, almost routinely—restricting delegations of power in such fields as energy, education, election campaign finance, financial aid to New York City, foreign aid, military arms sales, and international trade.

During this period, the veto became much too convenient a device, in the view of executive branch officials and many congressmen as well. For no purpose more noble than to give members of Congress and their staffs a role in the administrative process, veto provisions were attached to grants of power that, in previous decades, would have been freely made on an unrestricted basis. Yet, if the device was overused, it nevertheless remained valuable as a bargaining chip to enable the executive branch to win delegations of authority that it could not have gotten otherwise. Thus, in 1979, the Congress became hopelessly torn among competing regional and occupational interests in trying to write criteria for the executive to follow in preparing a standby gasoline rationing plan. Finally, President Carter asked the Congress to let him resolve the conflicts and prepare a plan, and the legislators in either house could veto it if they did not like it. On that basis, they were happy to make the delegation, and when the administration plan was sent to Capitol Hill, they thought better than to reignite the earlier conflict. By simply not acting, both houses allowed the plan to take effect. Ironically, at the time that Carter was proposing the legislative veto as the most practical way of getting a gasoline rationing scheme adopted, he and his administration had been officially on record for a year—and would remain on record—as determined to win a Supreme Court decision outlawing the veto in most, if not all, of its applications, and it was his Justice Department that brought the *Chadha* case before the high tribunal. . . .

At its worst, clearly, the legislative veto did contain serious potential for abuse. But at its best, it was of great utility in winning for the executive branch delegations of power it could not otherwise receive. It was a means of resolving conflict between the branches and establishing satisfactory working relationships that would enable the government to act. It was developed not by strict constructionists of the Constitution, obviously, but by practical politicians and statesmen. Their responsibility was not to divine what the founding fathers had in mind in the eighteenth century but, rather, to make the constitutional system work in the twentieth. How could the inefficiencies, delays, hiatuses, conflicts, and deadlocks inherent in a government of separate and competing branches be overcome? For this purpose, the legislative veto came to be what Justice White called it in his dissent: "an important if not indispensable political invention."

What Happens Next?

The immediate consequence of the Court decision is that 207 legislative veto provisions are invalidated, but no one knows how many of the 126 laws containing those provisions are constitutional in their entirety. That turns on the question of severability. In the case before it, the Court held that the veto provision was severable, and the rest of the law was therefore unaffected. The executive branch thus received an enhanced grant of power—all the discretion with none of the restraint.

But whenever the veto clauses are found not to be severable, entire laws will fall.

To decide whether a veto provision is severable, the judges have to determine congressional intent. If the Congress had understood the proper limits on its power then as it does now, would it have enacted the law without the veto or would it have withheld the delegation? To divine what 535 congressmen would have done in hypothetical circumstances in more than two hundred separate instances is surely one of the most prodigious tasks of mind-reading ever assigned to anyone.

But the Congress will not just sit still awaiting judicial pronouncements. It will be proceeding case by case to clarify its intentions for the future, if not the past, by passing fresh legislation establishing new executive-legislative relationships—or reestablishing old ones—in disputed areas. . . .

Having lost its veto over arms sales, for instance, will the Congress respond by granting a blanket power to the president to sell arms to anybody, including Saudi Arabia or Jordan? Or will it tell the president: when you have a deal worked out, bring it to us and we will authorize it if we choose? The latter would appear to be the better bet. It will be the likelier course, too, on reorganization of the government (in fact, it is the present course, because President Reagan never won reorganization power even subject to a veto) and on deferral of expenditure of appropriated funds. . . . Similarly, as under the Levitas amendment to the [Consumer Product Safety Commission] bill, some regulatory agencies will be turned into advisory bodies, at least for certain types of regulations.

When the Congress adopts two-stage procedures, the need for it to act by statute at the second stage (instead of allowing actions to happen by simply not vetoing them—that is, by doing nothing) will add to the workload of an already overloaded legislative branch. Government executives will have to spend even more of their time dealing with, and bickering with, the Hill. All this the Chief Justice recognized. The processes of government, he acknowledged in his majority opinion, "often seem clumsy, inefficient, even unworkable," they often result in "cumbersomeness and delays," and "delay, untidiness, and potential for abuse" are "obvious flaws." But the flaws and inefficiencies were "consciously" accepted in 1787, he argued, in the greater interest of making sure that "arbitrary governmental acts" would not "go unchecked."

There is irony in the Burger reasoning, for it is precisely to check arbitrary governmental acts—by the executive branch—that the legislative veto was devised. What prevents arbitrary government is not the independence of the branches that Burger was intent on upholding. It is just the opposite—the "checks and balances" by which an act of one branch is made dependent on approval by another. The legislative veto is an additional check and balance that the founding fathers did not think of. If it violated the Constitution's language, it actually served to reinforce the very constitutional principle the chief justice chose to cite in striking it down.

In many instances, the almost-all and almost-nothing alternatives reflected in the two CPSC amendments will still appear to the Congress as an unhappy, or even unworkable, pair of choices. In particular, whenever the government must be empowered to act quickly a two-stage procedure is not suitable, and yet the Congress may consider an unrestricted delegation to the executive quite out of the question. Here the War Powers Resolution of 1973 is the prime example. The Congress concluded that it could not deny to the president altogether the power to send military forces into combat situations without specific authorization, for crises arise and must be dealt with instantly, whether in the middle of the night or on a Sunday afternoon or when the Congress is on vacation. On the other hand, the legislators were adamant against relinquishing their constitutional power to declare war, through an unrestrained grant of power to the president. Giving the president the war power—but limiting it to sixty days—was an ingenious middle course that the legislative veto device made possible. In such situations, the Congress is still likely to regard some middle course as a practical necessity, and it will be searching for a new device that will survive judicial scrutiny. . . .

In the immediate aftermath of the *Chadha* decision, some members of Congress searched for a universal response that will fit all the 207 cases. Some suggested that a "summit conference" between the branches be held, to work out a new pattern of relationships. But the quest for a broad, uniform solution will be unproductive, because the range of veto provisions is too broad and the types too diverse. The 207 delegations of power now subject to the veto will have to be reviewed one by one, piecemeal, and assigned to their proper category—those to be granted, those to be withheld, and those to be subjected to an equivalent of the old legislative veto restriction, through an appropriations rider or similar device. Predictably, the Congress will delegate power to the president in the relatively unimportant areas while retaining control over actions that are significant and controversial.

Looking further ahead, legislators will need to decide whether their veto was a mechanism of such practical indispensability, as Justice White suggested it was, that the Constitution should be amended to make it legal. At least one proposed amendment has already been introduced in the House, and the question will no doubt be on the agenda of constitutional reformers for years to come.

Specific Proposals:
Text and Analysis

A. DISSOLUTION AND SPECIAL ELECTIONS
(CONSTITUTIONAL AMENDMENT)

Section 1. At any time during the first three years of a presidential term, the president shall have power to issue a proclamation of no confidence in the Congress, and the Congress shall have power to adopt a resolution of no confidence in the president. The affirmative vote of an absolute majority of the members of each house shall be necessary to adopt a resolution on no confidence, and the president shall have no power to veto such a resolution. A resolution of no confidence proposed by one-third of the members shall be privileged in the House of Representatives and shall have precedence over all other bills, resolutions, and motions in the Senate.

Section 2. A proclamation or resolution of no confidence shall fix a date for the calling of special elections for the appointment of electors for president and vice-president, and for the offices of senator and member of the House of Representatives. The date for such special elections shall not be sooner than 110 days nor later than 130 days from the date of issuance of the proclamation or adoption of the resolution of no confidence. The clerk of the House of Representatives shall notify the chief executive of each state and of the District of Columbia of the date of such special elections, and each state and the District of Columbia shall provide for the choosing of electors, and the election of representatives and senators, on that day. The convening and balloting of electors for president and vice-president and the transmittal of the ballots to Congress which shall count them shall be in the manner specified in the twelfth and twentieth articles of amendment. Such convening and balloting of electors shall be at a date specified by Congress, not later than twenty days after the date of special elections.

Section 3. A proclamation or resolution of no confidence shall specify a date for the commencement of the terms of president, vice-president, senator and representative, which date shall be not later than twenty days after the convening and balloting of electors for president and vice-president. The term of office for the president and vice-president chosen in any special elections shall be four years. The term of office for representatives chosen in any special election shall be [two years] [four years]. The term of office for senators chosen in any special election shall be [two years for members elected to seats of the first class specified in Article I, four years for members elected to seats of the second class and six years for members elected to seats of the third class] or [four years for members elected to seats of the first class specified in amendment _____ and eight years for members elected to seats of the second class]. All such terms shall extend to the next following January 3 in the case of the House of Representatives and the Senate and until the next following January 20 in the case of the president and vice-president.

Section 4. No person shall be elected to the office of the president more than twice, including election in a special election pursuant to this article, *provided* that any person may be elected a third time to the office of the president in a special election held pursuant to a resolution of no confidence if such person has served in the office of president for less than six years before the adoption of such resolution of no confidence.

Section 5. The Congress shall have power to enforce this article by appropriate legislation.

Analysis

The proposed amendment allows for the dissolution of the executive and legislative leadership and the holding of new elections. Both the president, by proclamation, and the Congress, by a resolution not subject to veto, may declare their lack of confidence in the other branch, thereby triggering new special elections for president, vice-president and Congress. Special elections would be held not later than 130 days and not fewer than 110 days from the issuance of a proclamation or resolution; primaries, caucuses and party conventions could be held during this period under rules and at dates left to the choice of the states and the political parties. The proposed amendment also provides for the convening and balloting of the electoral college following elections triggered by a proclamation or resolution of no confidence.

The proposed amendment could be adapted to provide that the terms of office for those elected in any special election would be the same as the existing terms or to longer terms if other amendments lengthening terms are also adopted. To prevent a permanent departure from November elections and terms beginning the following January, the terms of those elected in special elections would automatically be extended to the January following the last year of the term. To preserve the principle of the Twenty-second Amendment, the proposed amendment bars persons from election to the presidency more than twice (including special elections), with an exception for persons who have served as president for less than six years at the time Congress adopts a resolution calling for a special election. To avoid unnecessary special elections, a proclamation or resolution of no confidence would not be permitted during the fourth year of a presidential term.

A provision could also be added to limit the number of times a proclamation or resolution of no confidence could be issued or adopted during the first three years of a presidential term.

The proposed amendment squarely addresses the increasingly serious problem of deadlock between the executive and legislative branches. If conflict between the executive and legislative branches prevents the government from responding to national concerns, either Congress or the president would have the power to appeal to the electorate by calling for new elections. Voters would have the opportunity to break an impasse by electing a president and majorities of both houses pledged to break the deadlock one way or another. The fact that all congressional seats, as well as the presidency and vice-presidency, would be filled in a single special election would increase the likelihood that voters would choose one major party or the other to control both the executive and legislative branches. Voters, of course, would remain free to reelect all incumbents and permit the deadlock to continue.

The proposed amendment would also provide a mechanism for cutting short the term of a president who has lost the confidence not only of the majority of the House and Senate, but also of the majority of the voting public. The impeachment process serves, at best, to remove only those presidents who can be shown to have committed criminal violations of the public trust. The proposed amendment would enable Congress to call for new elections to confirm its judgment that the incumbent president, while not guilty of an impeachable offense, is unable adequately to fulfill the duties of the office. To do so, however, Congress would have to put its own seats at risk in the same special election.

The proposed amendment would help to prevent deadlocks as well as to break them. The mutual risk of dissolution and removal should encourage both Congress and the president to cooperate in fulfilling their governmental responsibilities while the longer presidential and congressional terms could allow such cooperation the time needed to produce results. There is little risk that the amendment would be invoked excessively, because incumbent presidents and legislators would be most unlikely to risk their incumbent status except in the gravest of circumstances.

Opponents of the amendment raise numerous objections to the proposed reform. Common to many objections is the concern that the amendment unwisely moves towards a plebiscitary government. In the words of *The Federalist, # 71*:

"The republican principle demands that the deliberate sense of the community should govern the conduct of those to whom they entrust the management of their affairs, but it does not require an unqualified compliance to every transient impulse which the people may receive from the arts of men, who flatter their prejudices to betray their interests." They also point out that the present system of biennial elections provides a periodic equivalent of the parliamentary vote of no confidence, and that giving Congress the right to call for new presidential elections undermines the constitutional authority and independence of the president.

Critics of the proposed amendment also argue that it could lead to the type of governmental instability experienced under certain parliamentary regimes, such as Italy. Proponents of the amendment reply that in countries with two major political parties, such as the United Kingdom and the Federal Republic of Germany, governments continue on average for four years or so as in the United States. Proponents also point out that under the present system, deadlocks on major issues (e.g., the budget) do indeed persist, and that, as the recent experience of Germany shows, dissolution offers a practical method of breaking such deadlocks.

B. ONE-HOUSE OVERRIDE (CONSTITUTIONAL AMENDMENT)

Two-thirds of either house of Congress shall have power to present any bill, previously passed by that house and thereafter not passed by the other house within 120 days, to the president. The president shall sign the bill or return it to the house in which it originated within thirty days. If the president signs the bill, it shall be a law.

Analysis

This amendment is designed to provide a remedial process, short of reconstituting the government, for breaking deadlocks on major policy issues. The amendment permits the president and one house of Congress, by a two-thirds majority, to override the other house—just as two-thirds of each house presently may override a presidential veto. Much of the discussion regarding the national referendum process [see next proposal] is also relevant here.

C. REFERENDUM (CONSTITUTIONAL AMENDMENT)

Section 1. The president shall have power by proclamation to submit any bill passed by [a majority] [two-thirds] of the Senate or House of Representatives, but not passed by the other house at the same session of Congress, to a national referendum. The president [may] [shall] fix a date, not less than [thirty] days or more than [one hundred twenty] days from the date of proclamation, on which the referendum shall be conducted.

Section 2. The national referendum shall permit votes in favor of or against the submitted bill. Any citizen of the United States registered to vote in general elections in any state shall have the right to vote in general elections in any state in the national referendum. If a majority of those citizens voting in the referendum vote in favor of the submitted bill, it shall be law.

Section 3. No more than [two] bills shall be submitted to national referendum in any presidential term.

Section 4. The Congress shall provide by appropriate legislation for the conduct of national referenda.

Analysis

This amendment empowers the president, if supported by either a majority or two-thirds of either house of Congress, to submit a bill to popular decision in a nationwide referendum. If a majority of the electorate support the bill, it becomes law. No more than two bills may be submitted to referendum in any presidential term.

The amendment is designed to provide a remedial process, short of reconstituting the government, in situations involving governmental deadlock over a major policy issue. The amendment might offer better chances for breaking such limited deadlocks than would presidential dissolution of Congress and calling for new elections. New elections might simply return to office incumbents skilled at appealing to parochial constituencies, rather than persons supporting or opposing the president's programs. The amendment would permit direct popular resolution of policy questions without this danger.

The amendment would also reduce the influence of parochial and other special interests over legislation dealing with major policy issues. The president would require the support of only one house of Congress in order to call for a referendum, and no referendum could be held unless he so proclaims. Both these features of the proposal would restrict the ability of interest groups to attach special favors to or win special exceptions from bills. The referendum process could be used to present to the voting public issues which are deadlocked in ordinary legislative channels because of single-interest groups.

Three principal objections may be raised to the proposed amendment. First, the referendum process might work to the detriment of minority groups, by reducing present checks on legislation supported by popular majorities. Second, the electorate arguably lacks the time, experience and desire to make an informed decision on specific legislative proposals. Third, the temptation to break a deadlock by referendum would circumvent the healthy system of compromise inherent in the present legislative process.

It is worth noting that the French constitution permits the president alone to propose adopting legislation by referendum in a very limited class of cases such as ratifying treaties and reorganizing the executive branch of government. President Mitterand has recently proposed a constitutional amendment widening the scope of legislation by referendum to cover any bill involving civil liberties.

D. ITEM VETO (STATUTE OR CONSTITUTIONAL AMENDMENT)

The president shall have power to disapprove any items of a bill making appropriations of funds while approving the remainder of the bill. Any items of a bill so approved shall be law, and any items so disapproved shall not be law. If the president disapproves any items of a bill, he shall append to the bill at the time of signing it a statement of the items disapproved, together with the reasons for such disapproval. The house in which any bill containing items disapproved by the president originated shall have power to reconsider such items and if, after such reconsideration, two-thirds of that house shall agree to pass a bill containing any such items, to send this bill to the other house. If approved by two-thirds of that house after reconsideration, such bill shall become a law. But in all such cases, the votes of both houses shall be determined by yeas and nays, and the names of the persons voting for and against the bill shall be entered on the journal of each house respectively.

Analysis

This proposed constitutional amendment grants the president power to veto individual items of appropriations contained in bills presented to him by Congress. Items vetoed by the president do not become law, while the remainder of the bill does. An explanation of the reasons for any such item veto by the president is required. The amendment also provides for a legislative override of any item veto by a two-thirds vote of each house. The amendment could be modified to permit the reduction, as well as the elimination, of individual items.

The proposed amendment is intended to serve a number of ends. First, an item veto would increase executive influence in Congress, thereby reducing the dangers of governmental deadlock. Clinton Rossiter has remarked: "The president often feels compelled to sign bills that are full of dubious grants and subsidies rather than risk a breakdown in the work of whole departments. While it salves his conscience and cools his anger to announce publicly that he would veto these if he could, most congressmen have learned to pay no attention to his protests." Second, as the foregoing quotation suggests, the amendment would enable the president to veto—or, through the threat of a veto, prevent the passage of—individual appropriations plainly not in the national interest. The proposed amendment could also enhance the president's power to administer the federal government by giving him control over the content of the federal budget, both as a whole and with respect to individual programs. Proponents of the item veto, including President Reagan, note that more than forty states permit their governors to veto individual items in appropriations bills, and argue that the historical experience under such provisions has been favorable.

Opponents of the proposed item veto have argued that such a provision would unduly expand executive powers. A president might place extreme pressure on individual legislators by threatening to veto appropriations in that person's district or state. Legitimate appropriations, which also were of local political importance to a senator or representative, might be held hostage for votes on entirely unrelated subjects. The effect of the item veto might even be to increase overall expenditures, if a president threatened, for example, to veto a favored project unless a legislator agreed to support some large expenditure dear to the president's heart. As President Taft said, "It is wiser to leave the remedy . . . to the action of the people in condemning at the polls the party which becomes responsible for [irresponsible appropriations] than to give, in such a powerful instrument, a temptation to its sinister use by a president eager for continued political success." Opponents also argue that an item veto would grant what are in effect legislative powers to the president, permitting him to sign into law only individual parts of what Congress intended to be a single, interdependent set of appropriations. This objection is made with particular force in connection with proposals to authorize the president to reduce, as well as eliminate, individual appropriations.

Proponents of the item veto respond that the device merely restores the veto power to the president. The increasing tendency of appropriation bills to be omnibus affairs, passed late in the session, seriously constrains the executive's traditional veto power. Authorizing the president to veto individual items of appropriations, it is argued, merely restores to the executive the veto power the framers intended the president to wield. Moreover, it makes the president accountable to the public for legislative actions he can now blame on the Congress because he presently has no practical power to veto them. If he is given the item veto power and fails to exercise it, he could no longer transfer the blame to Congress.

E. LEGISLATIVE VETO (CONSTITUTIONAL AMENDMENT)

The Congress may by legislation provide for expressions of congressional intent by concurrent resolution regarding actions taken under such legislation.

Analysis

Major confusion and uncertainty have resulted from the Supreme Court's 1983 decision that the legislative veto is unconstitutional (*INS* vs. *Chadha*). The majority opinion by Chief Justice Burger proclaimed that not only the one-house but also the two-house legislative veto violate the separation-of-powers doctrine in general and the "presentment" clause of Article I in particular.

> **Section 7.3.** Every order, resolution, or vote to which the concurrence of the Senate and House of Representatives may be necessary (except on a question of adjournment) shall be presented to the president of the United States; and before the same shall take effect, shall be repassed by two-thirds of the Senate and House of Representatives, according to the rules and limitations prescribed in the case of a bill.

A review by the Justice Department has identified 207 instances of legislative veto provisions in 126 statutes over the past fifty years. The Department contends that the "separability" clauses in these statutes permit the legislative veto feature to be deleted in most cases, without violence to the rest of the statute. Many members of Congress feel, however, that the legislative veto feature was central in the often-sensitive negotiations on such legislation and cannot be removed without adjusting other features of the packages. The House Judiciary Committee counsel contends that each such case will have to be adjudicated before the status of thousands of actions taken under these acts, many of them major, can be clarified. The prospect is thus for years of legal wrangling and uncertainty about programs.

Several congressional "remedies" have been introduced or proposed since the decision. They tend to fall into two categories:

1. authorizing two-house vetoes by legislation which provides for amendment of proposed actions within stated periods by joint resolution (with a two-thirds vote required in each house if the president vetoes the resolution); and

2. legalizing one-house vetoes either by (1) legislation providing that the measures in question will take effect within a stated period only if approved by a joint resolution (which the president presumably would not veto) or (2) a constitutional amendment specifically recognizing the one-house veto.

Looking forward as well as backward, therefore, and denied the use of a proven device for sharing powers, Congress and the president could spend many more years groping for a new formula.

The proposal here would minimize this period of costly confusion by a constitutional amendment with three main features:

1. preserving the two-house (concurrent resolution) veto used and widely accepted over the past fifty years as a sensible way of achieving coherent action on subject-matter too technical or transient to be appropriate for regular legislation but too important or sensitive to be appropriate for outright delegation;

2. clearing up the cloud cast by *Chadha* over the use of the concurrent resolution in general; and

3. letting stand the Court's elimination of the one-house and committee vetoes since these do not make Congress, in Woodrow Wilson's phrase, "efficient without suffering it to be meddlesome."

F. REDUCED MAJORITY FOR TREATY RATIFICATION (CONSTITUTIONAL AMENDMENT)

Approval by Three-fifths of the Senate

The president shall have power to make treaties, provided three-fifths of the Senate concurs.

Approval by a Majority of Each House

The president shall have power to make treaties, provided a majority of each house of Congress concurs.

Analysis

These proposed amendments remove the existing requirement, in Article II, section 2, that two-thirds of the Senate approve any treaty negotiated by the president. John Hay described this rule as "[t]he irreparable mistake of our Constitution," and many scholars and public figures have agreed. One principal evil resulting from the two-thirds rule is that it permits a small number of senators—motivated perhaps by wholly parochial considerations arising from the composition of certain constituencies, or even by personal animosity—to block treaties backed with overwhelming national support and possessing great international significance, or to extract unreasonable and often unrelated concessions (e.g., the appointment of a protege to high office) in exchange for their support. Second, the president, aware that a small group of senators possesses such power, may refrain from proposing or pursuing negotiations in areas where a treaty might serve compelling national interests, simply from fear of a costly defeat on Capitol Hill. Finally, even if the support of two-thirds of the Senate can be won, this feat takes considerable amounts of time; in an age in which increasing international interdependence demands bilateral and multilateral agreements on a host of questions, the inertia resulting from the two-thirds requirement is extremely costly.

The principal justifications for the two-thirds requirement are that it reduces the danger of presidents unwisely entering into treaties. Moreover, the requirement forces the president to educate both the Senate and the public thoroughly as to the wisdom of proposed treaties. Supporters of the existing process argue that because of the importance of treaties (unimportant international agreements typically take the form of executive agreements), the dangers of deadlock are outweighed by the value of checks on unwise treaties and incentives to educate the public. Proponents of the change reply that the existing requirement often induces the executive to convert possible treaties into executive agreements, thereby bypassing the constitutional requirement of Senate ratification anyway.

The proposed amendment replaces the two-thirds requirement with two alternatives, namely approval by three-fifths of the Senate or a majority of each house of Congress. The former proposal continues the special role of the Senate in foreign policy, justified by the less parochial concerns of senators as compared to representatives. The latter proposal would permit treaties to be entered into in the same manner that war is declared and foreign assistance is dispensed. This procedure is a well-tested one, familiar to all the actors, but it still requires a constitutional amendment.

Part 5

The Amending Process

Many of the reforms outlined in this book can be achieved by means other than constitutional amendment. The political parties, by adopting new rules, could nominate their candidates at bicameral conventions and require their nominees to finance their campaigns solely with money channeled through the party treasury. Campaign financing limits could be set by agreements between the major parties. Other changes, such as the option of voting a straight party ticket in all federal elections or holding presidential elections two weeks before congressional elections, could be accomplished by statutes. Still others might be brought about by changes in customs and conventions, such as a determination by the president to use his party's leaders in Congress as an informal but binding council of advisers.

Many of the changes proposed here, however—changes in the terms of office for members of Congress and the president, appointing legislators as heads of executive departments, dissolution and special elections—would require constitutional amendments.

The traditional way to amend the Constitution, outlined in Article V, is for Congress to adopt specific language by a two-thirds vote of each house (no need for the president's signature), and for the legislatures, or special ratifying conventions, of three-quarters of the states to ratify the amendment proposed by Congress. This mode is difficult, as the framers intended, but not impossible, as the successful adoption of twenty-six amendments shows. It requires a strong consensus in Congress and widespread support among the states. It can be blocked by one-third-plus-one in either house of Congress or by simple majorities in a single house (or in the ratifying conventions) in just thirteen of the fifty states.

The Constitution does provide another way. Article V says that, if two-thirds of the states make application, Congress shall call a national convention for proposing amendments, and if three-quarters of the states ratify the results, the amendment or amendments shall be adopted. The framers' purpose in providing this alternate mode was to prevent Congress from blocking amendments which large popular majorities were determined to make. Though this method has never been used, its availability helped to persuade the Senate to approve the seventeenth amendment, providing for the direct popular election of senators.

More recently, this method has been pursued by advocates of a balanced budget amendment. This modern drive, which is apparently close to fruition, has occasioned a discussion of the ambiguities in this provision of Article V. In this Part of our collection, we present a thorough discussion by C. Herman Pritchett of the pros and cons of using this method.

Also included are a paper by Austin Ranney on popular opinion toward various proposed constitutional amendments, and an analysis by A. E. Dick Howard of recent constitutional changes at the state level. The states have often served as laboratories of government in the American federal system. Professor Howard's article presents an instructive analysis of different ways to fashion revisions and of the means for building a popular consensus in support of them.

C. Herman Pritchett

36. Why Risk a Constitutional Convention? (1980)

C. Herman Pritchett, an authority on constitutional government and former president of the American Political Science Association, taught for many years at the University of Chicago and is now on the faculty on the University of California at Santa Barbara. This article appeared originally in The Center Magazine.

Article V of the Constitution provides two methods for amending that document. First, Congress may propose amendments by a two-thirds vote of each house, which must then be ratified by three-fourths of the states, either by the state legislatures or conventions, as Congress may direct. All twenty-six amendments to the Constitution have been proposed in this way, and all except one have been ratified by state legislatures. Conventions were mandated by Congress for ratification of the twenty-first amendment, because of a belief that gerrymandered, rural-dominated state legislatures did not accurately reflect public attitudes toward prohibition.

Second, the legislatures of two-thirds of the states may make application to Congress to call a convention for proposing amendments. From 1789 to 1974, at least 356 applications were filed with Congress for the calling of a convention, but in fact none has ever been held. Consequently, a discussion of the operation and possible consequences of a convention necessarily requires a certain amount of speculation and prediction.

Today's interest in the convention method of amendment arises from the effort to secure an amendment to require balancing the federal budget, by the convention route if necessary. At present writing, apparently some twenty-eight or twenty-nine state legislatures have approved applications to call a convention for this purpose. Attention was

Reprinted by permission from *The Center Magazine*, March, 1980.

previously centered on the convention device in 1966 when, after the Senate had defeated a proposed amendment to overturn the Supreme Court's one-person one-vote decision, Senator Everett Dirksen undertook to secure the same result by convention applications from two-thirds of the states. His campaign fell short by only one state, thirty-three of the necessary thirty-four legislatures responding.

It appears that in only one case have the necessary number of states ever filed applications for a convention. In the early part of this century some thirty-one states, meeting the two-thirds requirement at that time, submitted petitions for an amendment to provide for direct election of senators. Congress failed to heed this call for a convention, but eventually proposed the amendment itself.

A study by Barbara Prager and Gregory Milmoe in 1975 for the American Bar Association revealed that actually seventy-five applications for direct election of senators had been filed at various times, the largest number ever received by Congress on one issue. They noted fifty-four petitions on apportionment, forty-two on federal tax limitation or repeal of the Sixteenth Amendment, thirty for the outlawing of polygamy, twenty-one for revenue sharing, and nineteen for revision of Article V. Applications in this last category were stimulated by the Council of State Governments, which in 1962 inaugurated a campaign for three so-called "states' rights" amendments.

The Drafting of Article V

Discussions at the constitutional convention in 1787 throw some light on the thinking of the framers concerning the amendments process. They took for granted that the states should have the right to set the amending machinery in motion. In fact, it was the role of Congress that was in dispute at the time. The original draft of the Virginia Plan (Resolution XIII) read:

> Provision ought to be made for the amendment of the articles of union whenever it shall seem necessary; and that the assent of the national legislature ought not to be required thereto. (Farrand, I, 22)

In the committee on the whole on June 11, George Mason approved:

> It would be improper to require the consent of the national legislature, because they may abuse their power and refuse their consent on that very account. The opportunity for such an abuse may be the fault of the Constitution calling for amendment. (Farrand, I, 203)

The committee on detail, reporting on August 6, revised the language of Resolution XIII, but retained the state monopoly on the amending process:

> On the application of the legislatures of two-thirds of the states of the union, for an amendment of this Constitution, the legislature of the United States shall call a convention for that purpose. (Farrand, II, 188, 557)

But on September 10, Elbridge Gerry moved to reconsider this provision, with the support of Alexander Hamilton and James Madison. Hamilton said that the plan, giving the states a monopoly of the amending process, was "not adequate."

> The state legislatures will not apply for alterations but with a view to increase their own powers. The national legislature will be the first to perceive and will be most sensible to the necessity of amendments. . . . (Farrand, II, 558) 558)

Madison joined in the attack, raising prophetic questions about the role and operation of the amending convention. He "remarked on the vagueness of the terms, 'call a convention for the purpose,' as sufficient reason for reconsidering the article. How was a convention to be formed? by what rule decide? what force of its acts?" (Farrand, II, 558). He then proposed the dual amendment plan which, with some modifications in wording and the addition of two provisos, became Article V. In *The Federalist*, # 43, Madison looked at the language on amendments and found it good:

> It guards equally against that extreme facility, which would render the Constitution too mutable; and that extreme difficulty, which might perpetuate its discovered faults. It, moreover, equally enables the general and the state governments to originate the amendment of errors, as they may be pointed out by the experience of one side, or the other.

Experience with Congressional Monopoly

Madison's favorable appraisal of Article V has been generally supported by subsequent experience. The amending process has proved to be neither too easy nor too hard, given a real consensus. Excluding the first ten amendments, which must be regarded as really part of the original Constitution, amendments have been adopted at the rate of less than one per decade. Following the Civil War amendments, there was a period of more than forty years during which the Constitution appeared unamendable. This was an era of agrarian discontent, industrial unrest, and growing interest in political and economic reforms. The conservatism of the Supreme Court—symbolized by its invalidation of the income tax in 1895—made constitutional amendment seem a necessary step toward achieving liberal legislative goals.

Under these circumstances, there was much talk about the necessity of easing the amendment process. In 1913, however, the long liberal campaign for the income tax and direct election of senators succeeded with adoption of the sixteenth and seventeenth amendments respectively. Adoption of the eighteenth amendment in 1919 revealed the possibility of a small but dedicated pressure group exploiting the amending machinery successfully. The women's suffrage amendment (nineteenth amendment) came in 1920. With six amendments added to the Constitution between 1913 and 1933, the amending process no longer seemed so formidable. Moreover, the liberalization of the Supreme Court's views by President Franklin D. Roosevelt's appointees substantially eliminated liberal interest in further amendments.

After the nineteen-thirties, pressure for amendments came principally from conservative political quarters. The increase in executive power and congressional expenditures, the federal government's acceptance of new welfare functions domestically and new responsibilities internationally, the reduced role of the states, and liberal tendencies on the Supreme Court stimulated conservative recourse to the amendment process. During the nineteen-fifties, the Bricker amendment to limit the federal government's power to enter into international agreements and a proposal to place a ceiling on federal income taxation were conservative measures that failed of adoption. In the nineteen-sixties, efforts to override the Supreme Court's decisions on one-person, one-vote and Bible reading in the public schools were defeated. The nineteen-seventies saw an organized effort to reverse the Court's abortion decision. Thus far, the only amendment secured by conservative forces was the twenty-second, limiting the president to two terms. In contrast, the four amendments adopted since 1961 have had a generally liberal character; three of the four extended the franchise. However, the probable defeat of the equal rights and District of Columbia amendments suggests that the era of liberal amendments may be over and the temper of the country more favorable for conservative amendments.

Problems with Amendment by Convention

There can be no question that over the years the great weight of informed opinion in the United States has opposed the use of Article V conventions. Much opposition, of course, is *ad hoc*, engendered by dislike of the purpose of the particular amendments proposed. But there are more principled objections to amendment by convention.

First, there are the practical types of queries that occurred to Madison in 1787, when he asked: "How was a convention to be formed? by what rule decide? what force of its acts?" No convention has been held since 1787, and after two hundred years that experience has little relevance. Many questions can be raised concerning the organization and powers of a constitutional convention. Here are some of them:

1. How is the validity of applications from the states to be determined?
2. How specific must the state legislatures be in asking for amendments?
3. Must all the applications be in identical language?
4. Within what time period must the required number of applications be received?
5. Can Congress refuse to call a convention on demand of two-thirds of the states, and if it does, can it be compelled to act by the courts?
6. Who are the delegates, and how are they to be chosen?
7. Can the convention act by simple majority vote, or will a two-thirds majority be required, as in Congress, for proposing an amendment?
8. How is the convention to be financed, and where does it meet?
9. May the convention propose more than one amendment?
10. Is there a time limit on the proceedings, or can the convention act as a continuing body?
11. Can controversies between Congress and the convention over its powers be decided by the courts?

An even more serious case against the Article V convention invokes the specter of "Pandora's box." A parade of horribles—which some contend are imaginary and others insist are very real—has featured arguments against a convention. The possibility of a "runaway" convention is supported by the experience of the 1787 Convention, which had been authorized by Congress to meet for the "sole and express purpose of revising the Articles of Confederation." The convention promptly ignored these instructions and proceeded to draft an entirely new Constitution based on a fundamentally different principle of union. Could not this happen again? Could not a convention claim to be a truer representative of the popular will than Congress, superior in authority, and justified in defying any restrictions placed upon it by Congress? Could it not proceed to redraft the Constitution, repeal provisions of the Bill of Rights, reverse unpopular Supreme Court decisions, and generally remake the constitutional system in its own image?

Convention proponents dismiss such concerns as hypothetical hobgoblins. They contend that, in the unlikely event of a runaway convention, three-fourths of the states would never ratify its proposals.

The dangers can be overdrawn, but the contents of Pandora's box have been frightening, not only to liberals worried about the Bill of Rights, but also to some conservatives favorable to the budget-balancing principle. Senator Barry Goldwater wants a budget-balancing amendment, but not by the convention route. In the Senate on February 26, 1979, he said he was "totally opposed" to a convention. It might run wild, he warned, adding, "We may wind up with a Constitution so far different from that we have lived under for two hundred years that the republic might not be able to continue." Though Howard Jarvis later succumbed to pressure to support a convention, his initial reaction was strongly and characteristically against opening up the Constitution to "weirdos" who might write their own "screwball" version of the document.

Preventing a Runaway Convention

It does seem altogether possible, given the current political temper of the country, that a convention called to draft a budget-balancing amendment might go further afield. Is there any way to guard against this possibility?

Former Attorney General Griffin Bell has said that he "absolutely" believes that Congress can set limits on what kind of amendments a convention can propose. The same position has been taken by former Senator Sam Ervin, by Senator Jesse Helms, and generally by those favoring the convention approach. Legislation for the purpose of exercising such control has been before Congress since 1967. At that time it appeared that Senator Everett Dirksen might succeed in securing the required applications from thirty-four state legislatures for a convention to repeal the Supreme Court's legislative apportionment decision. Senator Ervin, who supported Dirksen's effort, recognized the widespread fears of an uncontrolled convention and sought to allay them by drafting a Federal Constitutional Convention Procedures Act (S. 2307, 90th Cong.). The Senate failed to take action when the Dirksen threat faded. But in 1971 another convention proposal surfaced, as some nine state legislatures petitioned for a convention to propose a revenue-sharing amendment. This time Ervin's bill, after some amendments to make it more acceptable to liberal senators, passed the Senate by a vote of 84–0 on October 19, 1971 (S. 215, 92nd Cong.), but the House took no action.

In 1977, an almost identical bill was proposed, sponsored in the Senate by Helms, Goldwater (in spite of his opposition to conventions), and Senator Richard Schweiker, and in the House by Henry J. Hyde, Republican from Illinois (S. 1880 and H.R. 7008, 95th Cong.). The sponsors were advocates of a constitutional amendment outlawing abortion, and again the purpose was to quiet various objections that had been lodged against the convention device. The bills had not, by March, 1979, emerged from the judiciary committees of either house.

These bills have been drafted on the assumption that Congress does in fact have power to control and specify the powers and procedures of an Article V convention. If that is true, then the Ervin-Helms bills, if adopted, would dispose of many of the concerns about runaway conventions. The principal provisions of the bills are:

1. State legislatures can call for a convention for the purpose of proposing "one or more" amendments to the Constitution.
2. Legislative adoption of resolutions calling for a convention are to follow the regular state legislative rules of procedure, except that the governor's approval is not required.
3. Applications for a convention are to remain effective for seven calendar years, but rescission would be possible up to the time that two-thirds of the state legislatures had presented valid application.
4. When applications from two-thirds of the state legislatures have been received, the two houses of Congress must by concurrent resolution designate the time and place of the meeting and "set forth the nature of the amendment or amendments for the consideration of which the convention is called." The convention must meet within one year.
5. Each state is to have as many delegates as it is entitled to senators and representatives in Congress. Two delegates are to be elected at large and one from each congressional district "in the manner provided by law." Vacancies are to be filled by the governor. Delegates are to have the same immunities as members of Congress, and the concurrent resolution shall provide for their compensation and all other expenses of the convention.
6. The convention is to be convened by the vice-president of the United States and would then proceed to elect permanent officers.
7. Each delegate is to have one vote. In Ervin's original bill, the vote was by states as in the convention, each state having one vote.
8. Amendments are to be proposed by "a majority of the total number of delegates to the convention." This is the only substantial point on which the 1971 Ervin and the 1977 Helms drafts differ. While

the Ervin bill originally provided for majority vote, it was amended on the floor of the Senate to require a two-thirds majority. The Helms bill goes back to a simple majority.

9. Three provisions undertake specifically to guarantee against runaway conventions. Section 8(a) requires each delegate to take an oath "to refrain from proposing or casting his vote in favor of any proposed amendment . . . relating to any subject which is not named or described in the concurrent resolution of the Congress by which the convention was called."

10. Then Section 10(b) provides that "no convention called under this Act may propose any amendment or amendments of a nature different from that stated in the concurrent resolution calling the convention." Finally, Section 11(b)(1) permits Congress to disapprove the submission of any proposed amendment to the states if "such proposed amendment relates to or includes a subject which differs from or was not included among the subjects named or described in the concurrent resolution . . . by which the convention was called," or because the procedures followed by the convention were not in conformity with this act.

11. As required by the Constitution, ratification is by vote of three-fourths of the states. Congress retains its Article V right to direct whether ratification shall be by state convention or state legislative action. State legislatures shall adopt their own "rules of procedure" in voting on ratification, which must be completed within seven years of submission of the amendment to the states. A state may rescind its ratification prior to ratification by three-fourths of the states.

12. To avoid the possibility of judicial review of any issues raised by the convening of a convention or the exercise of powers by that body, the bills provide that any questions concerning the adoption of state resolutions calling for a convention shall be determined by Congress, "and its decisions thereon shall be binding on all others, including state and federal courts" (Section 3[b]). Likewise, questions whether proposed amendments are of a nature differing from that stated in the concurrent resolution "shall be determined solely by the Congress of the United States, and its decisions shall be binding on all others, including state and federal courts" (Section 10[b]).

The intention of the Ervin-Helms bills is to settle in advance any question as to the organization and powers of an Article V convention and to guarantee against a runaway body. When the Ervin bill was before the Senate in 1971, it won praise from different quarters of the political spectrum. *The New Republic* said: "Ervin's bill is sound insurance against a runaway rewrite job by latter-day founding fathers. Congress should adopt it." The columnist James J. Kilpatrick wrote: "This is a wise and prudent bill."

For whatever a measure of this sort may prove to be worth, it can do no harm. The only significant point in controversy would seem to be whether action of a convention should be by simple or two-thirds majorities. Even the most adamant opponents of constitutional amendment by convention might well regard such legislation as insurance against a future disaster.

But Will It Work?

The premise that Congress can control a convention and prevent any wayward tendencies assumes that Congress has the will to enforce limits such as those imposed by the Ervin bill. But is that necessarily so? Suppose that a convention, called to write a budget-balancing amendment, goes on to draft amendments providing criminal punishment for abortions, forbidding busing to remedy *de jure* or *de facto* racial segregation, authorizing Bible reading in public schools, or abolishing the exclusionary rule in the federal courts—all purposes that a congressional majority might approve. In this situation, Congress might have no interest in enforcing the Ervin statutory limits. The oaths which the bill requires of convention members are probably not legally enforceable, and the legislation makes all congressional decisions pertaining to disputes with the conventions final and not subject to appeal to the courts. In any case, ever since 1939, the Supreme Court has taken the position that the amending process is, in its entirety, a political issue in which the courts will not intervene.

Even if Congress had the desire and the courage to lasso a runaway convention, what would be the effect? Suppose a convention, called to act on budget-balancing, also proposed an abortion amendment, which Congress then refused to submit to the states because it was unauthorized by the concurrent resolution. The abortion amendment would be killed, but at what cost? Paul J. Mishkin, who proposes this scenario (*Newsweek*, March 5, 1979), suggests that supporters of the abortion amendment would see the congressional action as a subterfuge, "a betrayal of trust by their opponents, Congress, and 'the system.'" He concludes that "the convention route will inevitably precipitate issues that will strain the network of trust on which a free democratic society depends."

Laurence H. Tribe, the Harvard law professor and author of the book *American Constitutional Law*, also stresses the dangers of a confrontation between Congress and a convention, whether "by treating some applications as invalid, or by withholding appropriations until the convention adopted certain internal reforms, or by refusing to treat certain amendments as within the convention's scope. As a result of any of these decisions, the nation might well be subjected to the spectacle of a struggle between Congress and a convention it refused to recognize— a struggle that would extend from the convention's own claim of legitimacy to disputes over the legitimacy of proposed amendments."

Already there is disagreement over how many valid applications have been filed with Congress for the budget-balancing convention, though Senator Birch Bayh says that, considering the climate of the country, "I for one am not going to look at the crosses on the t's and the dots on the i's."

Tribe also sees the possibility of the Supreme Court's involvement in disputes between Congress and the convention or the states. Some of the requirements of the Ervin bill might be challenged as unconstitutional interference with the internal procedures of an Article V convention. According to Tribe, even if the Court declined to intervene on the ground that the issues were political and nonjusticiable, "a decision to abstain would amount to a judgment for one side or the other . . . and leave the Court an enemy either of Congress or of the convention and the states that brought it into being."

Election of Delegates

One of the most frightening aspects of a constitutional convention, which has been little discussed, concerns the election of delegates and the character of the election campaigns. The Ervin bill says simply that the delegates shall be elected "in the manner provided by state law." Conceivably states might set up some special method for nonpartisan election of delegates. But much more probably the regular election laws would be used, with nominations by party primaries or petitions, and general election contests between two major party candidates and perhaps others from minor parties.

The possibilities of the nation tearing itself apart in such election free-for-all contests are mindboggling. A normal partisan election campaign is structured to some extent by party loyalties and allegiances, incumbencies, and voting patterns, the issues often being subordinated to candidates' personalities. But in an election for delegates to a constitutional convention, with no incumbents, and with issues paramount, the pressure of interest groups on candidates would be crushing. Every big or little pressure group would want commitments from candidates, and they in turn would seek votes by embracing as many causes as possible. It is inconceivable that candidates would campaign simply on the degree of their commitment to a balanced budget, or that they would be permitted to avoid discussing other issues. It is inconceivable that they would not be asked to take stands on abortion, gun control, busing, regulation of religious cults, exemption of religious schools from state educational regulations, coddling of criminals, or any other currently controversial public issue. Positions taken on these extraneous problems might well determine which delegates were elected; and delegates who had won election on these issues would be expected to carry them onto the convention floor, making it unlikely that the convention could be confined to its assigned subject.

The Folly of a Budget-Balancing Amendment

There is too much chance that a constitutional convention would be, in Justice Potter Stewart's vivid phrase, "a loose cannon." Calling a convention for budget balancing or any other purpose is playing Russian roulette with the Constitution. If an amendment requiring budget balancing is desirable and wise public policy, it should be drafted and proposed by Congress in the manner by which the previous twenty-six amendments have been added to the Constitution.

But should budget balancing be in the Constitution at all? This is not the place, nor am I the one to discuss the economic arguments for and against budget balancing. But as a political scientist and a former student of public administration, I can raise questions about the practical implementation of a public policy; and I suggest that a budget-balancing amendment would be unenforceable. There is no possibility of framing an amendment that would be able to control expenditures in the real world of national finance.

Budgets are forecasts. Even if they are in hypothetical balance at the beginning of a fiscal year, they can be thrown out of balance by unanticipated developments—a defense emergency, a depression (a one-per-cent rise in unemployment costs twenty billion dollars), a natural calamity, an oil embargo. There are no feasible sanctions to enforce budget balancing. A deficit cannot be made up out of the president's salary. Presumably the amendment would direct Congress to raise taxes or reduce expenditures when a deficit threatened, but the members of the Ways and Means and Appropriations committees cannot be man-damused or put in jail.

The fact is that the drafters of a budget-balancing constitutional amendment would face an impossible task and find themselves on the horns of an inescapable dilemma. Either the amendment will require a balanced budget with no ifs, ands, buts, or escape clauses, in which case it will be as futile as King Canute and as unenforceable as the eighteenth amendment. Or it will be supplied with enough escape clauses so that it becomes nothing but a moral preachment to Congress.

Even if it were possible to draft a practical budget-balancing amendment, its inclusion would be a violation of the spirit and purpose of the American Constitution. Fiscal policy has no place in the fundamental law of the republic. State legislators and others who are familiar with state constitutions, some of which run to almost one hundred thousand words, are incredibly detailed, and are amended at every election, may not see an issue here. But the strength of the Constitution and the foundation for much of its mystique has been that it was limited to fundamentals—government structure, governmental powers and their limitations, and individual rights. Loading the Constitution with policy preferences cheapens the document and freezes policies where alternatives should remain available.

As Tribe points out, "Slavery is the only economic arrangement our Constitution has ever specifically endorsed, and prohibition the only social policy it has ever expressly sought to implement." Madison said that the purpose of amendments should be to correct the "discovered faults" and "errors" in the Constitution. The only two amendments that did not have this purpose were the eighteenth and the twenty-first.

The Hidden Case for the Convention

It is well to recognize that reasoned arguments against a convention will not necessarily relate to the motivation of many convention advocates. Many proponents admit, more or less frankly, that they do not really expect or even want a constitutional convention. For them, the campaign is simply a way to force Congress to pay attention to the problem of budget deficits and to draft its own constitutional amendment. It is a ploy, a two-by-four to hit the congressional mule over the nose. This is not true of Governor Jerry Brown of California, however. His strategy appears to go well beyond this limited purpose, or even 1980. James Reston, following an interview with Brown, reported that "his call for a constitutional convention to compel a balanced budget is only one means of changing the political dialogue," and is somehow connected with the exploration of outer space in the twenty-first century.

Again, there are those who back a convention as a way of expressing their distrust for Congress and, indeed, their alienation from the entire political system. For many, budget balancing has become a code word to express resentment against the spenders, the bureaucrats, the government regulators, the welfare cheats. They are fed up and they aren't going to take it any more. Any stick to beat a dog.

The American Constitution is, in a sense, the victim of its own success. Veneration of the Constitution has resulted in an "amendment mania." Constitutional amendments are attractive to reformers and propagandists of all persuasions who want to give their cause status and glamour and place it beyond the reach of legislative challenge or later change of national mind.

A constitutional amendment is sought by the budget balancers because they want to invoke the prestige and the finality of constitutional language. But the surest way to drain the Constitution of its prestige and its finality is to make it a hostage in quarrels over explosive social issues. Peter McGrath's warning in a *New Republic* article in 1976 is eloquent and timely:

> Illegitimacy is one thing that a constitution can never risk, for it is the main agent of legitimacy for substantive policy decisions. This is why it is unwise for us to force our Constitution too far into the bitter controversies of the moment, such as those over busing and abortion. Each time we do so, we demystify it a little, which even in this secular age is not necessarily a good thing. The Constitution is an organism, and when you kick it, it kicks back, as Richard Nixon found out to his sorrow and surprise. But like any living thing, it can be worn down, burdened with work it was never made for.

Austin Ranney

37. What Constitutional Changes Do Americans Want? (1984)

Austin Ranney taught at Yale, Wisconsin and the University of California, Berkeley, before assuming his present position as senior fellow at the American Enterprise Institute in Washington. He has written several books on American and British politics.

Although some forums looked seriously at the heritage of American independence, many of the activities inspired by the 1976 bicentenary of the American Revolution fitted Webster's definition of "celebrations": they "held up for public acclaim" and "demonstrated satisfaction by festivities." There were no conferences, articles, or books asking whether American independence has been a good thing, or whether it fits the conditions of the twentieth century, or whether we should rejoin the British crown.

In sharp contrast, many of the activities now being generated by the approaching bicentenary of the Constitution are cerebrations. Scholarly undertakings, such as Project '87 and the American Enterprise Institute's study of the Constitution, are holding conferences and producing books and articles (such as this) asking how and why the constitutional system of today differs from the system designed in 1787. In addition, a number of more activist groups, such as the Committee on the Constitutional System co-chaired by Lloyd Cutler and Douglas Dillon, are considering what changes need to be made in the Constitution to make it better able to cope with today's problems. And at least eleven proposals for

Reprinted from *This Constitution: A Bicentennial Chronicle*, Winter, 1984, published by Project '87 of the American Historical Association and the American Political Science Association.

amending the Constitution, ranging from equal rights for women to a mandatory balanced federal budget, are now at various levels on the nation's agenda. Indeed, the balanced budget amendment needs the support of only two more state legislatures to require Congress to call the first national constitutional convention since 1787. Accordingly, while we may commit some sins in observing the Constitution's bicentenary, they are not likely to include smugness or mindlessness.

Most of the current cerebrations focus on what constitutional changes *should* be made, and pay little or no heed to how much popular support particular proposals are likely to attract. Such a focus seems entirely appropriate for scholars who wish only to describe, analyze, and explain the existing constitutional system. But scholars and other citizens who wish to *change* their system cannot escape considerations of how much popular support their proposals have now and how much more can be mobilized. This article is intended to be a modest contribution to discussions of constitutional change by reviewing some relevant data from public opinion polls; for, with all the perils of biased questions, skewed answers, and misleading interpretations that bedevil the polls, they still provide the best evidence we have on how our mass publics feel about proposals for changes in the Constitution.

A first glance at the poll data quickly shows that survey respondents are receptive to some proposals for constitutional change, divided on others, and resistant to still others. Hence it seems useful to proceed by identifying the main types of current proposals and seeing what the polls reveal about the level of popular support for each.

Proposals to Institute Substantive Policies

Some of the most prominent current proposals for constitutional amendments do not seek fundamental changes in the structure of government or the processes by which public policy is made. Rather, they attempt to change certain policies made by the president, the Congress, and/or the courts; or they seek to institute policies that those policymakers are unwilling to adopt. Until recently the equal rights amendment received far more attention than any other in this category, and the polls have shown consistently that about two-thirds of the public approve the amendment. However, after its passage by Congress in 1972, its proponents were unable to persuade the legislature of three-fourths of the states to ratify it, falling short by three states. Since the most recent ratification deadline expired in 1982, one effort to get Congress to re-propose it has failed, and it has recently received less attention from the national news media.

It has been replaced on center stage by the balanced budget amendment. By July of 1984, the legislatures of thirty-two states—just two fewer than the two-thirds required by the Constitution—have submitted petitions to Congress requesting that a constitutional convention be held to propose an amendment requiring the federal government to adopt balanced budgets except in times of national emergencies. It is too early to say whether two more states will join the petitioners, or whether the courts will regard the petitions already submitted as binding on Congress (many of them differ from the others in one respect or another), or whether Congress will respond by calling a convention or by submitting its own amendment to the states, or whether thirty-eight states would ratify such an amendment however proposed. Be that as it may, it is clear that the general idea has strong public support: for example, a 1983 Gallup poll showed 71 percent in favor and only 21 percent opposed, and other polls have produced similar results.

Another amendment in this category that has aroused strong passions is the proposal, which has a number of variants, to reverse a Supreme Court ruling by allowing states to hold organized prayers, on public school property during school hours, for children attending public schools. (Perhaps we should note in passing that Herbert Stein, the well-known economist, has proposed that the two amendments be consolidated into one providing that all school children be required to pray for a balanced budget.) This general idea also has strong public support: an NBC/AP poll in 1982 showed 72 percent in favor of "allowing organized prayers in public schools" and 28 percent opposed. However, in 1984 a proposed amendment to that end received the support of only 56 senators, 11 short of the necessary two-thirds majority, and for the moment the proposal is dormant (as is a related proposal to allow "silent prayers" during school hours).

Another well-publicized amendment intended to reverse a Supreme Court decision is one that would prohibit, or allow the states to prohibit, abortions except when necessary to save the mother's life. This is the only one of the amendments strongly supported by conservative and Moral Majority leaders that is opposed by the general public: a Louis Harris poll in 1982 showed 33 percent in favor and 61 percent opposed. Moreover, perhaps in keeping with this sentiment, an amendment recommended by the Senate Judiciary Committee in 1984 failed to win the necessary two-thirds majority from the whole chamber.

Proposals to Increase Direct Popular Control of Government

In their capacity as scholars if not citizens, most historians, political scientists, and legal scholars are likely to be more interested in the pending proposals to change one aspect or another of the Constitution's decision-making processes. One group includes proposals that seek to increase direct popular control of the national government in various ways. One of the most familiar items in this category is the perennial proposal to abolish the electoral college and institute direct popular election of the president. A 1981 Louis Harris poll showed 77 percent in favor of such an amendment and 21 percent opposed. Yet when such a proposal, strongly backed by President Jimmy Carter, was voted on by the Senate in 1979, it was supported by only 51 senators—well short of the number needed to submit it to the states.

A number of amendments are also being proposed to "democratize" the presidential nominating process, although none has yet gotten past the committee stage in Congress. Several proposed amendments would replace the present gaggle of state presidential primaries, caucuses, and conventions with a series of regional primaries. A recent Gallup poll reported 66 percent in favor of such a change and 24 percent opposed. Another proposal would go even farther by mandating that both parties choose their presidential nominees in one-day national primaries. This proposal has received less attention recently, but a 1980 Gallup poll showed 66 percent in favor and 24 percent opposed.

Perhaps the most radical of the "democratizing" amendments is one proposed by former Senator James Abourezk and Representatives Guy Vander Jagt and James Jones in 1977 to establish legislation by popular initiative on the national level comparable to the systems now operating in many of the states. Their amendment failed to get out of committee in either chamber, but a Gallup poll at the time showed 57 percent in favor and 21 percent opposed.

One other proposal that might be placed in this category is the amendment to give the District of Columbia two senators and at least one representative, all with full voting rights, in Congress. This proposal received the necessary two-thirds approval by both houses of Congress in 1978, but by July 1984 it had been ratified by only sixteen states; it requires twenty-two more by the end of August 1985. I have been unable to find a national public poll on the proposal, but the leaders of the "D.C. voting right" movement have apparently given up on it and have shifted their efforts to getting the District admitted to the union as a full-fledged state.

Proposals to Make Government Less Political and/or More Efficient

While not uninterested in many of the proposals for constitutional change in the first two categories, scholars have generally conferred, lectured, and written considerably more about proposals in a third category—those that seek, in one way or another, to overcome the fragmentation of power, internal antagonisms, and weakness of leadership they see in our constitutional structure so as to make it capable of developing, adopting, and implementing truly coherent and consistent policies. These proposals, in turn, can be divided into four main subgroups:

1. *By limiting tenure in office.* A number of people believe that one of the worst aspects of our present constitutional system is the fact that the terms of some or all of our national elected officials are so short that they are forced to spend most of their time and energies in office on running for reelection and thus have too little time to develop and work for long-range programs. Accordingly, one much-discussed proposal, advocated by former President Jimmy Carter, among others, would change the president's term of office from four years to six and make him ineligible for reelection. The public, however, is apparently torn between the desire to have a president "above politics" and the desire to have a president they can turn out of office in less than six years, if they do not like him: a Gallup poll showed 49 percent in favor of the single six-year term and 47 percent opposed.

They are less divided about proposals for limiting the terms of members of Congress: a 1982 Gallup poll showed 61 percent in favor and 32 percent opposed to an amendment to limit both representatives and senators to a total of twelve years in office.

2. *By giving the president an item-veto over appropriations.* Despite the reformed congressional budgetary process adopted in the mid-1970s, the polls show that most people blame Congress more than the president for the soaring expenditures and deficits of recent years. It is therefore not surprising that a proposed amendment to give the president the power to veto individual items in appropriations bills—a power now enjoyed by the governors of forty-four states—was shown by a 1983 Gallup poll to be approved by 67 percent and opposed by 25 percent.

3. *By bridging the separation of powers.* A number of eminent reformers believe that the greatest deficiency in our constitutional system is the separation of powers between the president and Congress and the consequent endemic discord in their dealings with each other. Few reformers propose to remedy this congenital incapacity by the root-and-branch substitution of a British-style parliamentary system, but many advocate the construction of a series of bridges between the two branches comparable to those in Westminster. For example, some urge that cabinet members be given seats and voices in Congress. Others propose that the president be required by choose cabinet members

from among members of Congress and call a new election whenever necessary to break a deadlock.

It would be illuminating to know how ordinary Americans feel about the specific proposals and about the general idea of substituting British-style concentration of powers for our traditional separation of powers. Unfortunately, I am unable to find recent polls that bear directly on these questions, but perhaps public attitudes on the fourth sub-group of proposals can cast at least some indirect light on whether Americans want a more coherent and disciplined constitutional system.

4. *By establishing responsible party government.* Ever since the 1870s a succession of distinguished American writers—Woodrow Wilson, Frank Goodnow, E. E. Schattschneider, David Broder, and James MacGregor Burns, among others—have argued that America badly needs a more effective and responsible governing system, one that is capable of developing and carrying out coherent programs of public policy and accepting the responsibility for the programs' consequences. Most of them have agreed that formally replacing our presidential system with some version of the Westminster model is not only politically impossible but institutionally unnecessary. They say that we can get the same results much more easily by developing outside the written Constitution a system of "responsible party government." That system has three basic requirements. First, after each election one party must be in control of both the presidency and the Congress. Second, all the majority party's members in both branches must act together cohesively on all policy matters. And third, at each election the governing party must be held fully responsible, *as a party* and not as a collection of independent officeholders, for how well or badly the party has exercised its stewardship. With such responsible parties, these writers say, we can achieve truly coherent and democratic government without changing a word of the written Constitution.

How do the American people feel about responsible party government? I have been able to find only one piece of direct evidence from the public opinion polls, and the circumstances in which the questions were asked are worth recalling. As the 1976 election approached, the United States had had divided party control of the national government (a president of one party and a Congress controlled by the other) for sixteen of the thirty years since World War II. The Louis Harris organization wanted to know whether the public thought that, aside from the individual merits of Gerald Ford and Jimmy Carter, it would be good to have both the presidency and the Congress controlled by the same party. So they asked their respondents a question bearing directly upon the first condition of responsible party government—one-party control:

In general, do you think it is better for the country to have Congress under the control of one party and the White House under the control of another party, so that there is a way for each to keep the other under control, or do you think it is better to have the Congress and the White House under the control of the same political party, so that the business of the federal government can be done more effectively?

They asked the question in August and again in November after the election. On both occasions the respondents divided almost evenly:

	August	November
Favor divided control	40%	39%
Favor same-party control	38	45
Not sure	22	16

Harris reported that those who preferred same-party control gave as reasons, "Real problems of the country will be neglected in the stalemate that takes place between the White House and Congress"; and "real reforms to make the federal government more efficient won't be enacted." Respondents favoring divided control commented, "It's a good way to be sure that one party can't get away with corruption and misuse of power in office"; and "the growth of big government and big federal spending can be prevented better."

The voters' choices in national elections since World War II provide additional evidence. From 1946 to 1982 there were a total of nineteen congressional elections and therefore nineteen opportunities to choose Congresses controlled by the president's party. Only nine produced same-party control of both houses of Congress and the White House. So it seems that divided party control, not same-party control, has been the more normal situation in American government.

This state of affairs is possible, of course, only if a good many voters regularly split their tickets, and that is just what they have done. Survey evidence shows that in the 1960 election only 35 percent of the voters voted split tickets, but in 1964 the proportion rose to 57 percent, in 1968 it was 66 percent, and in 1972 it was 67 percent. I estimate that the level remained at about two-thirds in the 1976 and 1980 presidential elections. Evidently, then, achieving same-party control of the national government's three elective agencies is not highly valued by well over half of the American electorate.

Conclusion

Neither the polling nor the voting data provide conclusive evidence about what kinds of constitutional change Americans want, but the survey answers are suggestive. For example, it is clear that survey respondents are considerably more receptive than members of Congress to constitutional change. We have reviewed eleven proposed constitutional amendments that have recently been introduced in Congress. Substantial majorities of the general public have favored nine of the eleven (ERA, balanced budgets, school prayers, direct election of presidents, regional presidential primaries, a national presidential primary, national initiative, limiting terms of senators and representatives, and presidential item veto). Popular majorities have rejected only one proposal (outlawing abortions), and respondents were evenly divided on another (a single six-year presidential term). By contrast, Congress has sent only one of these proposals (ERA) to the states for ratification; it has given two others less than the necessary two-thirds majorities; and it has taken no action on the others. On this showing, then, there is considerably more resistance to constitutional change in the Congress than in the general public.

Be that as it may, is there any common theme underlying the changes survey respondents favor and reject? I believe there is. They approve proposals to require a balanced federal budget and to give the president the power to veto individual items in appropriations bills, both of which are intended to restrain federal spending. They approve leaving it up to each state and locality to decide for itself whether it wishes to have school prayers. They *dis*approve a federally-imposed ban on abortions, evidently preferring to leave the matter to private decision.

They also approve a number of proposals to give the people more direct power over national public officials, by direct nomination and election of the president, by limiting congressmen's tenure in office, and by giving the people the power to bypass Congress and legislate by popular initiative.

These proposals are all intended to limit the reach and power of the national government in one way or another. It should not surprise us that survey respondents favor them, for they are entirely in keeping with what the polls have been telling us is the prevailing popular mood since the late 1960s. It remains to be seen whether that mood will persist and, if so, whether it will become strong enough to overcome the continuing reluctance of Congress to make very many or very drastic constitutional changes of any kind. And that, in turn, will determine whether the United States will celebrate the bicentenary of the Philadelphia convention mainly by celebrating and cerebrating about the Constitution or by changing it.

A. E. Dick Howard

38. When States Amend Their Constitutions (1974)

A. E. Dick Howard, who has taught constitutional law at the University of Virginia since 1964, was executive director of the Virginia Commission on Constitutional Revision, which led the drive that produced a new constitution for the commonwealth in 1970. This article, which summarizes that experience and compares it with that in other states, appeared originally in the University of Richmond Law Review.

"The earth belongs always to the living generation." So said Thomas Jefferson in developing a constitutional theory which included the belief that Virginia's constitution should be revised at regular intervals "so that it may be handed on, with periodical repairs, from generation to generation. . . ."

Despite such advice, some generations of Americans have shown more interest than others in revising their state constitutions. For about a quarter of a century—from the 1920's into the 1940's—no American state adopted a new constitution. By midcentury, however, interest in revising these fundamental laws had burgeoned. So widespread was the movement for constitutional revision that by 1970 a leading student of the subject commented that there was at that time "more official effort directed toward revising and rewriting state constitutions than at any time in the nation's history, with the possible exception of the Civil War and Reconstruction era."

Some of these revision efforts were notably successful, for example, the rewriting of the Hawaii constitution which was approved by the people of the state in November, 1968. Other revisions ended in failure, perhaps the most conspicious instances being those of New York in 1967 and Maryland in 1968. Indeed, in modern times, many states have

Reprinted by author's permission from the *University of Richmond Law Review,* 1974.

found it more difficult to secure popular approval of a revised constitution. When Virginians went to the polls in November 1970 to vote on a new constitution for the commonwealth, those who hoped the result would be favorable had before them the unfortunate experience of a number of sister states. Although some states had succeeded in at least partial revision, since 1967 the voters of New York, Rhode Island, Maryland, New Mexico, Oregon, Arkansas and Idaho had rejected proposed new charters for their states. Yet when Virginia voted on four questions comprising a revised constitution, each one passed, and by percentages ranging from a low of 63% to a high (on the main body of the constitution) of 72%. . . .

That Virginia's voters would approve a new constitution was not a foregone conclusion. Defeats of new constitutions in other states— perhaps the most publicized being that in Maryland in 1968—would make one cautious about predicting the success of any constitutional revision. That major political and civic leaders had endorsed Virginia's new constitution was no guarantee; the backing of a "who's who" of such leaders in Maryland had not saved the proposed Maryland constitution. The new Virginia charter was attacked on many of the same grounds, including regional government and governmental spending, which had been used in Maryland. One opposition pamphlet reminded its Virginia readers, "Marylanders have done it. . . . Virginians can do it too." Moreover, if Maryland's proposed constitution was hurt by extraneous events—notably the riots of April 1968 in Washington and Baltimore—Virginia's political climate in 1970 was hardly uneventful, especially when there was a U.S. Senate race without precedent, featuring Senator Byrd running as an independent against nominees of the two major political parties. And while enough private money was raised to run a respectable informational campaign, money was tight enough that some important items had to be cut—there was, for example, no television advertising in northern Virginia.

Despite the problems, the final vote was overwhelmingly "yes." A number of factors played a part in producing the highly successful outcome, and Virginia's experience may usefully be compared with that of other states to shed some light on reasons why constitutional revisions succeed or fail.

To begin with, how the groundwork for revision is laid, and by whom, is a significant factor. Constitutional revision in Virginia was, from start to finish, a highly deliberative process. Having the groundwork laid by a blue-ribbon study commission meant that when the general assembly met, the issues which it would debate had already been sharply defined by the commission's report and commentary. Conscientious preparation may seem a simple enough goal to achieve, yet in New

York and Rhode Island a lack of planning and issue-sharpening have been suggested as reasons for defeat of revised constitutions. The New York study commission lacked neither funding nor talent nor time, but it failed to produce sharply drawn issues and recommendations for the New York convention to focus on. Instead the New York commission provided large quantities of information and arguments on both sides of the issues, even when it had to strain to find arguments on one side and even when it had to avoid analysis in order to appear neutral. As a result the delegates were bewildered by the vast amount of information confronting them. The task of lobbyists for special interests—who were always ready to supply answers even if the commission was not—was thus made easier. In Rhode Island the convention got bogged down in discussion of trivial issues to the neglect of larger ones, and in both states, the poor image that resulted, in part from the lack of planning and organization, hurt the ratification effort. In addition, both conventions had an image of being dominated by politicians. Those who comprised the Virginia commission, on the other hand, were widely recognized as among the most talented, respected, and nonpartisan figures in the commonwealth. Their prestige helped to put the General Assembly in an affirmative and responsive frame of mind when the legislators received the commission's report.

There are two major methods by which states typically revise a constitution—by constitutional convention or by the state legislature. Either vehicle is usually preceded by a study commission. Whichever means, convention or legislature, is used, a keynote of the revision process must be political realism. One of the lessons to be gleaned from a study of constitutional revision among the states is that a new constitution can be killed by an overdose of partisan politics—partisanship that divides the revisors and voters alike. Equally a new constitution can be killed by too little politics—a process which, through an excess of idealism or naivete, can be insulated from political reality.

One of the simplest lessons the Virginia revisors learned was that it was dangerous to make unnecessary enemies. A proposed change should be weighed to be sure that the benefits to be derived sufficiently outweigh the cost in terms of alienation of those who may oppose the change. A change of largely theoretical value may not be worth the electoral price paid for making it. For example, many state constitutions contain unenforceable, hortatory language in their bills of rights. Reformers often scoff at such language and urge that it be removed. The reformers who comprised the Maryland convention did excise the hortatory language of Maryland's Declaration of Rights. Having done so, they found themselves saddled with the opposition charge that the rights of Marylanders were being taken away. It is hard to conclude that the change—of theoretical value at best (and even that can be argued)—was worth the cost.

Another rule often found in the textbooks is that only policymaking offices should be filled through popular election. Following this precept, the Maryland revisors stripped many of that state's constitutional officers, such as the clerks and the registrars of wills, of their constitutional status. It is doubtful that this step was worth the price of creating a vigorous and vocal source of opposition to the new Maryland charter in every courthouse in Maryland. Not only did the local officials oppose the constitution, but many citizens, in rural areas especially, considered it important that such officers be elected rather than appointed by other politicans.

Another costly move by the Maryland convention was the decision not to require that a local referendum be held before legislative creation of regional governments. There are valid policy reasons why regional government should not invariably be subject to local veto, but it is evident that the Maryland convention's decision badly hurt the revision effort in Baltimore County. The regional government provision made it easy for opponents to appeal to racial fears in the area around Baltimore city, and the resulting negative vote in the county has been termed by one demographic analyst to be a principal cause of the statewide rejection. Ordinarily these suburbanites could have been relied on to support the constitution, just as did those in the Washington suburban counties of Montgomery and Prince George's.

In Virginia, by contrast, the revisors retained the philosophical language of the Bill of Rights, they avoided any direct assault on the constitutional status of local officers such as sheriffs and clerks (though making it possible through local referendum to abolish or alter such offices), and, while recognizing the concept of regional government, they wrote in a requirement of referendum in the localities affected. As the *Washington Post* observed at the close of Virginia's 1969 legislative session, "The political realism so painfully missing in retrospect in Maryland a year ago and so prominent in Virginia's new effort gives the proposals a healthy chance of survival."

How are the prospects for success in constitutional revision affected by the form the revision process takes? Specifically, are there reasons to prefer a convention on the one hand, or legislative revision on the other? Having a prestigious study commission prepare a draft and then having the legislature refine the document in the perspective of their own understanding of the political process was one of the greatest strengths of the approach to revison in Verginia. But Virginia's experience may or may not be the best guide for other states.

Much has been written on the relative merits of having revisions undertaken by conventions or having legislatures tackle the job. Conventions are thought to be more representative of the people, are frequently composed of highly able, civic-minded citizens, are less political (because they are less highly structured than are legislatures), are more focused on the task of constitutional revision (because they are called into being for that specific task), and are likely to be more willing to make fundamental changes. On the other hand, they may be out of touch with political reality or may be dominated by ambitious politicians. Commissions, being smaller, may be able to work faster, and they may have more expert talent because they can be appointed from among the state's ablest citizens. Commissions are commonly more acceptable to legislatures than wide-open conventions, because their proposals can be vetoed by the legislature if it wishes. When the legislature, composed of politicians, has the final say, there is the risk, however, that the majority party will seek advantage for itself, or at least that the legislators as a body will try to gain advantage over other branches of government.

Generalization about the relative merits of conventions or legislatures as revisors is difficult, because an examination of the behavior of conventions and legislatures in a number of states indicates that the circumstances of the particular state are crucial. In Maryland, to be sure, the convention operated in a political vacuum, producing a document that took insufficient account of what the people or the interest groups would think of their work. Though they produced an excellent model constitution, they lacked that very closeness to the people which is considered one of the major advantages of using a convention. The same tendency was present in the Connecticut convention, but more realistic delegates managed to curb the reformers and achieve a reasonable document which the voters accepted.

In other state's conventions, there has been the danger of partisanship. In Michigan, though the convention began in a bipartisan spirit, it ended with the Republicans, who formed a majority of convention delegates, agreeing among themselves on a constitution and producing a straight partyline vote on the document. Though that document was approved, partisan conventions in New York and Rhode Island found the people repelled by their behavior. On the other hand, in such diverse states as Pennsylvania, New Jersey, and Hawaii, conventions have met in a bipartisan spirit, recognized the need to compromise in order to achieve success, and produced documents which satisfied the major interests in those states. Indeed, in Pennsylvania, though the Republicans controlled the convention, the Republican president insisted upon equal representation for Democrats on all convention committees. Strong, conciliatory leadership has been suggested as one reason compromise was possible in some of these states; conversely, weak leadership was a factor in producing a convention that bogged down in partisan wrongdoing. The representativeness of the delegates, their responsiveness to the constituency, and their willingness to compromise their own wishes and those of their parties in order to win others over to the revisions have also been factors in successful revision efforts by conventions in Missouri, Pennsylvania, and Hawaii. These revisions stand in contrast to the unrepresentative character and consequent unresponsiveness of the Maryland convention and the partisanship displayed by New York and Rhode Island delegates.

In Virginia the General Assembly proved that a legislature is not incapable of reform. It did not fall prey to the evils of partisanship. It put its understanding of the citizenry into the effort, deciding, after much debate, to eliminate the potentially divisive handicapped children and capital city boundary amendments, which could have provoked sectarian and racial feelings, respectively. The General Assembly approached its task with an understanding of the difference between constitution-making and ordinary legislating.

It seems, then, that given favorable conditions either a convention or a legislature can undertake a successful constitutional revision. Equally, given the wrong conditions, either can fail. As one observer has noted:

> With favorable prevailing winds and strong cooperative leadership, each structure appears capable of performing successfully in both the drafting and marketing stages. . . . Theoretical advantages, in brief, do not appear to have the political muscle that would make an extended comparative analysis of these structures very meaningful.

The comparative lessons to be learned from other states' revisions seem to lie not so much in the particular method chosen (though this can be crucial in a particular state) as in factors of leadership, both within the body that shapes the revision and in the state at large when the proposals are laid before the people.

Political realism and a spirit of bipartisanship are important in creating an atmosphere of consensus. The absence of emotionally charged issues in Virginia made possible a consensus of political leadership backing the new Constitution. This spectrum of support was a key factor in the document's success at the polls. Not within memory have political leaders of such divergent views—indeed, often the bitterest of enemies in the political arena—combined so cordially and publicly in a common political undertaking. The symbolism of the liberal, moderate, and conservative factions of both major parties uniting behind the revised Constitution could not be lost on anyone with even a passing understanding of Virginia's political scene. . . .

Factors like bipartisan and grass roots political support, the endorsement of major newspapers of such disparate philosophy as the *Washington Post* and the *Richmond Times-Dispatch*, and the deletion of disruptive controversial issues indicate that the compromises made by the Virginia constitution-makers were widely accepted. Proposed constitutions in some states have been defeated because of the opposition of important blocs of voters whose interests were not protected. Experiences of other states have shown that offending one of the major parties can hurt, and that local officeholders can have an important impact as well. Conservation groups (New Mexico), the Civil Liberties Union (New York), and civic leaders and newspapers alienated by the self-interest shown by legislative draftsmen (Rhode Island) have also been instrumental in the defeat of new constitutions. Of course, the political and economic interests of a state have much to do with who takes part in drafting a constitution, and the relative strengths of each no doubt have an effect on whether compromises are made.

An aggressive campaign for ratification was another important factor in the result in Virginia. An observer of the Maryland experience has noted that the campaign there tended to be intellectual and sober, not the sort of campaign likely to roll away the ennui with which most voters will regard a constitutional referendum. The Virginia proponents set out, like those in Hawaii, in the spirit that ignorance and apathy were likely in the end to be greater enemies than overt opposition. This was particularly a problem in Virginia because a commission and the legislature, rather than a more highly publicized convention, had drafted the document. An early start, organized along the lines of a statewide gubernatorial or senatorial campaign, and adequate (though by the standards of a statewide race for office, laughably modest) funding were components of the successful campaign in Virginia.

A catalyst of Virginia's referendum effort was the superb work of the local campaign committees. In some communities, one or more individuals were the spark plugs. In others, a local organization— oftentimes the League of Women Voters or the Jaycees—made the local campaign go. Some of the variation in votes from one community to another turned on predictable demographic characteristics, but in many cases a highly favorable vote in a community (especially in areas thought less receptive to innovation) was in good measure a function of an active local committee.

The Virginia campaign also succeeded in getting more usable information before the voters than is customary in a referendum effort. Not only was such a massive educational campaign probably without precedent in Virginia, a special effort was made throughout the campaign to translate the rather dry abstractions of constitutional revision into issues which touched the lives of individual citizens—education, environmental quality, consumer protection, and taxes. And there is reason to think that the central theme which evolved in the campaign—"Bring government closer to the people"—struck a responsive chord in citizens. In contrast, the Arkansas proponents never successfully translated the dry abstracted dealing with the structure of state and local government into terms the voters could understand. They never made the voters see that the new constitution would mean something to them personally. Observers have assigned this as a major reason for the defeat in that state.

The form of the ballot was unquestionably a factor in the outcome in Virginia. There is general agreement that putting a revised constitution on the ballot as a single question was a central factor in the defeat of both those proposed in New York and Maryland. One of the less well-known bits of political lore about former Vice-President Spiro Agnew is that, while still governor of Maryland, he told the Southern Governors' Conference in 1968 that the "principal difficulty" which brought about the defeat in Maryland was the submission of the revised constitution to the people on a "take it or leave it" basis. . . .

In Virginia, by contrast, the General Assembly sought to identify those questions—five of them as of the time of the 1969 session—which might be most controversial and to make it possible for the people to vote separately on them. This action meant that a voter would not have to vote against the entire Constitution if his disapproval was confined to one of the questions posed separately. Moreover, separating the questions on the ballot avoided the "take-it-or-leave-it" stigma and thus made it less likely that the voters would approach the revisions in general in a mood of distrust or apprehension.

Take-it-or-leave-it ballots have met with occasional success, as shown in Michigan, where voters approved a constitution submitted in that form in 1963. But the experience of New York, Maryland, and Rhode Island indicates that many citizens are likely to vote against an entire constitution when they dislike a particular provision, rather than vote for it because of the things they like. Not only in Virginia but also in Florida, Hawaii, Pennsylvania, and Connecticut, submission of more than one question led to adoption of most or all of the revisions.

Some observers have suggested that submission of a series of proposals rather than a single package tends to confuse the voters and leads to an incoherent constitution if some but not all of the proposals are adopted. If the number of proposals is very large, this argument may have merit, but when, as in Virginia, there are only four separate questions on the ballot, or, as in Connecticut, where only one controversial issue was separated (and defeated), the possibility of confusion does not appear great.

The road to constitutional revision is rarely without its perils. To some extent the lessons learned in one state are of value in another, yet every state has its own unique political climate which calls for a tailored approach. Revisors will want to consider the form which the revision process will take (convention or legislature), which changes are really worth fighting for, how the revision will appear on the ballot, how the state's leadership and political forces can be enlisted in seeking ratification, how a campaign should be organized to reach the grass roots level, how to combat the twin evils of voter apathy and opposition distortions, and how, when all is said and done, to ensure that a state's fundamental law is revised and presented in such a way that in reality it reflects the best aspirations of the state's citizenry.

A state constitution is more than a legal document; it is a repository of cardinal ideals and goals toward which a state's citizenry aspire. It embodies the tradition of the social contract developed by philosophers such as John Locke and given application by American constitution-makers, among them the men who met at Williamsburg in 1776 to draft Virginia's first constitution.

"Reform, that you may preserve," said the British statesman Macauley in urging passage of the Reform Bill of 1832. That advice may be apt for constitution-makers. The experience of one state is, of course, no sure guide for another. But Virginia's success in pursuing constitutional revision may have some useful implications for those setting out to revise the constitutions of other states. The ability of American states to adopt fundamental law which permits effective responses to contemporary and future needs is, after all, one test of the viability of the states in the federal system.

Part 6

Other Constitutions

For most of our nation's history, we Americans have been reluctant to admit that we could learn anything useful about modes of government from other countries. If the American constitutional system was not perfect already, it could be corrected by Americans, working with American materials.

There have been a few exceptions to this generalization, perhaps the most prominent being Woodrow Wilson in his professorial days. (Wilson, by the way, was the only president to have an earned doctoral degree.) Wilson was fascinated by Walter Bagehot's brilliant analysis of parliamentary government in *The English Constitution* (1868), and sought, in his own book, *Congressional Government* (1885), to use Bagehot's methods and values in a critical analysis of the American system. In other writings, including the one printed here as in Part 3, he was even more explicit in urging Americans to adopt central features of the British system.

In general, though, these suggestions have met stiff resistance. Americans have traditionally been convinced that constitutional form should reflect the culture and experience of a particular people and that we have little to learn from the experience of other nations.

The bicentennial era may be a good time to take another look at this tradition. After all, the framers of 1787 were eager to draw on the teachings of philosophers and historians such as James Harrington, John Locke, William Blackstone, David Hume and Montesquieu. James Madison, James Wilson, Alexander Hamilton, Roger Sherman, Gouverneur Morris and others combed the western tradition of political ideas and experience for insight into the nature of confederacies, the forms of representation, and the relationship between executive and legislative power. Other framers (Benjamin Franklin, Hugh Williamson, Pierce Butler, Charles Cotesworth Pinckney, John Rutledge) had travelled and studied abroad and drew lessons from what they had observed in other countries. Madison's Notes of the Federal Convention reveal that the framers were eager to discuss and learn from this foreign material.

The Committee on the Constitutional System has sought to follow the example of the framers. While there has been little disposition among Committee members to adopt the parliamentary system as such, there has been an eagerness to consider whether devices developed in foreign regimes might be helpful in the quest for ways to improve American governance.

Accordingly, when Lloyd Cutler, one of the Committee's co-chairs, had an opportunity in 1983 to study European constitutional systems at All Soul's College, Oxford, he was asked if he might summarize some of his findings for the Committee's benefit. We publish his memorandum here, including a table that compares certain provisions of the French, West German and British constitutions. In addition, we present an address by Michel Debré, chairman of the committee that drafted the current constitution of France, in which Debre outlines recent developments in French constitutionalism, including the move toward "presidentialism."

39. Modern European Constitutions and Their Relevance in the American Context (1984)

Lloyd N. Cutler is co-chair of the Committee on the Constitutional System.

During the 1983 Michaelmas term at All Souls College, Oxford, I had the opportunity to study the constitutional systems of the Federal Republic of Germany, France, Ireland and the United Kingdom. As part of my research, I met with a number of German politicians and constitutional experts, with former Premier Michel Debré and Professor François Luchaire, the chairman and principal draftsman of the committee which prepared the 1958 constitution of the Fifth Republic, and with John Kelly, former attorney general of Ireland and the author of the leading treatise on the Irish constitution. I also taught a joint seminar at All Souls on the American and British political systems with Geoffrey Marshall of Queens College and the Oxford politics faculty, in which a number of other Oxford politics and legal scholars took part.

Attached as Appendix A is a comparative summary of the German, French, and British constitutional systems, with special attention to the relationship between executive and legislative power, methods of election, and procedures for fixing accountability and breaking deadlocks.

Several features of these European systems are of considerable interest for the work of our Committee. The most interesting aspects are set forth in this memorandum, along with two ideas for strengthening party legislative cohesion, one based on the German "second ballot" and the other on conducting congressional elections in presidential years a few weeks *after* the presidential election.

Why Do European Legislators Maintain Party Cohesion?

The most obvious difference in how the European and American political systems work is the much higher degree of party cohesion in European legislatures, as compared to the United States Congress. In the European parliaments, the members almost always vote as their party leaders ask them to, while American congressmen and senators frequently do not. If one were to take the twenty most important items of legislation per session and compute the individual rate of deviation from the position of the party's leaders, most observers agree that the rate of deviation in Congress would probably be several times higher than in the European parliaments.

Much less obvious is why this is so. When this question was put to scholars and practical politicians in Europe, there was wide agreement on two main factors:

a. In the United Kingdom, Germany, France and Ireland, the party organization—national or local—plays a much greater role in nominating candidates and renominating incumbents than in the United States. The same is true as to a candidate's source of funds. In contrast, our primary system and our method of campaign financing force candidates to fend for themselves, and make them— especially incumbents—substantially independent of the national or local party organizations as far as election and reelection are concerned.

b. In the British, German, French and Irish parliaments, there is an enormous difference in status and power between being a member of the majority and a member of the minority. The opportunity to hold a high post in government (in the U.K., about 25 percent of the Conservative MPs have ministerial posts in Prime Minister Thatcher's government), to assist constituents and to influence legislative decisions depends almost entirely on being a member of the majority. Opposition members can make speeches, but they cannot rise in government, help constituents or affect legislative outcomes unless their party (or their coalition of parties) wins a majority of seats in the next election. This gives members of both the majority and the opposition a very strong incentive to vote as their respective party leaders request, since the key to power is to demonstrate the kind of loyalty that is essential to achieve status and power.

In Congress, however, being a member of the minority is only marginally less rewarding than being a member of the majority. The ranking minority member of a Senate or House committee has almost as much power and almost as many perquisites as the chairman, and the same is true of less senior majority and minority members. As a result, minority members can help their constituents almost as much as majority members, and because most major legislative actions are taken by differing cross-party coalitions, minority members have substantial impact on legislative outcomes. For all these mutually reinforcing reasons, and because the party organizations have little impact on nomination or renomination, or even on a member's chances to run for president, senators and congressmen have much less incentive than their European counterparts to vote as their party leaders ask. If greater party cohesion in Congress would be desirable, the above comparison may point a way to achieve it.

Fixing Accountability and Breaking an Impasse

All of these European systems allow a government to resign and call new elections. In the United Kingdom, Ireland and France, this can be done at any time. In Germany, it can be done only if the government loses a confidence vote in the Bundestag, but shortly after Helmut Kohl became chancellor, he was able to manufacture an ersatz vote of no confidence in order to call new parliamentary elections in which he won a larger Bundestag majority. In addition, the British, French and Irish systems *require* a government to resign if it loses a vote of confidence, and the German system does so if, after voting in favor of a no confidence motion, the Bundestag is able to elect a different chancellor.

The French constitution provides several other methods, short of resignation and dissolution, by which the government can avoid or break an impasse:

1. If the government "pledges its responsibility" for a bill, it is automatically deemed enacted without any legislative vote unless the opposition introduces a motion of censure and prevails. If the motion prevails, the government must resign.
2. The president can submit certain major bills (government reorganization, EEC agreements, treaties) directly to a popular referendum instead of to Parliament. Although many critics branded it unconstitutional, President de Gaulle successfully invoked this device for a constitutional amendment (direct popular election of the president).
3. The president can dismiss the premier at will and name another (who must win the support of the Assembly majority). The Constitution does not expressly provide for dismissal at will, but

Presidents de Gaulle, Pompidou and Giscard d'Estaing have exercised this power.

All these European systems also provide for breaking deadlocks between the upper and lower houses of the legislature. (In Italy, the consent of both houses is required, as in the United States.) Under each system the upper house can delay, but not prevent, the passage of national legislation. In Germany, however, bills that directly affect the states, or Lander, as they are called (taxes shared between federal and Lander governments, regulatory laws administered by and grants distributed via Lander), require the approval of the Lander-controlled upper house (Bundesrat) as well as the Bundestag.

Shifting the Legislative-Executive Balance

In the British, German and Irish systems, of course, the executive is elected by the legislature, and there is no legislative-executive balance to shift. The French system, however, provides for a strong president, even stronger than ours.

The French president has several powers not available to the American president.

- He is elected for a seven-year term, with no limit on the number of terms, and has much more time to carry out his program.
- He has the "sole power" to conduct foreign relations and negotiate and ratify treaties (except for certain types that require parliamentary approval).
- He can appoint the premier, equivalent to appointing the House and Senate leaders.
- As noted above, he can dissolve parliament and call new elections (but cannot do so again until after one year).
- As noted above, he can by-pass Parliament by passing laws via a national referendum or having the government "pledge its responsibility."
- In times of grave national danger, he can govern by decree.

Improving Party Legislative Cohesion

Our Committee has considered the merit of suggestions by Woodrow Wilson and others that the president's cabinet be selected from sitting members of Congress who would retain their seats.

The European systems vary widely in this respect. Members of the British cabinet must be members of the House of Commons or the

House of Lords, and while in the cabinet, they retain their seats. At the opposite extreme, the French premier and his cabinet may not serve in Parliament while members of the government, although many of them are chosen from the members of the Assembly. When they resign their Assembly seats to join the cabinet, their places are taken by party alternates elected in the general elections for that very purpose. Members of the German government can be, but need not be, members of the Bundestag, and on joining the government usually retain their seats. In Ireland the prime minister, the deputy prime minister and the finance minister must be sitting members of the lower house (the Dail) and the other cabinet members must be members of the Dail or the Seanad.

The German system includes an interesting feature that helps to build party consciousness and legislative cohesion, and that might (in sharply modified form) perform a similar function in the American system. That feature is the "second ballot," which is used to elect half of the Bundestag. Of the 496 Bundestag seats, half are filled on a constituency election basis. The other half are filled at large in the same election according to the result of the second ballot. In the second ballot, voters select the political party they prefer to form the government. The distribution of the at-large seats is in proportion to the percentage of second ballot votes cast for each party, with a minimum of five percent (or the winning of at least three constituency seats) necessary to receive any second ballot allotment. But—and this is an important but—the at-large seats are allocated so that the total percentage of Bundestag seats held by each party, including its constituency seats, correspond to that party's percentage in the second ballot. The at-large seats awarded to each party are filled from a party list in order of preference. Constituency candidates can also be included on the party list, and if they win the constituency election, the next person on the party list is awarded the party's next second ballot seat.

With our strong American tradition of a two-party system, it is probably not desirable, as well as not feasible, to elect the members of Congress on a proportional representation basis such as the German second ballot system. Nor is it desirable or feasible either to cut the number of congressional constituencies by half, or to double the size of Congress, in order to fill half the seats by means of a German-type second ballot. But there is a sharply modified version of the second ballot idea that might help us to build American party consciousness and legislative cohesion.

For example, we could amend the Constitution to provide for a "second ballot" in which voters, at the same time they voted for president, member of Congress and senator, would also vote for the party they preferred to have a majority in the House and Senate. For each percentage point by which the most preferred party led the second most preferred party (up to say ten percentage points), the most preferred party would be entitled to name five additional members-at-large of the House (up to a total of 50) and one additional at-large of the Senate (up to a total of 10). The at-large seats would be filled in order from a party list published by each party before the election. As in the German system, constituency candidates could also be included on the party lists and could fill one of their party's at-large seats if defeated in the constituency election. To satisfy the prohibition in Article V of any constitutional amendment that alters the equal suffrage of the states in the Senate, the second ballot percentages would be calculated on a state-by-state basis for the Senate at-large seats, so that each state, regardless of population size, would have an equal voice in electing the at-large senators. If this solution does not satisfy the test of Article V, the second ballot could be used only to fill at-large seats in the House.

Such a plan would not have the two main disadvantages, in American perception, of the German system:

- It is not a proportional representation plan. To the contrary, it provides *additional* legislative seats for the majority or plurality party.
- It would not reduce the number of constituency seats at all, and would increase the total size of each house by only ten percent.

At the same time, it would preserve the principal advantages, again in American perception, of the German system:

- It would raise party consciousness among voters and candidates, and draw greater attention to party policies and platforms.
- It would give the majority (or plurality) party a significant bloc of additional votes in the House and Senate, and enhance its chances to build party cohesion behind a coherent legislative program. Since the additional at-large members would have no constituency responsibilities, they would be more likely than constituency members to vote with their party leaders.
- The party list would enable the winning party to find places in Congress for some of its leading members who happen to lose their constituency elections, or who have previously distinguished themselves in executive positions or state governments rather than in Congress.

A first working draft of such an amendment is attached as Appendix B.

Some French Suggestions

As a result of his work on the French constitution, Michel Debré is quite familiar with our Constitution and its history. He has also had extensive practical experience as premier and minister in dealing with the American government. His view of the most useful changes to consider in our Constitution are as follows:

- He favors a six- or seven-year presidential term with no limit on the number of terms, or at most a two-term limit. In addition to the familiar arguments for a six-year term, he makes an impressive additional argument. He points out that the United States is one of the two superpowers and needs a political system adequate for its role as a superpower. The leaders of the other superpower have effective terms of office that are measured by decades. With this longevity they can afford to outwait an American president who, at any given moment, has less than four years remaining in his term. The other superpower's leaders would give more weight to the positions of an American President who has a six- or seven-year term, particularly if he were eligible to be reelected for second term.
- He believes it would be useful for the American president to have a prime minister responsible for carrying out the details of the legislative and administrative program, while the president concentrates on major policy issues at home and abroad. This would permit the president to stay above the daily legislative battle, to avoid symbolic defeats, and to replace a prime minister who had lost the confidence of Congress or the country.
- He favors simultaneous, rather than staggered, elections for president and members of Congress and, if possible, for the Senate. In any event, he would favor a longer term, perhaps four years, for members of the House.
- He favors granting the president the right to dissolve Congress and call for new elections, as the French constitution now provides.
- He also sees merit in authorizing the president to enact certain types of legislation and treaties (*e.g.*, arms control agreements) by putting them to a national referendum rather than to Congress.

Professor Luchaire offered another suggestion of considerable interest. He believes we should consider the advisability of conducting the presidential election one to three months before we conduct the election of representatives and senators. In this way, the voters could decide on whether to elect a Republican or Democratic candidate for Congress *after* they had decided whether to elect the Democratic or Republican candidate for president. This would enhance the likelihood of electing a majority in each house of the same party affiliation as the president, and thus enhance that party's chances of "forming a government" that could frame and execute a coherent set of policies.

Luchaire points out that the French presidential election occurs at a different time than the parliamentary elections, that President Mitterrand was elected at a time when the majority of the Assembly was held by the opposing center-right parties, that after his election Mitterrand promptly dissolved Parliament and called for new parliamentary elections, and that his party won an absolute Assembly majority large enough so that he did not even require the votes of the Communist Party members of his coalition to maintain his majority.

Such a change in the timing of American elections could be accomplished by an act of Congress, without need of amending the Constitution. Under Article I, section 4, and Article II, section 1, Congress may determine the time for holding both presidential and congressional elections and is not required to set the same time for both.

APPENDIX A

Federal Republic of Germany	France	United Kingdom
1. *Constitutional source*	1. *Constitutional source*	1. *Constitutional source*
Basic Law, adopted by the Lander (states) 1949	Constitution of the Fifth Republic, ratified 1958	Acts of Parliament, common law, and custom
2. *President*	2. *President*	2. *President*
Yes	Yes	No—hereditary monarch
a. Election	a. Election	a. Election
By the federal assembly, consisting of equal numbers of representatives from the Bundestag (federal lower house) and the Lander legislatures.	By popular vote. If no candidate receives over 50 percent of the vote, run-off election between top two fourteen days later.	(not applicable)
b. Powers	b. Powers	b. Powers
Largely figurehead.	Greater than U.S. president.	Monarch's power largely figurehead.
(1) If Bundestag fails to elect a chancellor, president can appoint chancellor or dissolve Bundestag.	(1) Appoints premier and, if government loses vote of confidence, can dismiss premier. (Although constitution does not expressly authorize, presidents have exercised power to dismiss premiers at will.)	

(2) Can veto ministerial appointments by chancellor (rarely done except for criminal or nazi record).

(3) Can scrutinize laws and refer them to constitutional court to determine their validity.

(2) No veto power, but can ask parliament to reconsider passage of laws.

(3) Can submit certain major bills (reorganization of government departments, EEC agreements, treaties) to popular referendum instead of to parliament.

(4) Sole power to conduct foreign relations, negotiate and ratify treaties (certain designated treaties require approval by parliament). Commander-in-chief of armed forces.

(5) Can dissolve Assembly with new elections 20–40 days later. No further dissolution for one year.

c. Term
5 years, two term limit

c. Term
7 years, no limit on number of terms

c. Term
(not applicable)

d. Impeachment
For willful violation of Basic Law or other federal law on motion of ¼ of Bundestag or Bundesrat and decision by ⅔ of members of the impeaching house. Apart from impeachment, federal constitutional court can forfeit president's office if it finds him guilty of willful violation.

d. Impeachment
For high treason only with impeachment by majority vote of the Assembly and Senate and trial by the High Court of Justice (composed of members of parliament elected equally by the Assembly and Senate).

d. Impeachment
(not applicable)

3. *Parliament*
a. Bicameral
Bundestag and Bundesrat

3. *Parliament*
a. Bicameral
National Assembly and Senate

3. *Parliament*
a. Bicameral
House of Commons and House of Lords

b. Lower house
(Bundestag)

b. Lower house
(National Assembly)

b. Lower house
(House of Commons)

(1) Elected by people. Method and number not entrenched but subject to parliamentary law.

(1) Elected by direct suffrage. Method, number and term not entrenched but subject to parliamentary law.

(1) Elected by direct suffrage. Method, number, and term not entrenched but subject to parliamentary law.

(2) Under present law 496 members, of whom 50 percent are elected by constituency; other 50 percent on the basis of "second ballot"

(2) Under present law 478 members are elected by constituency. If no candidate gets 50 percent+ in first election, run off 2 weeks

(2) Under present law 635 members elected from separate geographic constituencies on a plurality basis.

for preferred party, with members selected according to rank on party list. Adjustments are made so that each party percentage of entire house corresponds to its percentage of second ballot vote, with 5 percent minimum or 3 constituency seats required to earn any allotment of second ballot vote.

later between 2 highest candidates.

(3) Four-year term unless earlier dissolution, in which event new election in 60 days for new 4-year term.

(3) Five-year term under present law unless earlier dissolution, in which event new election must be held within 20–40 days thereafter for new full term.

(3) Five-year term, unless earlier dissolution.

c. Upper House (Bundesrat)

c. Upper House (Senate)

c. Upper House (House of Lords)

(1) Consists of members of Lander governments which appoint and recall them. Each Land has at least 3 members, with 4 if over 2 million population and 5 if over 6 million. Each Land delegation votes by bloc.

(1) Elected by indirect suffrage to insure representation of territorial units of the republic and Frenchmen living outside France. Number, method of election and term not entrenched but subject to parliamentary law.

(1) Over 1,400 members consisting of hereditary peers appointed by monarch on nomination of prime minister.

(2) Term indefinite

d. Relation between houses.

(2) Term same as Assembly

d. Relation between houses.

(2) Term: life.

d. Relation between houses.

All legislation involving Lander in collection or sharing of taxes, making of grants and transfer payments, and administration or execution of law must be passed by a majority of the Bundestag and consented to by a majority of the Bundesrat. All other legislation is enacted by majority vote of Bundestag alone, but only after giving Bundesrat an opportunity to object by simple majority or two-thirds vote. Despite objection, Bundestag may proceed by same simple majority or two-thirds vote.

All legislation must be passed by both Assembly and Senate, but if they disagree and conference does not resolve issue, Assembly may enact legislation by majority vote if government (see below) asks it to do so.

Legislation must be passed by majority of both houses but if House of Lords does not pass, Commons may then enact by its own majority.

4. *Forming the government*

• Consists of the chancellor and ministers

• Chancellor is elected by a majority of Bundestag on proposal of president. If president's nominee rejected, majority of Bundestag can elect anyone else. (In practice, president nominates leader of majority party or coalition.)

• Presidents appoints and dismisses ministers on proposal of chancellor.

4. *Forming the government*

• President appoints premier and terminates premier's functions when premier presents resignation of government. (In practice deGaulle and subsequent presidents have appointed and dismissed premiers at will.)

• On proposal of premier, president appoints and dismisses other members of cabinet.

• President presides over council of ministers (cabinet).

• Premier and ministers cannot hold seats in parliament. (In practice, most are chosen from parliament and resign seats in favor of alternate.)

4. *Forming the government*

• Monarch asks leader of majority party or of majority coalition to be prime minister and form a government. Prime minister picks all other government ministers (about 90).

• Prime minister designates executive committee or "cabinet" consisting of about 20 members of the government.

• All ministers must be members of Commons or Lords.

5. *Governing and resigning*

• Chancellor determines general policy.

• Minister of defense commands armed forces in peace; chancellor in event of attack.

• Chancellor and ministers need not be (but usually are) members of Bundestag.

• Bundestag can dismiss chancellor only by majority vote electing a successor ("constructive vote of no confidence").

• If chancellor seeks a vote of confidence and fails to obtain majority, president may dissolve Bundestag at request of chancellor; but right to dissolve lapses if majority of Bundestag have elected another chancellor.

5. *Governing and resigning*

• Premier Direct operation of government. Government determines & directs policy of nation. (In practice, presidents frequently intervene to assume direction themselves.)

• Certain types of government action require laws passed by parliament (civil rights, draft, nationality, criminal law, taxation, nationalization, education, labor, property rights, appropriations). In other fields government may issue regulations by decree.

• Even where law is required, government can bypass parliament by pledging government's "responsibility," in which event proposed law is deemed enacted unless majority of

5. *Governing and resigning*

• Cabinet has "collective" responsibility; meetings are secret; cabinet members must support government policy or resign. (In practice, prime minister usually can insist on prevailing. Some prime ministers have bypassed consulting full cabinet—e.g. Churchill's use of inner "war cabinet" and Eden's decision to invade Suez.)

• On defeat of major bill or at request of prime minister, cabinet must resign as a group.

• Virtually all legislation is initially proposed by cabinet. If parliament fails to pass any "major" item, modern custom is for government to resign.

assembly adopts a motion
of censure.

• Majority of assembly may
adopt a motion of censure
at any time in which event
premier must submit resignation of government.

6. *Amendment*

Requires two-thirds majority
of Bundestag plus two-
thirds of Bundesrat. No further action by Lander or
electorate.

6. *Amendment*

Requires majority vote of
both houses plus majority
vote in popular referendum.
No referendum required if
president proposes amend-
ment to both houses "in
congress" and obtains 60
percent majority of com-
bined Assembly-Senate vote.
(President deGaulle arguably violated this procedure
in 1962 when he proposed
amendment for direct popular election of President to
replace original 1958 provision for indirect election
and successfully submitted
it directly to a referendum
without prior passage by
parliament.)

6. *Amendment*

Under doctrine of suprem-
acy of parliament, parliament by statute may alter
any rule established by
prior statute, common law
or custom. Subject to being
overridden by parliament,
judges may also vary rules
established by common law.
Some customs simply
change over time (e.g. in
mid-19th century govern-
ment was not obliged to
resign if Commons rejected
a major bill).

APPENDIX B

A SECOND PARTY BALLOT: OUTLINE OF PROPOSED CONSTITUTIONAL AMENDMENT

Article _____

1. At all congressional elections, each voter shall be entitled, in addition to casting a ballot for representative and when applicable for senator, to cast a second ballot for the political party the voter chooses to have a majority of the House of Representatives and of the Senate.
2. The results of the second ballot shall be tabulated separately, on a national basis and on a state-by-state basis.
3. The respective shares of the parties having the largest and second largest number of second ballot national votes shall be calculated as percentages of the aggregate number of second ballot national votes for the largest and second largest parties only. For each percentage point (or major fraction thereof) of difference between the respective shares of these parties, the party with the larger share shall be entitled to designate five additional at-large members (but no more than a total of fifty such members) of the House of Representatives party list referred to in paragraph 5.
4. The party receiving the largest number of second ballot votes in each state shall be determined. The respective percentage shares of states won by the parties winning the largest and second largest number of states shall be calculated. For each percentage point (or major fraction thereof) of difference between the shares of these parties, the larger party shall be entitled to designate one additional at-large member of the Senate (but no more than a total of ten such members), to be selected in the order of the Senate party list referred to in paragraph 5. (No more than one at-large member of the Senate may be a resident of the same state.)
5. Before each congressional election, each political party desiring to participate in the second ballot shall compile a separate party list in order of preference of the persons it designates to serve as at-large members of the House of Representatives, and a separate such list for at-large members of the Senate, in the event the party becomes entitled to designate at-large members as set forth in paragraphs 3 and 4. The list may include persons standing for

election as a constituency member of the House of Representatives or Senate, but if elected as a constituency member, any such person shall be stricken from the party list and the next person shall be designated to serve as an at-large member.

6. The term of all at-large members of the House of Representatives and Senate shall be the same as the term of a constituency member of the House of Representatives.
7. Congress shall have power to enforce this article by appropriate legislation.

Michel Debré

40. Reflections of a Modern Framer (1978)

By analogy with James Madison, Michel Debré could be called the "father" of the constitution of the Fifth French Republic. Having worked through writings and speeches since the end of World War II to propound correct doctrines of modern constitutional government, he was named chair of the drafting committee in 1958. When the new government was inaugurated, he served for three years as its first prime minister. In this address, delivered at a conference sponsored by the State University of New York at Brockport in June, 1978, he relates the structure and processes of the constitution to the needs of the Fifth Republic and comments on the interplay of parties and the presidency in a modern republic.

A parallel is often drawn between the American Revolution and the French Revolution; but it is important also to understand how they differ.

In the United States, events at the end of the eighteenth century created a legitimacy. The citizens of the first states wanted order; the members of the constitutional convention in Philadelphia gave it to them. Order was born of the Constitution, society was created and power emerged.

In France, events outwardly similar, at least in the early days, brought down a legitimacy that was several centuries old. Order, society, and power in France were changed by the political rupture. And the entire nineteenth century attests to the aspirations of modern times.

This effort was made more difficult still by the fact that France's relative power declined as a result of the Napoleonic wars and the

Reprinted from *The Fifth Republic at Twenty*, edited by William G. Andrews and Stanley Hoffman, published by the State University of New York Press, Albany, N.Y. Copyright 1981.

slower growth of its population. On a European scale it remained a country capable of greatness, of making its presence felt in distant lands; but at the world level it had lost its supremacy.

In 1870, a few years after the War Between the States which ushered in the rise of American power, there occurred the first of three wars between France and Germany. The defeat of the empire and the upheaval of the commune—a brief, terrible tragedy—resulted in a republic whose constitutional laws were drafted without republican zeal or democratic fervor. The sole concern was to counter "personal power" until a conservative parliamentary monarchy patterned after the British could be restored.

As it happened, the fundamental political rules that were instituted on a provisional basis endured unchanged until 1940, creating a quite special type of system that I labeled some thirty years ago the "assembly system."

It looked as if there were separation of power, but in reality it was different. A mercantile bourgeoisie and a landed aristocracy succeeded, either by fighting each other or pooling their efforts, in becoming the dominant political class, resulting in a system of parliamentary sovereignty. The only check on the all-powerful chamber of deputies was the senate, whose task was to cool the passions of the former. The tribute to Montesquieu concealed the triumph of Rousseau's ideology.

The chief of state was elected by both chambers. This rule of law came to mean, in fact, that the majority in parliament chose as the person to head the executive a man who would never take a major initiative and who would, above all, respect the authority of parliament.

The cabinet was responsible to the chambers. The electoral system chosen for the election of members of parliament was not the British or American one nor the majority vote sought by the early republicans. It was an election in two rounds that made it difficult to have a cohesive majority. The cabinet, which was formed from a coalition of parties, became vulnerable. Its responsibility to the assembly became submission. This submission generated crises and instabilities which—with few exceptions—were the hallmark of the republic.

Laws were the expression of parliament's will. Parliament was not checked by constitutional rules simply because those who had adopted the laws wanted them to be temporary and so had not set forth any principle that legislators had to respect. To top it all off, there was silence about the judiciary, whose independence lay more in the judges' minds than in the statutes.

The Third Republic had a hard time establishing its legitimacy. In the nineteenth century, France was deeply divided between monarchists and republicans, who in turn were divided among themselves. Moderate republicans opposed radical republicans, and the moderates and radicals opposed the socialists.

Nevertheless, the republic gradually won recognition through its regulations, laws, and leaders. It was helped by a vigilant patriotism that emphasized the reconquest of Alsace and Lorraine; that wanted, through education and social legislation, to put leadership within reach of the people; and by a spirit of adventure and expansion which, in less than thirty years, increased France's presence in Africa, Asia, and the Pacific.

The republic was badly shaken by a series of major events occurring within. The most important of these was the Dreyfus affair, which in the long run served the cause of the republic's legitimacy by imposing on the institutions and on the men who ran them, in addition to their obligation to serve the nation, the obligation to respect the rights of the individual.

Thus, in 1914, first the *union sacrée*, then victory, endorsed the national legitimacy of the republic. The Third Republic had remodeled France, had recovered Alsace and Lorraine, and had set the country on the path of modernization and social progress.

But, as is often the case in history, the consolidation of a political system coincides with the intimations of its downfall. The tragic effects of the weakness of the administration, long hidden by the quality of the civil service, began to increase.

The price of victory was heavy: politicians were slow to perceive the significance of a million-and-a-half dead and another million-and-a-half wounded. A decline in the population—whether due to a decline in the birth rate or a rise in mortality—lowers the quality of the population. This was especially true after a long war in which the youngest, bravest, and most dedicated had fallen. Twenty years later, when the generation sacrificed would have reached the age of responsibility, the burden of their absence could be felt.

Politicians in Europe, whether British of French, found it no less difficult to understand the return of the United States to isolationism or Russia's turning inward on itself when once it had proclaimed itself the bastion of socialism.

A few years later, there was no greater perception about the consequences of the American crisis for Europe than there was courage to confront the rise in dictatorships, or the tyranny Hitler installed in Germany and around it.

In 1933, the seeds of doubt were sown first—unfortunately in too few people's minds—about the political capability of the Third Republic. No one doubted its moral legitimacy. Human rights were respected. The effort to promote human advancement and dignity went on. But moral legitimacy is not enough. There must be political legitimacy, that is, the ability to ensure the survival of the nation and the security of its citizens. In the face of economic difficulties, growing unemployment, and threats from a bloodthirsty and criminal regime, France of the 1930s looked decidedly pallid: divided at home, naive abroad.

The disaster of 1940 confirmed its impotence. The republic went down in defeat. And for France there emerged a new crisis of legitimacy. A semblance of legal power was installed in Vichy. In a few months, it ceased to be legitimate. A semblance of illegal power was installed in London. In a few months, General de Gaulle came to embody the legitimacy of institutions.

In August 1944, General de Gaulle arrived in Paris. Wholly determined to restore France to the ranks of victorious nations, he was confronted at home with the prestige of the Communist Party, the after-effects of Vichy high-handedness, and the haste of a political establishment impatient—to use the words of an illustrious parliamentarian of the time—to demonstrate its capacity for democracy through its capacity for ingratitude.

General de Gaulle seemed omnipotent. With his attention turned toward his principal goal, he kept silent on institutions. On the strength of his personal legitimacy, he wanted to gain time before giving France a new constitution. The German surrender brought a torrent of different opinions. Some urged him to return to the institutions of the Third Republic. That might have been a solution, providing it were done fast and with a few drastic changes. It was not done fast and, apart from a small number of people who had thought about it in the final months of the resistance, there was no general agreement on what changes should be made. So General de Gaulle convened a constituent assembly and at the same time held a referendum repealing the constitutional laws of 1875.

Then General de Gaulle committed, in my opinion, the error of not presenting a draft constitution—doubtless out of concern for democracy. I would like to interject a personal word here: I was one of the people who had thought about the institutional requirements of modern France, and when I was called to assist General de Gaulle in mid-1945, I used my earlier thoughts to prepare the text of a constitution based on the three points I believed had been revealed by the inadequacy of the Third Republic. For the stability and authority of the executive I used an idea that found favor later, the idea of a republican monarch. In the second place, a genuine parliamentary system was needed, that is, a cabinet that directs the actions of the government and the work of parliament but is responsible to this body; a parliament whose activity is organized and whose will is not all powerful. And finally, a method of election which, while ensuring as cohesive a majority as possible, permits solid cooperation between the cabinet and parliament, and thus greater government stability.

These ideas were never translated into facts. The return of political parties that accompanied the rebirth of democracy resulted in a conflict which General de Gaulle predicted would have serious consequences on the political history of France. He did not want to jeopardize his legitimacy in quarrels he viewed as secondary compared to the state of the world. He withdrew. From the standpoint of institutions, he did, nonetheless, make one innovation: the use of the referendum which, thus, made a furtive entry into the constitutional life of the republic and which soon became an element of its legitimacy.

Left to itself, that is, to the parties, the constituent assembly was subject to strong Socialist and Communist influence and produced a poor constitution. Underneath apparent changes—to wit, the solemn reaffirmation of the principles of democracy, the new organization of parliament with the power of the second chamber considerably diminished in relation to the first, and rules of procedure that were supposedly designed to give the government more staying power—underneath, it was a return to the assembly system, the system of the Third Republic. In many respects its mechanisms were even worse, and consequently so were its drawbacks.

These, then, were the roots of the illegitimacy of a regime which, as the French people gradually came to realize, had as its sole aim setting up what General de Gaulle later called the party system. By this he meant the system in which virtually all the political power reverted to a coalition of parties which, although clever enough to get their leaders into power, were not strong enough to lead the country.

On two occasions, the people showed their impatience and distrust. The first time they rejected the text of a constitution prepared and adopted by the constituent assembly. The second time, they adopted a text which was scarcely any different from the first, but which had the support of the parties, especially since General de Gaulle had announced his opposition to it. It was approved by only one third of the votes, with slightly less than one third of the people voting against it and a little more than one third staying away from the polls. Even this lukewarm response was obtained only after assurances were given on all sides that the draft could be revised quickly. Actually, the people never really gave the institutions their backing since they saw all too clearly how close they were to the ones that had made France ineffectual politically between the two world wars.

I said this at the time, and events proved that my fears were justified. The institutions of the Fourth Republic were unable to set up a legitimate regime because the assembly was elected by proportional representation.

Under this system, the executive, legislative, and administrative power is shared by the leadership of the parties, no one of which can ever obtain a majority and consequently ever feels responsible for the general interest. It is really a coalition of party interests which sets up camp in the state and shares its spoils. Let me add an important point, which is that this system of voting gives the Communist Party a great deal of weight.

Individual merit was not much help: those leaders who were former members of the Resistance, many of whom were my friends and comrades-in-arms, were on the whole courageous and sincere. But when it came to dealing with world events and especially the trials awaiting France in Indochina and North Africa, this system, without a stable executive power and dominated by the all-powerful impotence of a divided assembly, demonstrated its inability to decide on a national policy, its inability even to ensure respect for human rights.

The Fourth Republic can claim some successes, which were due to the fact that deep down the French people wanted to avenge the circumstances that had brought them to such depths: the birth rate did climb and industry began to grow. The French joined in the postwar euphoria. It was not a citizenry the republic was missing—it was leadership.

General de Gaulle immediately perceived the weakness of the new republic. In 1947, he founded the Rally of the French People. It had immediate success both in the municipal elections and in the elections for the second chamber, later named the Council of the Republic.

Popular reaction against the parties of the Fourth Republic was so strong that in order to defend itself, the administration, just prior to the decisive legislative elections of 1951, instituted an unheard-of voting system: it was proportional representation coupled with the so-called *apparentements* method in which the various parties, by combining the votes received by their tickets, could obtain a majority and thus divide the seats among themselves. In fact, that explanation was for outsiders only. The real aim was to keep General de Gaulle from returning to power by means of an election. The results were as desired. The Rally of the French People got more votes than any other party by a large margin, but its representation in parliament came to only 130 deputies out of nearly 600.

A legitimate regime that is not successful rapidly ceases to be legitimate. It was to preserve his stature that General de Gaulle withdrew a few month after this defeat.

It did not help make the Fourth Republic more legitimate; quite the contrary. Unconsciously for some, consciously for others, the Fourth Republic sought a new kind of legitimacy by trying to build a European superstate. Many were pleased by this until the plan for a "European army" came up. The great controversy over this European Defense Community provoked a national crisis and resulted in 1954 in rejection of the proposal by the National Assembly. The Gaullists and some moderates, the Communists, and half the Socialists joined together in rejecting the political prospects of integrating France into Europe. Sustaining a military defeat in Indochina and, close on its heels, becoming bogged down in a military situation in Algeria were the final blows to a failing regime. The government could neither bring about victory by arms nor negotiate with the rebels. Confronted with the threat of civil war, President Coty summoned General de Gaulle, and in a historic meeting in June, 1958, even though the number of Gaullist deputies had been drastically reduced by the preceding elections, de Gaulle obtained the backing of all those political groups, except the Communists, that had fought so hard against him for ten years.

So, legitimacy was once more, for a few months, embodied in a man, General de Gaulle. Guided by experience, despite pressing economic and financial problems, despite the difficulty of the Algerian problem, General de Gaulle made it his first priority to draft a new constitution. It took one summer.

The drafting began early in July and was completed at the end of August. The 1958 constitution was approved by a referendum in September. The aim of the new constitution was to build a legitimate republic by creating a state that was effective with regard to national exigencies while remaining faithful to the principles of democracy.

For twenty years, I have read and heard it said that this constitution was made for General de Gaulle. For twenty years, I have alerted professors of political science to the fact that this is a major analytical error. Most certainly this constitution, in the minds of those who conceived and wrote it—and I myself was foremost among them—did allow General de Gaulle to assume responsibility for French affairs for the longest period of years possible. How could we have considered doing otherwise when in every respect of our domestic state of affairs, the needs of Europe, and the exigencies of the world scene called for a kind of government that only General de Gaulle could lead and ensure? But in spirit, the constitution was not tailored to an individual. Its aim was to correct the inadequacies of the republic's institutions which had been apparent for nearly a century, inadequacies which, because they were so ill-suited to national exigencies, led to the disasters of the post-World War I period and to the dangers of the decolonization period.

When summarizing my thoughts, I have often repeated an idea that I think is still true: 'The republic had to acquire the attributes of government.' What did it need to succeed? . . .

The executive first of all had to be a chief of state worthy of the name. What do I mean by "worthy of the name"? Well, above all he should not be a nonrepresentative college in which alliances could be made. Then, he should have powers that guarantee him the ability to take responsibility for the nation's fate. Finally, he should have control over the functioning of institutions, if not directly, then in any case through his right to appeal to arbitrating bodies.

One such body is the Constitutional Council, which ensures primarily that the rules determining jurisdiction in constitutional matters are respected. But the most important arbitrating body is public opinion itself, expressed in referendum or in elections when the assembly is dissolved.

All this went into the Constitution.

The parliamentary system means above all that the cabinet is based on a majority in Parliament and is responsible to that majority. The tragedy for the republic had been its instability because the administration could constantly be challenged over any issue. This was corrected by specific measures, such as controlling parliament's agenda, setting a strict procedure for the motion of censure, and making it incompatible to hold a seat in parliament and hold a cabinet position. Parliament, which is active for two three-month sessions each year, is completely free to bring matters up for consideration and put questions to ministers, but it cannot challenge the responsibility of the cabinet without using a formal procedure and this procedure cannot be invoked frequently: the motion of censure. Parliament had the right to change things, but within its jurisdiction. One major innovation in the 1958 constitution was defining legislative limits so that the administration can keep the Assembly from infringing on the administration's action, something as harmful as ministerial instability. These two phenomena—infringing on administrative action and ministerial instability—are the two main problems with the assembly system compared with a true parliamentary system. The parliamentary system was instituted.

I would have liked the principle of election of deputies by majority vote to be written into the constitution. I did not win on this point. The French tradition of the vote as a political instrument rather than a principle is very strong. Proportional representation was abolished but, also by reason of France's political sociology, the ordinance changing the voting method reestablished the two-ballot system, under which an absolute majority was needed to win on the first ballot. The reform was not as strong as I would have wished.

Four years after the 1958 constitution, General de Gaulle wanted to make a major change and succeeded in doing so despite opposition by the leadership of all the political parties. Whereas the original text of the constitution had called for election of the president by a college of 100,000 people representing first and foremost the cities, towns, and departments, de Gaulle held a referendum which approved election of the president of the republic by universal suffrage. This measure unquestionably reflected a personal idea of General de Gaulle. His legitimacy came from the people and, faced with the prospect of new presidential elections, he thought that as far as he was concerned he could not request renewal of his mandate without appealing to the people as a whole. But this personal idea was reinforced by two other ideas, each of them of fundamental importance. One was an idea regarding national defense. Since 1959, France had wanted to become a nuclear power and base its defense on deterrence. One of the elements of deterrence is the credibility of an authority who would carry out the terrible threat should the need arise. This credibility assumes that the chief of state has legitimacy in his own right, independent of the legitimacy of institutions. He therefore had to have the support of universal suffrage.

The second idea had to do with institutions. France is still a country where it is difficult to picture the formation of two parties which alternate in power and thus ensure the democratic functioning of the state. Extreme groups in France contest the legitimacy of the republican form of government. Because of this, the republic still lives under the threat, despite the merit of its institutions, of once more falling into the system of coalitions of various parties which dominate the government. Basing the authority of the chief of state on universal suffrage is a safeguard against this eventuality.

The 1962 referendum, which approved election of the president of the French Republic by universal suffrage, is interesting in another respect. Four years previously, the 1958 referendum had given the new constitution an unusually broad popular base. With the exception of the Communists, every party had recommended voting for it and it was possible to deduce that this support by the political parties had been a determining factor in shaping the vote to the wishes of General de Gaulle.

In 1962, the situation was completely different. General de Gaulle stood alone. The Communist Party opposed him but he was also opposed by the Socialists, the Radicals, the Christian Democrats, and the moderates. Only the Gaullists supported de Gaulle, and they seemed so isolated that when I began to campaign in support of him, people thought that I showed an exceptional amount of courage! The referendum was more than 60 percent in favor. Nearly two-thirds of the French voted for General de Gaulle and, above and beyond the man, for the legitimacy of a republic that could free itself of the grip of the parties in times of major importance. This shows the extent to which the leadership of the parties can act as a screen. And the nature of the step taken by the Gaullist authors of the constitution must be clearly understood: it was to reveal the truer political reality by appealing to the people through universal suffrage. It is not a right to be abused, moreover. De Gaulle learned this cruel lesson in 1969.

Twenty years have elapsed. General de Gaulle is dead. Succeeding him for five years was one of his prime ministers, then on his death, a man who had been one of his ministers for a few years, a man whose political commitment had never been to Gaullism. The personal position of the current president is much more favorable to the old parties.

Whereas the institutions of the Third Republic acquired legitimacy only belatedly and those of the Fourth Republic never, the elections early in 1978 actually revealed the extent to which the present institutions have become established. Twenty years after 1958, the French people see them as a reflection of themselves, and the immediate and total acceptance of the results, and therefore of the state, is very significant. The institutions of the Fifth Republic have given the republic its legitimacy. This is what I am most proud of, though I am not overlooking that, France being France, that is to say a country that has scarcely changed since Julius Caesar or Richelieu passed judgment on it, everything could still be brought into question again. The sanctity of institutions, which is what the public needs, is all too easily exposed to criticism, sometimes on ideological grounds, sometimes from self-interest.

Certain gains, very important ones, seem to be permanent now. Among them are the election of the president of the republic by universal suffrage, the elimination of the danger of governmental instability and the ruling on the constitutionality of laws by the Constitutional Council. In other words—and this is what is important—the rules that check the excessive power of an assembly have become legitimate and so cannot be contravened without a veritable disruption of legitimacy.

But over and above the legitimacy that has now been acquired, it is important to consider three things that may influence for better or worse its ultimate evolution. The first, which is not unusual, is that there are two possible readings of the constitution, that is, two ways of interpreting it; the second, more disturbing, is the desire to move either closer to the presidential system or closer to the assembly system; the third, totally undesirable, is the trend on the part of numerous party leaders to seek proportional representation in election to the National Assembly.

The president of the republic chooses a prime minister. The prime minister must have the confidence of the National Assembly. An arrangement such as this leads to two interpretations of the constitution, both completely correct.

One interpretation makes government more particularly the affair of the president. The other interpretation gives the prime minister considerable personal authority due primarily to the support of the parliament. These two interpretations have each been employed in turn.

In the early years of the present constitution, during the three years when I was prime minister, the head of state enjoyed an indisputed preeminence in all matters pertaining to defense, foreign affairs, and Algeria, matters in which the prime minister, as his name indicates, was the principal collaborator of the head of state. Regarding all else: the whole range of internal affairs, the economy, finance, administration, education, social questions, and so forth, I, the prime minister, had a free hand. Then came another prime minister and General de Gaulle saw to the general operation of things. He was able to do this all the better because the elections gave his supporters an absolute majority in the National Assembly.

In 1966, after his term of office had been renewed—not the easy victory he had expected—he gave greater freedom of action to the then prime minister, Georges Pompidou, and the minister of economy and finance that I became. Our greater freedom was confirmed after the legislative elections in 1967, which marked the resurgence of the opposition. After the events in May, 1968, the National Assembly was dissolved, and in the ensuing elections, the Gaullists won a large majority. The new prime minister, Maurice Couve de Murville, became a very strict and loyal top aide of General de Gaulle, who remained at the helm until the unfortunate referendum that caused him to withdraw from public life. The presidency of Georges Pompidou lasted for five years. His first cabinet, that of Prime Minister Chaban-Delmas, had considerable autonomy regarding the management and general direction of national affairs. However, this was not the case with his successor, Mr. Messmer. The government then became more "presidentialized," as they say in politico-legal jargon. It has continued to be so with the cabinets designated by the current president, who would have been obliged, as he acknowledged during the 1978 election campaign, to alter his line of conduct completely had the elections been won by the opposition. On the contrary, the success of the majority has enabled him to strengthen the presidential side of the constitution.

I have grave political disagreements with the current leadership of my country. In no way does that influence my constitutional judgment. The presidential system is not prohibited by our constitution, and when the majority that has elected the president is the same as the one that has elected the Assembly, this division of power does not run counter to the constitution.

Nevertheless, I favor France having a more parliamentary application of its constitution. Too much concentration of power in the hands of the president at the expense of the cabinet diminishes parliament's ability to play a proper parliamentary role and runs the risk of paralyzing it in its main function, which is to be a trusted intermediary between the government and the people. At the same time, the administration may be run less effectively by ministers who feel no personal responsibility to the Assembly.

For this reason, I have serious doubts about the trends toward presidentializing the constitution in the manner of the United States. To strengthen these powers would require shortening the length of the presidential term. At the risk of shocking some, perhaps all of you, I must say that I find a four-year term rather short in a century in which nations are struggling for survival. Not to mention the fact that an increase in presidential powers is promptly countered by an increase in the powers of elected assemblies. Without dwelling on the paradox, it is important to see that the presidential system tends to be balanced by an assembly system. The United States, which is a powerful country, can combine the power of the president with that of Congress. This is a gamble you can take because of your strength and also your wealth. I do not think that France, a medium-sized nation with less wealth and constantly exposed to danger, can allow itself this luxury. There has to be a link, and also a buffer, between president and assembly; this role falls to the prime minister, or to the cabinet, on whom falls a very large share of the executive power, who is responsible to parliament and whose work he must also direct.

The possibility of a return to proportional representation for deputies to the National Assembly disturbs me deeply. I can see no point in giving the Communist Party maximum representation. Were this method of election followed in a country where the tradition of a multi-party system has long been established, it would achieve a real transfer of sovereignty from the people to party leaders. It would alter the parliamentary system by doing away with the concept of a united majority responsible to the electorate. In vain I proposed to my countrymen that we should follow the British and the Americans, who praise this system of election all the more since they have decided never to use it themselves. I am not always heeded, and I suspect I will have to continue the fight for the next several years.

The founding fathers of democracy, inspired by the noble idea that right should prevail over arbitrary rule, perhaps placed undue emphasis on institutions. To be sure, institutions are an important element of every republic. Throughout my life I have taken pains to say so and to make an often skeptical political establishment understand this. The definition of responsibilities, the chances of success of our leaders' initiatives, the length of time they are in office, the equilibrium of functions to circumstances are all equally essential elements in combining public well-being with public freedom, which is the supreme task of the republican state. The method of election cannot be left to circumstance; it is a fundamental element not only in the choice men make but in the general tenor of the seat of power.

Another feature that enhances the value of a constitution is its capacity to face crises—external crises, of course—but internal ones, which make for the greatness and the liability of the regimes founded on universal suffrage. Opposition between the executive and the legislative, change in the ruling majority, social crisis, are all inevitable when power comes from a regularly consulted electorate and when the functions of government are shared among independent authorities.

Through government stability and the principle of majority vote, the 1958 constitution reduced the number of crises. When they did occur, the ability of the head of state to consult the people made it possible to solve them democratically. But the institutions are only one part of public life. People are also involved, and they change. There are ideas, customs, the mood of the times, and these change, too.

During difficult periods, though public opinion can be mistaken, men and women are more ready to turn to those who can talk and act in the general interest. When times are less threatening, the art of theater, which is partly necessary in that phase of public life which is the quest for power, sometimes engenders illusions. Likewise, a generation of men and women that has gone through great trials is susceptible to the appeal of candidates who talk of responsibility before history. Generations that have not experienced these trials are more apt to look to flamboyant personalities, drawn by the possibility of being able to play a personal role. As for new ideas, it is sometimes difficult to separate those that are sincere aspirations from those concealing other interests. In our present age, which has been caught up in a whirlwind of innovation, as they claim to be—are not always consistent with the interests of the republic, which itself is permanent.

For example, among the politically aware in France, some are drawn to the idea of a so-called integrated Europe, without assessing either the political individuality of France on the continent or the dramatic requirements of the national state. Coupling public well-being with public freedom postulates the existence of a solidarity that has sprung up naturally. The mechanism that ensures authority through the law of the majority is a delicate instrument. It is not given to just any group to defer to the authority of one man designated by virtue of a margin over his competitor that may be less than one percent of the votes cast, or to a law adopted by one vote, as the Third Republic was. What I am saying is that legitimacy is not decreed. It is a sign of social consensus, which is a feature of nations in general and France in particular. France has given this legitimacy its own form, highly different from the Latin, Germanic, and Anglo-Saxon world that surround it.

Another example of the new ideas that are more widespread in the political establishment than among the people of France is the concept of dividing sovereignty among the regions. Administrative decentralization, as long as it is complemented and supported by political, financial, and social solidarity, is a good idea, but the dismemberment of power is disastrous.

In a country such as France, inequality in the distribution of income together with the profusion of local interests would quickly lead to fractured solidarity and a dispersal of power which would be the ruin of the institutions of the republic. My satisfaction with the progress made since 1958 is tempered by my concern over the all-too frequent failure to perceive the exigencies of the legitimacy of power in France.

I have dwelt at length on the word "legitimacy" in the course of these remarks. It is a difficult and fundamental issue that touches the very soul of the community. Nothing in public life is ever achieved permanently. But the unprecedented advance in our knowledge, like the progress in our technical capacity, does not affect the eternal behavior of men, societies and nations. The viability of institutions is an essential element in the success of this continuous struggle, the political struggle in which thought is the basis for action.

Legitimacy is loyalty to moral principles and the public interest, while respecting national sovereignty. Legitimacy requires simplicity. Everything in institutions that fosters the simple appeal to the truth of things and feelings strengthens legitimacy: a head of state elected by the people, deputies elected by majority vote, the right to dissolve parliament in the event of conflict between the cabinet and the assembly. On the other hand, everything that tends to obscure—a complicated electoral method, power-sharing with the regions, delegations to supranational communities—erodes legitimacy. The great merit of the Fifth Republic is having restored to the French people their right to decide their future. Never has France voted on so many issues and, what is more important, never have people gone in such numbers and so freely to the polls to cast their votes. They should now take care not to lose what they owe to tragic circumstances, which established a personal legitimacy for one man, General de Gaulle, which he, a good republican, used to restore the legitimacy of the republic.

May those who lead our country, and educate and inform its citizens, refrain from tampering with the principles of our society, with the public interest, and with our nation's sovereignty.

Suggestions
for Further Reading

The most basic requirement in considering whether the American constitutional system needs reforming is to understand the existing document. The first book to study for that purpose is *The Federalist**. These brilliant essays by Alexander Hamilton, James Madison, and John Jay are not an infallible guide to the intentions of the framers, but they do provide a coherent rationale for the Constitution, and they have exerted a great deal of influence as that meaning has evolved.

To get more directly at the intentions of the framers, one must turn to Madison's Notes of the 1787 convention. They are available in several editions, the most authoritative being the first two volumes of Max Farrand, ed., *Records of the Federal Convention of 1787** (Yale, 1911, 1935).

There are several good expositions of the convention, including Max Farrand, *The Framing of the Constitution** (Yale, 1913), Carl Van Doren, *The Great Rehearsal* (Viking, 1948), and Clinton Rossiter, *1787: The Grand Convention* (Macmillan, 1966). Gordon S. Wood, *The Creation of the American Republic, 1776-1787** (Norton, 1969, 1972), traces the development of constitutional ideas during the founding period. Scholars may consult the bibliographical essay in Professor Wood's *The Confederation and the Constitution** (University Press of America, 1979) for a guide to the secondary literature on this period.

Our understanding of the founding period has been greatly enriched by the effort of scholars to appreciate the ideas of the opponents of the original Constitution. Herbert J. Storing, *What the Anti-Federalists Were For** (University of Chicago, 1981) presents a sympathetic, though not uncritical, account of these ideas. For the documents themselves, introduced by an interpretive essay, see Cecelia M. Kenyon, editor, *The Antifederalists** (Bobbs-Merrill, 1966).

[* means available in paperback edition.]

Though there has been little hesitation, beginning with the Progressive period, to criticize the federal convention and assail the framers' motives, there are remarkably few studies which offer sustained critical analyses of the structure of government established by the Constitution. As James Sundquist has remarked, the great debate of 1787-1788 has never reopened, despite the expectations of the framers.

Nevertheless, there are a few books which reflect an effort to keep the tradition of critical thinking alive. Woodrow Wilson's *Congressional Government** (Johns Hopkins, 1981), originally published in 1885, during the heyday of congressional power, is no longer descriptively accurate, but it is powerfully written and still suggestive. Wilson, the only political scientist ever to serve as president, modelled his analysis (both as to method and standards of judgment) on Walter Bagehot's classic interpretation of parliamentary government, *The English Constitution** (Cornell, 1966; originally published in 1868). Another classic is Walter Lippmann, *The Public Philosophy* (Mentor, 1955), especially Part 2, which presents a powerful argument for responsible executive leadership.

Several recent studies have focussed on the relation of Congress and the presidency. James Sundquist, *The Decline and Resurgence of Congress** (Brookings, 1981), Louis Fisher, *President and Congress** (Free Press, 1972), and Louis Fisher, *Constitutional Conflicts Between Congress and the President** (Princeton, 1985) trace the ebb and flow of power between the two branches through recent events. Sundquist gives explicit consideration to various proposed reforms. The latter book by Fisher contains an extensive bibliography on executive-legislative relations.

James M. Burns, *The Deadlock of Democracy* (Prentice-Hall, 1963), traces the travail of the parties to its root in the constitutional structure. Stephen Horn, *Cabinet and Congress* (Columbia University Press, 1960), focusses on the cabinet as a link in the system. Charles O. Jones, *Every Second Year* (Brookings, 1967), analyzes the argument, pro and con, over a four-year term for House members. *The President, Congress and the Constitution**, by Christopher Pyle and Richard Pious (Free Press, 1984), contains the texts of a number of Supreme Court cases and other primary materials that bear on executive-legislative relations in the making of foreign policy.

Many books concentrate on the place of the presidency in the system. Charles Thach, *The Creation of the Presidency, 1775-1789* (Johns Hopkins Press, 1923, 1969), is the best analysis of the intentions of the framers. Edward S. Corwin, *The President: Office and Powers** (New York University Press, 1984), has recently been issued in an new edition. Arthur M. Schlesinger, Jr., *The Imperial Presidency* (Houghton Mifflin, 1973), examines the constitutional strains induced by the preoccupation with national security. "A Presidency for the 1980s," a report prepared for the National Academy of Public Administration by a panel headed by Rocco Siciliano and Don K. Price, analyzes the travail of the executive in light of the demands of modern administration; it has been published, along with some of the background studies, in Hugh Heclo and Lester Salamon, editors, *The Illusion of Presidential Government** (Westview Press, 1981).

The role of parties in the constitutional system has been a preoccupation of many political scientists since World War II. The debate began with an analysis and program of reform, *Toward a More Responsible Two-Party System* (Rinehart, 1950), produced by the Committee on Political Parties of the American Political Science Association. Austin Ranney, *The Doctrine of Responsible Party Government* (Illinois, 1962), traces the history of the idea. For a critical study of the original CPP report, see Evron M. Kirkpatrick, "'Toward a More Responsible Two-Party System': Political Science, Policy Science, or Pseudo-Science?" *American Political Science Review*, LXV (December 71), 965–990; and, for a more sympathetic account, Gerald Pomper, "Toward a More Responsible Two-Party System? What, Again?" *Journal of Politics*, vol. 33 (November 1971), 916-40.

Only a handful of books have set forth full-blown plans for constitutional revision. William MacDonald, in *A New Constitution for America* (B. W. Huebsch, 1921), proposed to center the government on a cabinet made up of legislators, reducing the president to a ceremonial head-of-state. MacDonald's model was squarely based on the British parliamentary system. William Yandell Elliott, a Harvard professor, in *The Need for Constitutional Reform* (Whittlesey House, 1935), reflected a desire, as the New Deal began to take shape, to facilitate national planning by strengthening the constitutional position of the executive. Henry Hazlitt, a conservative journalist, argued in *A New Constitution Now* (Whittlesey House, 1942) that the exigencies of war demanded a parliamentary form of government. Thomas K. Finletter, serving at the time as assistant secretary of state, in *Can Representative Government Do the Job?* (Reynal and Hitchcock, 1945), wrote that the post-war era would require unified government, which could best be attained by coordinated terms, a joint executive-legislative council, and the possibility of presidential dissolution. (Elliott's and Finletter's books are excerpted herein.)

The 1970s saw two other book-length proposals for constitutional revision: Charles Hardin's *Presidential Power and Accountability* (University of Chicago Press, 1974), and Rexford G. Tugwell's *The Emerging Constitution* (Harper's Magazine Press, 1974). Hardin's book is excerpted herein. Tugwell taught at Columbia and the University of Chicago and was a leading framer of the New Deal. His constitutional ideas were refined in dialogues at the Center for the Study of Democratic Institutions, in Santa Barbara, California.

The strains of the Vietnam War and the Watergate scandal stimulated interest in constitutional revision. Congressman Henry Reuss offered various proposals for closer collaboration between the executive and legislative branches. His plan for dissolution and new elections was the subject of a symposium in 1974 at George Washington University. Papers delivered at that meeting were published in the university's *Law Review* (vol. 43, no. 2, January, 1975); several are excerpted herein. In November, 1983, as chairman of the Joint Economic Committee of Congress, Congressman Reuss conducted hearings on "Political Economy and Constitutional Reform"; the two-volume report of those hearings (November–December, 1982; 97th Congress, 2d session) is a valuable collection of materials on the whole question of constitutional reform.

Many who have considered constitutional revision have come to the conclusion that it would be a mistake. Among those who take the idea seriously before rejecting it are Harold Laski, *The American Presidency* (Harper and Brothers, 1940); Don K. Price, *America's Unwritten Constitution* (Louisiana State University Press, 1983); and Bob Eckhardt and Charles L. Black, Jr., *The Tides of Power* (Yale University Press, 1976). All three are excerpted herein.

Two scholars who have worked closely with CCS have published, or will soon, major analyses of the need for structural reform of the American political system. James Burns, *The Power to Lead* (Simon & Schuster, 1984) concentrates on the need to strengthen parties. James Sundquist, *Effective Government and Constitutional Reform* (Brookings, forthcoming 1986) closely examines the whole range of proposals for breaking deadlocks and encouraging effective, accountable government.

The approach of the bicentennial has stimulated a number of other efforts to examine the fitness of the Constitution for modern governance. Project '87, a joint undertaking of the American Historical Association and the American Political Science Association, has supported a number of significant scholarly projects, held several conferences, issued collections of papers, and publishes a valuable magazine, called *this Constitution*, which contains articles, documents, and announcements about conferences and other serious events relating to the bicentennial. Sheilah Mann is the editor; her office is at 1527 New Hampshire Avenue NW, Washington, DC 20036.

The American Enterprise Institute has published several studies that deal with the issues raised in this book. *The New American Political System** (1980), edited by Anthony King, contains essays on the changing role of major institutions under modern conditions. AEI's Constitutional Studies project has sponsored a number of conferences, from which volumes of essays have emanated. The most recent, to which several members of this Committee contributed, is entitled *Does Separation of Powers Still Work?* (1985).

The Jefferson Foundation seeks "to enhance the public's critical understanding of the Constitution . . . by involving citizens in debate and discussion of the fundamental principles of American government" and to study "constitutional reforms which have been endorsed by various groups as ways of improving the structure and functioning of government." To facilitate these discussions, the Foundation has produced pamphlets on such topics as terms of office, the executive veto, the amendment process, judicial independence, and the single, six-year term for presidents. (The latter pamphlet is excerpted herein.) Their address is The Jefferson Foundation, P.O. Box 33108, Farragut Station, Washington, DC 20033.

Finally, pursuant to the topic raised in Part 6 of this volume, we offer a suggestion or two in the vast field of comparative constitutionalism. A good place to start is with Carl J. Friedrich, *Constitutional Government and Democracy: Theory and Practice in Europe and America* (Little, Brown, 1941). Also valuable and interesting is Friedrich's little book, entitled *The Impact of American Constitutionalism Abroad* (Holmes and Meier, 1967). *Presidents and Prime Ministers*, edited by Richard Rose and Ezra N. Suleiman (American Enterprise Institute, 1980), contains essays on executive power in Great Britain, Canada, France, and other developed democracies in Europe. Arend Lijphart, *Democracies: Patterns of Majoritarian and Consensus Government in Twenty-One Countries** (Yale, 1984), in a little over 200 closely reasoned and empirically rich pages, examines "twenty-one democracies [including the United States] that have been in existence for a long time [which] have developed quite different formal and informal institutions for translating citizen preferences into public policies." Lijphart's footnotes offer a survey of the literature in political science that bears on constitutional form and practice.